"With beautiful detail, Shulman tells the tale of a city, however rich or poor, that has always wanted to eat well. From a Harlem numbers house that lured gamblers with city-grown produce to a hipster butcher transforming a corner of Williamsburg, *Eat the City* reminds us that New York's true foodies live in every corner, in every class, of every borough."

—Tracie McMillan, author of *The American Way of Eating*

"Robin Shulman shows the farms beneath the feet of New Yorkers . . . Hers is an industrial, social, political, and of course culinary geography of the city, with finely observed portraits of the people, young and old, who are intent on following the footsteps of forebears they might not know they had—not just in farming, fishing, butchering, and brewing, but in calling for social justice for everyone who produces food."

—Corby Kummer, author of *The Joy of Coffee* and
The Pleasures of Slow Food

"A lovely, well-written, and fascinating account of people who built and continue to build New York through its food production, cultivation and creation . . . Shulman moves seemingly effortlessly between past and present in order to set the amazing stories of the people she writes about within a historical context. That is an amazingly difficult thing to do well."

—Suzanne Wasserman, PhD, director of the Gotham
Center for New York City History/CUNY

EAT
the
CITY

CROWN PUBLISHERS
NEW YORK

EAT

the

CITY

a tale of the

fishers, trappers, hunters, foragers,

slaughterers, butchers, farmers, poultry minders, sugar refiners,

cane cutters, beekeepers, winemakers, and brewers

who built new york

ROBIN SHULMAN

Library of Congress Cataloging-in-Publication Data

Shulman, Robin.
Eat the city : a tale of the fishers, trappers, hunters, foragers, slaughterers, butchers, farmers, poultry minders, sugar refiners, cane cutters, beekeepers, winemakers, and brewers who built New York / Robin Shulman. — 1st ed.
p. cm.
Includes bibliographical references.
1. Food supply—New York (State)—New York—History. 2. New York (N.Y.)—Social life and customs—20th century. I. Title.
TX360.U63N49 2012
363.809747—dc23
2012000333

ISBN 978-0-307-71905-8
eISBN 978-0-307-71907-2

PRINTED IN THE UNITED STATES OF AMERICA

Interior map and illustrations by Chris Silas Neal
Jacket design and illustration by Chris Silas Neal
Jacket map by Historic Map Works LLC

1 3 5 7 9 10 8 6 4 2

First Edition

For my mother, Barbara, a nourisher,

and my father, Art, an improviser.

And for my grandparents,

Irv and Ruth, Sadie and Harry, and also Rose.

More grows in the garden than the gardener has sown.

—AN OLD SAYING

Together, as the architects of something perfectly ordinary—our own lives—we became builders of a city so big and various it is beyond knowing.

—KATHARINE GREIDER

CONTENTS

AUTHOR'S NOTE

I began gathering material for this book in 2005, and worked intensively from January 2010 to December 2011. I was not present for all of the events I describe. Interviews, published and unpublished letters, journals, reports and minutes of meetings, newspaper and magazine stories, census and other government records, maps, talks, and historians' accounts all helped to reconstruct events that happened long ago. For more recent events, I also interviewed multiple participants, visited sites, and viewed television stories, videos, social-media sites, and blogs.

One name in this book, a child's, has been changed, to protect her privacy.

Where a quote is not from my own interviews, I have included sources in the Notes at the end of the book.

While conducting research, I interviewed hundreds of people and read hundreds of books. For complete information on sources, see my website, www.robinshulman.com.

GUYANESE-STYLE NET FISHING

TOM MYLAN'S PIG ROAST AT THE QUEENS COUNTY FARM MUSEUM ·· →

Queens

FLUSHING MEADOWS CORONA PARK

MADANI HALAL SLAUGHTERHOUSE

JORGE TORRES'S SUGAR CANE

The Bronx

VAN CORTLANDT PARK

ROGER REPOHL'S BEEHIVES

Bronx River

LaGUARDIA

• THE MEAT HOOK,

• BROOKLYN GRANGE ROOFTOP FARM

JOHN RUFFINO'S FISHING SPOT ON GANTRY PIER

Harlem River

LATIF JIJI'S HOME WINERY

JACOB RUPPERT BREWERY

CENTRAL PARK

WILLIE MORGAN'S GARDEN

THE LAST MAJOR SLAUGHTERHOUSE

Hudson River

Manhattan

st River

THE HISTORIC BREWERY
WHERE JON AND JOSH
CONSIDERED BREWING

GREENHOUSE

THE HAVEMEYER-BUILT
DOMINO SUGAR REFINERY

Brooklyn

JON CONNER AND
JOSH FIELDS'S
HOME BREWERY

SAL MEGLIO'S WINE AT
THE RED HOOK VFW

DAVID SELIG'S HIVES
OF RED HONEY

THE RED HOOK WINERY

PROSPECT
PARK

JFK

BROOKLYN VI
PARTY BOAT
FISHING

MAR GONZALEZ'S AND
YOLENE JOSEPH'S
CRABBING SPOTS

THE OLD
MANISCHEWITZ
PLANT

CHINATOWN
CRABBING
AND FISHING

ANDREW COTÉ'S
BEEHIVES ON THE ROOF
OF THE BRIDGE CAFÉ

HENRY O. HAVEMEYER'S
WALL STREET OFFICES

Staten Island

CLAMMING, CRABBING,
AND FISHING CONTINUE

INTRODUCTION

ONE DAY WHEN I was seventeen, I turned onto my Manhattan block to see a man sitting on my stoop, his stringy brown hair falling into his face as he leaned forward to focus on the needle he was sticking into his arm. He was blocking the entrance to my building. I slowed my pace, so he could finish before I arrived.

"Um, excuse me," I said, pausing in front of the stoop. The man courteously took the syringe out of his bruised, punctured forearm and stood to the side. I turned my key in the lock, pushed inside, and pulled the door shut tight behind me. This was what my neighbors were complaining about at building meetings. This was the overflow from the drug mart on the vacant land next door.

It was 1993, and I was new to New York, attending college, and living during the summer on Fourth Street between Avenues C and D. On my block in that far east of Manhattan, buildings were black with char, windows punched out, and sidewalks were tilted and overgrown with weeds. Vacant lots were piled with house-hold detritus and scraps of wood and steel from tenements that had burned and been demolished. There was always a salesman standing in some shadow chanting the names of heroin brands like an incantation: "Roadrunner, Roadrunner, Roadrunner," or "Satan, Satan, Satan." Gunshots and sirens sounded almost every night. Video stores sold nothing but action and porn. Enormous portraits adorned with doves and flourishes were spray-painted onto brick walls to memorialize dead kids my own age.

The action took place beneath my bedroom window, where the demolition of twelve-odd adjacent buildings had created a grassy plain, stretching the whole depth of the block from Fourth to Fifth streets. I would peer out as people traded wads of cash for vials, or poked through the rubble before nodding off in the trash. Sometimes a regular would disappear, and I'd wonder if he or she was still alive.

Kids in my building knew not to even look as they walked around grown women and men passed out still clutching a syringe on the sidewalk outside the vacant land. The kids certainly knew not to venture into the no-man's-land of a yard.

Their childhood was unfathomably different from my own, in a small farming town where we picked wild blackberries and rhubarb and mint in the depths of unmowed backyards and swam in clay-bottomed ponds. Here in New York, I began to wonder how a whole society had allowed this wilderness of human neglect.

But one day, I noticed a dozen of my neighbors at work, shoveling up the vacant land. Venturing into the yard, I smelled earth, along with stale, spilt beer, and felt the high grasses brush against my calves, prickling like needles.

"We're going to clean the place up, fence it off, and plant it," said my neighbor, sweating and leaning on his rake. "Want to help?" I put on thick gloves to shovel loads of vials and syringes and broken glass into heavy-duty green garbage bags.

It took my neighbors all spring and most of the summer to

clear the space. When clean, the landscape, with its frayed, over-grown grasses and enormous size, had a weirdly bucolic look, like an unevenly balding country heath. New people started to venture in—a lady knelt in the dirt to plant seedlings, little kids kicked around a luminous blue ball, and a group of guys with guitars and drums played *bomba y plena* late into the night, their songs carry-ing on the breeze and lulling me to sleep. There was something savory about a slow, hot midsummer evening when the kids ran through the garden long past dark while their parents laughed around a card table. In a place surrounded by violence, taking up space with regular life seemed like an act of defiance.

Soon, I found myself waking up to the creaky call of a black-eyed, red-wattled rooster. I would see him strutting around the garden, his tough, reptilian talons navigating the broken glass around the central pathway and the soft black earth of the raised vegetable beds. My neighbors fed him kitchen scraps and regarded him lovingly—until one day he fell silent.

"Chicken soup," explained my seven-year-old neighbor, Caro-lina, cheerfully. Her dad had wrung the rooster's neck and fol-lowed a family recipe, adding cilantro from the herb beds. "He was delicious," she said.

Only when Carolina pointed out that the rooster had never been a pet did I realize that most of the people I saw in the garden were not planting decorative flowers, but engaged in the serious work of tending vegetables and livestock. In a few years, the far east of Fourth Street had gone from buildings to prairie to a small working farm.

All through the neighborhood, wherever people could find an empty patch of ground, they were planting tomatoes, squashes, and greens, raising chickens and rabbits and turkeys and ducks, living off the fat of the urban landscape. Just about every block had some kind of chicken, many of them strange, spiky-feathered exotics from Japan, their owners would tell you, or birds that laid blue or green eggs like Easter specials. The chicken keepers ranged from sentimentalists to casual slaughterers, variously interested in eggs, meat, cockfighting, and company.

In the early 1990s, the Lower East Side was a free-for-all where you could do anything you wanted in a vacant lot, and it turned out that a lot of people wanted to produce their own food. The farming felt somehow like an antidote to the fires, the drugs, and the death that had come before. In a place that had seemed bent on self-destruction, people had figured out collective action to sustain themselves with something as elemental as food. It was like an old-fashioned morality play, the destroyers against the producers, where the producers win—with the rooster as the stand-in for the phoenix rising from the ashes.

EVENTUALLY I left Fourth Street to work as a journalist in the Middle East. For years I trundled back and forth between various points in the U.S. and abroad, and in 2005, when I came back to New York for good, little was recognizable. Gardens had been bulldozed, vacant lots built into orderly new condos, murals painted over, gunshots stopped. Empty storefronts along Avenue C had turned into sweet little bistros and wine bars. Landlords were recruiting more high-rent professionals, and a lot of my former neighbors had moved away. Once or twice when I got out of the subway station and saw glimmering glass towers, I did a double take, thinking I'd exited at the wrong stop.

Already dispirited from reporting on war, terrorism, and

destruction, now I also felt unmoored in the place I had called home. Maybe, I thought, I should literally plant roots. I started with tomatoes and cucumbers and basil in the garden on Fourth Street, which had survived after my neighbors fought to change its status to an official city parkland. Soon I realized I was more fascinated by the stories of the other gardeners than I was patient with the solitary labor of coaxing life from soil.

A debate was raging over the latest batch of roosters in the garden. Newcomers complained to the city about the racket—one rooster seemed to think each bright light was a new dawn and crowed at every set of passing headlights, while the others would chime in when a car alarm went off or they heard the bass in a boom box. The roosters had their supporters. But a vocal new faction was convinced that the birds posed the threat of avian flu. Emails with the subject line "The Chicken Question" piled up in my inbox. Soon the roosters were hustled into a borrowed truck and dispatched to an upstate sanctuary.

Yet elsewhere in the city, chickens were suddenly showing up as the backyard pets of young professionals. In one family I met in the Red Hook section of Brooklyn—a real estate agent and a college administrator with three kids—the woman of the house rose early in the morning, went out to the chicken coop, fed the birds, gathered their eggs, and sold a cartonful to anyone who came knocking in response to the sign in the window promising EGGS FOR SALE. The family kept four Rhode Island Reds, good sturdy American chickens, layers of eggs, survivors of winter, busty purveyors of white-meat flesh; two Golden Polish, birds with a feathery waterfall of bangs over their whole heads; two delicate little Egyptian Fayoumis, descended from the Nile Delta; and four French birds: two black-bodied, blue-legged Crèvecoeurs, and two Cuckoo Marans that laid chocolate-brown eggs. The man of the house took overly aggressive roosters to a nearby slaughterhouse and then cooked them on the grill. The family dreamed of expanding into a full-fledged urban egg farm, of coming home from the office to clean chicken shit.

What was going on here?

"It's this new thing," a friend told me knowingly. "I think it's an urban back-to-the-land trend."

But I knew that producing food had already transformed at least one neighborhood in the 1990s: mine. And I wondered if it had happened before, throughout the city. I began to investigate.

MORE than a century ago, far away in the little villages of eastern Europe, tired mothers crooned to their wakeful children the Sholom Aleichem lullaby: *In America, there will be chicken soup in the middle of the week.* They fulfilled that promise when they arrived in the newly constructed yet already crowded tenement buildings of my neighborhood, where they kept chickens, ducks, turkeys, and geese. There was squawking and clucking in hallways, apartments, basements, and narrow airshaft yards. It's not hard to envision a mother walking up wood stairs in my building, carrying her young child past an occasional flapping and feathery flight to the windowsill. For how long has a rooster wakened the people of Fourth Street? A hundred years? Two hundred?

How did history bring us to where we are? In an enormous, overdeveloped city with millions of citizens and hundreds of years of momentum, how do people mark the landscape with their own personal hunger?

I decided to find out. I took the subway deep into the boroughs to meet people who grow vegetables and fruits and mushrooms, who fish and forage, who go clamming and trapping, who collect honey, who produce cheese and yogurt, who make beer, wine, hard liquor and liqueurs, who keep goats for milk, and quails, ducks, and chickens for eggs, and who butcher city-grown rabbits, turkeys, roosters, and pigs. They invited me to rooftops and basements, rivers and fish tanks, fire escapes, window ledges, warehouses, packing plants, storefronts, breweries, wineries, and community farms.

Some of them were misplaced rural folk dreaming farm dreams on the subway. They were next-generation foodies forever seeking a more complex and rustic thrill from the homemade. They were people of limited means looking to save or make money. They were eccentrics obsessed with process. They were sentimentalists chasing tradition; they were parents concerned with health. They were professional artisans, and they were manufacturers focusing on profit. They were philosopher-farmers trying to build a new American urban life. In the most heavily built urban environment in the country, they showed me an organic city full of intrepid people who want to make things grow.

In libraries and archives and private homes, I paged through stacks of books, letters, journals, drawings, and photos related to the sugar trade in the 1700s, beer brewing in the 1800s, meatpacking in the 1900s. In a growing global metropolis, pumping out wealth, I began to piece together a picture of a hidden city where people concerned themselves with food and drink.

Perhaps it's only natural that this behemoth of a port city early on became a center of commercial food manufacturing. At one time or another, the land that became New York City led national production of oysters, coffee, sugar, vegetables, milk, yogurt, ice cream, margarine, beer, and kosher wine.

Long past the golden age of agriculture in New York, some urbanites continued to make their own basic foods. Homemade food appeared during times of economic, political, and cultural crisis. When people have lost their jobs or endured wars and prohibitions—in times of scarcity—they have been pressed into production. They have grown vegetables on the fire escape, kept rabbits for stews, and crushed grapes to make wine. They have foraged their own greens and berries in parks and brewed their own beer. Often they have been newcomers who insist on their own vision of the good life, in which food comes from trusted hands: their own or their neighbor's.

Cities have resources that people can tap in surprising ways. Amid the concrete and glass and steel are untended bits of wildlife, where invasive Japanese knotweed can be gathered to use like rhubarb, beach plums can be picked by the water, tree ear fungus can be harvested for hot and sour soup, blackberries can be hunted in a shaded grove, and dandelion greens in the sun. Cities also have train depots and shipping docks, where grapes can be imported for making wine, hops and barley can be brought in for beer, and raw sugar for refining. Big warehouses and expansive rooftops provide space where people can innovate new ways of intensive farming. Unpoliced neighborhoods and genteel blocks will tolerate chickens; fish can be caught on piers and bridges and boats and in aquaponic systems and basement tanks. People will always find ways to summon these resources to survive and thrive. They will use the geography of the city, its soil, its water, its light, its space, its transportation connections, its human creativity and energy—and its hunger—to produce food.

Look at old maps and you'll find food written all over the city in names that recall personal and local preoccupations. Parts of Harlem have been known as Goatsville and Pig's Alley. Hog Island, meanwhile, had been named by the Dutch who raised pigs there; Pigtown was an area in the Flatbush section of Brooklyn where pigeon houses and chicken coops thrived as well as pigs; and Hog Town was a part of Midtown whose recidivist pig keepers resisted swine clearance efforts with guns. Various Bone Alleys grew up throughout the city near the homes of professional bone pickers; West Twelfth Street and West Thirty-Ninth Street were both once called Abattoir Place, after local businesses. On Skinner Street, now Cliff Street, butchers sold animal skeletons as well as hides still attached to horns and tails; people used the skulls to decorate their storefronts and carriages; and kids built animal-skin forts they would defend from other gangs. Pearl Street was named after the discarded oyster shells that littered it long ago. Sugar Loaf Street, today's Franklin Street, was named for a sugar house. On the Brooklyn waterfront, Java Street was named for the coffee unloaded from ships coming from the other side of the world. Mulberry Street, Cherry Street, Orchard Street, the Meatpacking District. Turtle Bay, where today you'd be hard-pressed to find turtle soup, and Coney Island, where few coneys— rabbits—survive. The Bowery is named after Peter Stuyvesant's old Dutch farm, or *bouwerij,* that it once traversed.

The first Europeans to land in what became New York Harbor found an eater's paradise: hillsides reddened with ripening strawberries; waters crowded with twelve-inch oysters and six-foot lobsters; walnut and chestnut forests and orchards of sweet apples and pears; skies darkened by throngs of blackbirds, quail, and partridges; grounds replete with gamboling deer, forty-pound wild turkeys, and Native American crops of squash, beans, and maize. For more than a hundred years after the Dutch settled Manhattan, Staten Island, Brooklyn, Queens, and the Bronx in the 1600s, most everybody raised their own vegetables, pigs, and goats, and the occasional cow. Even after the English took over, many people still brewed their own beer, made their own wine, and tended beehives for honey. But by the early 1800s, new ideas of urbanity and sophistication were at odds with the presence of pigs, goats, and dirt plots of vegetables. New York could not be a world-class city and also collect fertilizer from a manure pit.

The agricultural city became an industrial one; in 1865, Brooklyn had five hundred factories; by 1870, a thousand; by 1880, over five thousand. Suddenly, in a few quick decades at the end of the nineteenth century, the last of the farms became housing. The railroads had laid track for a national food network—no need to grow it all here. The subway and elevated trains allowed people to live farther from the city center, right on top of onetime crops. The idea of factory production became the norm, as sugar refineries, breweries, and wineries thrived throughout the city. Well-off city-born folk saw urban agricultural production as the sign of a dirty rube. New York was a food manufacturing city until after World War II, when planners began to view the city as too big, rich, and important to concern itself with such basic needs as food. The costs of land and labor rose and dirty industry was zoned out of city life. Food production receded from view.

· · ·

AS I continued to research this book, my conception of what I was writing changed. Taking the subway to meet people young and old, poor and rich, native-born and immigrant, I realized that I was uncovering an unseen city of thriving food production, full of practices that most New Yorkers don't share and aren't even aware exist. Unbeknownst to many chroniclers of the city, these practices have continued over time. I began to see how the history of food is geography, immigration, culture, urban planning, science, technology, education, health, real estate, economics: the history of the city itself. This book is about all of those things, but it is most of all about how people express and share the impulse to create and sustain.

People know this city for its ostentatious displays, its speed of life and change, its ability to tear things down and build back up. I was more interested in the intimate, homely city where food creates community, as among a few people netting tiny silvered fish near the mouth of the Bronx River, or founding a newfangled, old-style butcher shop where the butchers show the customers new cuts of meat.

Food, of course, is about hunger. We eat what we miss and what we want to become, the foods of our childhoods and the symbols of the lives we hope to lead.

And so many people continue to labor in a sometimes hostile environment to create something small, pure, odd, personal, transitory: food.

HONEY

SUNDAYS IN THE SUMMER, Andrew Coté likes to hive hop, collecting honey. Sometimes he takes the subway from his apartment on the Lower East Side, his smoker and his bag of hive tools banging against his thigh as he walks. But mostly he drives a white Toyota Tundra pickup abuzz with bees hovering over the truck bed, where their honey has been stashed. They will travel with the truck for hours, from one borough to another, seeking to reclaim what is theirs in a scene out of an urban *Winnie-the-Pooh*.

Andrew curses his way through traffic, flips one-handed through a giant ring for keys to the next rooftop hive building, and parks wherever he can find a space.

Much of city beekeeping is vertical work. Up a narrow stairway in the dingy darkness, carrying tools to hives on a roof in the shadow of the Brooklyn Bridge. Down six flights of stairs from rooftop hives on a different building on Second Avenue, balancing heavy, oozing frames of honey.

Back outside, truck full of honey, when someone pauses and stares at the buzzing bees still lingering above the truck, Andrew says, "We're out of here," and guns the motor. When a cruiser slows down and a cop yells out the window, "Is that honey?" Andrew cheerfully calls, "Legal since April 2010! Want to try?"

While hobbyist beekeepers usually maintain just a hive or two, Andrew practices a particularly muscular brand of urban beekeeping, managing forty hives on rooftops, terraces, and balconies, and in yards and gardens in Manhattan, Brooklyn, and Queens. A fourth-generation beekeeper, Andrew is a kind of honey lord with a petty honey fiefdom, supervising a network of hundreds of novices he has taught and mentored in the city. He sells boxlike hives he makes himself, along with packages of bees as starter kits. At the New York City Beekeepers Association that he helped launch, he presides over monthly meetings, which routinely draw the illuminati of the beekeeping world—great beekeepers, authors of books on honey, artists focused on bees.

To hear Andrew tell it, honey-making is a hustle. It's nothing like producing wine or cheese, where you mix careful quantities of ingredients together, monitor temperatures and chemical processes, and tend a thing while it becomes something else. In beekeeping, your job is observation, fraud, and theft. You set up conditions (a good clean hive, water, a supply of nearby flowers) so the bees feel equipped to plan for the future. Sooner or later, your bees will fly forth and suck nectar from flowers, spit in enzymes that thicken and preserve it, and construct cells of wax in which to store it as food for the long winter. Driven by instinct that looks like artisanal zeal, they will use their tiny wings as fans to cool the wax in summer and warm it in fall. Many die. You, on the other hand, just pry open the lid of the hive, which the bees, perhaps foreseeing such crimes, have sealed shut with a sappy glue they extract from plants. You knock out the bees with a dose of smoke and seize their waxen provisions. And then you're out, with nary a sting. You've got honey.

Of course, Andrew will tell you that in cities, beekeeping is more complicated. You've got to find a place to install a hive—perhaps some unused roof or flower-filled community garden—and lobby co-op boards and garden members to approve. You've got to make arrangements for access at least once every few weeks. You've got to carry around heavy protective clothing to keep from getting stung—many times—as a single bee stinging emits a scent that alerts other bees to join the attack.

In a crowded city, you have to work especially hard to prevent a swarm, a hive reproduction technique whereby half the bees in a colony fly off to find a new home and cluster for hours or maybe days in some tree—or, in the case of New York, one of many tree-like structures, such as a traffic light or a street sign in front of the Bulgari jewelry store on Fifth Avenue. It looks like the stuff of horror films: a ball of 30,000 bees flying through the air making a noise like a buzz saw, Andrew will say. People get scared. Nearby businesses can't operate, and crowds gather to stare. A beekeeper can head this off by dividing the hive in two when it's particularly populous and active—but the timing has to be right. In case of error, Andrew and other experienced beekeepers set up a swarm hotline where anyone can leave a voice message that gets sent as a text alert to phones including Andrew's. He will grab his beekeeping gear and rush over. Like a hooded superhero on a utility ladder, he will trap the swarm and spirit the bees away to a new hive.

New York City outlawed beekeeping in 1999, and for a decade afterward, a clandestine apiarist culture survived despite the risk of a $2,000 fine for an illicit hive. People put up screens and walls and grew foliage to hide the hives in their gardens. On rooftops, they painted hives gray to look like air conditioning units, or red, like chimneys. After removing frames of honey, they wrapped them in garbage bags and sealed them with duct tape before carrying them, quietly buzzing, into public view. They hosted underground honey tastings and sold their wares in boutique groceries. At most, there were a few dozen beekeepers in the city, and the hobby seemed to attract lone eccentrics, such as a Brooklyn drag performer who sold honey under his female alias, and a man in the Bronx who lived in a rectory and had learned beekeeping from a Trappist monk. Finally when beekeeping became legal again in 2010, new beekeepers emerged in force.

Often they're in it for the honey. City honey is an edible record of available nectar in the urban landscape, and a discerning palate can see and taste the distinctive flavors of different neighborhoods. A complex and nuanced South Bronx honey comes from bees feasting on flora at the nearby botanical garden. A Manhattan East Village honey, pale with a minty taste from bees working the linden trees, has hints of apple, peach, and rose, from the many community gardens. A Prospect Heights, Brooklyn, honey is heavy from the Echinacea flowers of a local garden and from Prospect Park itself. In some neighborhoods, the honey is so sweet, it's overwhelming: sharp, almost acid. In others, it is light, high, citrusy, and tangy. Elsewhere it's musky and indistinct—or nutty, spicy, with a bitter aftertaste. Hives near one another generally produce similarly flavored honeys, so that if you were to map a particular city's honey flavors, you would see gradually shifting regions determined by prominent nearby flowers. It's even easier to track the changing flavors of honey throughout the season as various flowers bloom and fade. Early honey, from clover and the spring-flowering trees, is light in color and flavor, and the later stuff from goldenrod in the fall has a deep hue with a heavy taste.

Some newer beekeepers have been moved to the hobby by tales of colony collapse disorder, the name for a phenomenon in which whole colonies of bees disappear. The cause has not yet been fully determined, but studies point toward systemic pesticides. Farmers and commercial beekeepers, whose bees pollinate agricultural crops, began to talk about a dearth of pollinators to produce fruits and vegetables across the country. Urban bees were less affected, and some city people began to tend their own hive in hopes that they could somehow bolster the species. A sense of crisis in beekeeping peaked just as New York City legalized the practice. Interest soared.

Urban beekeepers all over the country do what Andrew does: They are swarm wranglers, bee dealers, hive inspectors, club leaders, beekeeping teachers, honey sellers. But most major cities that allow beekeeping have a long-standing institution with a stable community to manage problems. In Chicago, a nonprofit cooperative contracts with City Hall to manage the hives on its roof. In San Francisco and Seattle, volunteer organizations have collected swarms for decades. But in New York, all this is new, and Andrew Coté is often the one to educate, mediate, and trap wayward bees. The recent legalization of urban beekeeping unleashed a wave of pent-up interest from aspiring beekeepers, fans of bees, and the media. These days, Andrew often works with a pack of acolytes in tow, a microphone clipped to his T-shirt and a lens trained on his face.

Andrew's own group for hobbyist beekeepers, the New York City Beekeepers Association, grew to 300 active members in just a few years following legalization. He alone trained 320 people in beekeeping in two years, while a competing beekeeping meet-up group trained another 400. Perhaps New York has become the city with the most interest in urban beekeeping in the history of beekeeping in American cities. But bees are wild creatures that cannot be tamed, and that can create unforeseen problems—interpersonal problems that require diplomacy not generally associated with keepers of honeybees. Problems that are, so to speak, sticky.

At thirty-nine years old, Andrew is fit, strong, and tightly strung. He's classically handsome enough that a modeling scout signed him up while he was working at his market honey stand, and he ended up starring in a Goldman Sachs ad. He has a flirtatious sparkle in his eye, a quick grin, a quicker wit, a handy touch, a low tolerance for error, and moods that shift as quickly and totally as a sudden storm. He has worked as a community college professor of English but also spent time in Iraq. He doesn't like to talk about what he did there, but he came back in 2006 with post-traumatic stress disorder and Monday-afternoon appointments with a shrink. Now he seems to lack the self-corrective feature that makes human interaction bearable. He can be incredibly dedicated: When a bus hit his cargo van last spring while he was delivering bees, the bloodied Andrew, covered in broken glass and lying on a gurney by an ambulance, phoned other beekeepers to come pick up their packages. Yet he also punches people when he's mad. He tears up when he's sad. He writes vengeful emails to strangers. Fellow beekeeper David Selig says, "He's like an angry bee."

.   .   .

ONE late-summer day in 2009, David Selig—shirtless, barefoot, hot—stepped out onto the deck off his bedroom, climbed a utility ladder up to the roof, coffee mug in hand, and tiptoed across the scalding silver surface to visit his bees. He had already collected early honey from two hives he had installed on his roof in the spring: It had been a pale tawny color, strained of all flavor but a newborn sweetness, like the first clover blossoms. But now, as he settled with his coffee, squatting near the entrance of the hive, he noticed something strange. The foragers flying back from gathering nectar were glowing in the late-afternoon light, incandescent, as though lit up by an internal red bulb.

Something unusual had clearly affected his bees. David is a calm person: He's thoughtful, low-voiced, he is not rash. He finished his coffee, noting the disconcerting beauty of his red bees in the sun, like living, moving warning lights. Then he stepped back down the ladder and went inside to Google "red bees." The search turned up nothing much—Red Bee comics, Red Bee crafts, Red Bee Media. When he went back to the roof to check the hives, the bees no longer looked red, the honeycomb seemed fine, and he chose to assume that whatever had been amiss, had passed.

David was in love with honey. Not just the sweetness, but the way it connects you with the place where you are, since bees, collecting nectar and pollen from flowers, skim what they need from any environment and transform it into something you can taste. When he traveled to Syria, Turkey, and Jamaica, he would taste the honey, seek out beekeepers, and find that often, through their bees, they noticed changes in botany and climate, industry and agriculture, that others did not. "I enjoy observing nature," David would say when he got stung and his skin swelled and reddened with a rush of blood. Bees had first fascinated him when he was a child helping to keep them during summers at his grandparents' farm in Ontario, Canada. More recently, David, a restaurateur with chains of successful eateries, had opened a kind of honey bar for wholesalers where people could sample single-varietal honeys on wooden blocks, such as wild lavender honey from Provence, fragrant and incredibly light and dry on the tongue. Ultimately, he sold the place after it was featured in a magazine and he was flooded with hundreds of orders a day. "Honey doesn't pour quickly," he said. "We just couldn't even keep up with orders."

When he finally decided to buy his own house with his girl-friend, it seemed natural to ask Andrew Coté to provide materi-als for two white wood-frame hives for David to install on the rooftop.

David didn't see a red bee again until the next year, during his second summer in the house, when day after day the thermometer edged over 90 degrees. Beekeeping had just become legal, and others with new hives in the neighborhood were worried about the heat. David's girlfriend, Cecilia Dean, a fashion muse and editor of an avant-garde magazine, parked herself under the ceil-ing fan, the dog, Mott, lolled with his tongue out, the two cats barely moved, and David went to check on his charges on the roof. He stepped through the threshold of Cecilia's museum-like walk-in closet—packed with vintage Helmut Lang and Martin Margiela suits, custom-made gifts from Karl Lagerfeld and Marc Jacobs, spiky stilettos from Nicholas Kirkwood and thigh-high boots from Balenciaga—and onto the deck. He climbed the lad-der to the roof, and as he sat with his soy latte to enjoy watching the bees, he noticed that they were again glowing red.

He jammed scraps of wood and twine for burning into his

beekeeper's smoker, a metal device like a bellows that breathes a cool, pleasant-smelling smoke that has a calming effect on bees. Then he banged away at the propolis, the sticky substance the bees use to close up the hive. He pried off the lid with a flat-headed tool, directed the smoke toward the bees within, and pulled out a frame from inside. Reassuringly, it was heaving with honey. But the substance looked unusually dark. And when he held it up to the morning sun, he saw that the honey was an untrue, electric shade somewhere between fuchsia and scarlet. He pulled out frame after frame of the second hive, only to find the same. And there were his bees, flying back to their hives, bright red lights themselves, to efficiently deposit the neon nectars of their labors, leaving blazing droplets like so many scattered pomegranate seeds on the white wood.

"Then you freak out," David said.

A bee's-eye view of New York City shows a landscape if not lav-ishly fecund, then sufficient. Whole dizzying blocks have been planted to produce the intensely sweet blossoms of magnolia trees, the fragrant florets of linden trees, the curling pink flowers of cherry trees, and the cloudlike white cluster blooms of orna-mental pear trees. In backyards of brownstones and row houses are azaleas and rhododendrons and lilacs; in apartment window-sill boxes and fire escape planters are impatiens and sweet alyssum and geraniums. Tiny blossoms stud Japanese knotweed plants in the alleys, and frilly flowers from mugwort growing out of the cracks of sidewalks beckon on burned-out, untended blocks. Even rubbled lots riddled with vials and syringes, Corona bottles and Red Bull cans, soon enough sprout fast-growing ailanthus trees, with blossoms the color of cream, in a kind of unattended urban renewal. Asters and goldenrod and early-flowering willows grow along the rivers, on the swamps, by the highways. Delicate blooms of Queen Anne's lace shoot out of the ballast at railroad tracks. Rooftop gardens and decks produce blossoms from tomatoes and mint, squashes and oregano, melons and lavender, cabbages and rosemary, kale and peppers and chives, all of them offering their nectar to the discerning bee. The lawns of the great parks teem with the go-to flowers of weedy white clover, dandelions in the spring, and napweed in August. Park beds foster black-eyed Susans, Echinacea, yarrow, sunflowers, sedums, wisteria. For a bee, guided by eyes that respond to ultraviolet light, and a sense of smell as powerful as a hound dog's, most every nook and cranny in the city blooms.

A bee needs to forage nectar all summer long, and, surprisingly, an urban landscape can offer bees a more diverse diet than a rural one. Contemporary rural landscapes are often dedicated to a single large-scale crop. If the only plant around is, say, soybeans, then bees can starve before the soybean plant opens its flowers. Commercial beekeepers whose main income generator is pollination regularly feed their bees high-fructose corn syrup as a dietary supplement in dry periods between work. Hobby beekeepers in isolated bits of California and Florida say that they have to supplement their bees' diet too, in times during the summer when there's no nectar or pollen for them to forage. This happens less in cities, because the flora are more diverse. Yet bees need volume, too, and city flowers may be hard to find in quantity enough to sate a hungry hive.

In the 1980s and early 1990s, as more people in New York City took up gardening in abandoned, burned, and industrial neighborhoods, some watched their flourishing flowers shrivel and die. They worried their plants were not being pollinated. So they fertilized their squashes and cucumbers by hand, snipping off all of the flower but the pollen tube on the male plant and nuzzling it against the newly open female. Roger Repohl, a community gardener who lives in the Morrisania section of the South Bronx, recalls that his own plants weren't doing as well as he wished. "The horticulturists came by and said, 'That's because the South Bronx is so devastated at this time, there's not enough pollinators,'" said Roger, who soon took up beekeeping. Across the city, various community gardens quietly installed illicit beehives behind a wall or in a bush, and a few knowledgeable people trained others in the care and maintenance of honeybees.

John Ascher, a bee expert at the American Museum of Natural History, says that fear of insufficient pollinators may have been unfounded. *Apis mellifera*, the honeybee, buzzes around alongside more than 240 kinds of wild bees recorded in New York City. The variety is enormous and includes tiny, bronze-colored sweat bees, longhorned bees, masked bees, carpenter bees, and bees that lay eggs in other bees' well-kept nests to consume their pollen and nectar. Any given community garden in New York is likely to foster as many as several dozen bee species, according to recent research. Though there might be a bad year or two for bees—too hot, too cold, too much rain—it's unlikely that any area of the city would go without pollination for long.

"We look at the city and think of it as being inhospitable to wildlife," said Kevin Matteson, an urban ecologist who has studied bees in New York City. "But when you look at it and think of what bees see and what they need—it is absolutely hospitable to wildlife."

. . .

"**POP** the smoker!" yells Andrew Coté to his disciples on a rooftop filled with wood planter boxes of basil, peppers, cardoons, chrysanthemums, and cleomes, and several white, gray, red, and yellow hives. The young beekeepers-in-training scramble for matches to burn burlap to produce smoke that causes bees to react as though under attack, and to fortify themselves by consuming stores of honey, rather than stinging interlopers. The apprentices work like surgical assistants, proffering each instrument as Andrew requests it. "Hive tool!" he says, and an arm stretches forth with the tool. "Paper towel!" he says, and the towel is there. Andrew hunkers down in front of what look like filing cabinets of bees, which is essentially what the hives are. They consist of stacked wooden boxes: a brood box at the base, where the queen lays her eggs, and honey boxes, or supers, above, which the workers pack with honeycomb. The supers are filled with frames, like hanging file folders, which themselves are made up of flat waxen sheets double embossed with hexagonal patterns on both sides, which the bees build up with their own wax and fill with honey. It's easy to lift out a full frame of honey and exchange it for an empty one for the bees to work next. It happens a few times a summer, so maybe the bees know what to expect. The longer you spend working in their hive, the angrier they get.

There are routine things to do to keep urban bees happy. You have to put out trays of water so the bees won't gather on windowsills to slurp the dripping beads of liquid condensation from air conditioners or crowd a public pool deck to suck from chlorinated puddles. A tar roof can get very hot and burn bees' legs, so it's important to keep it wet, or covered with a sheet, when opening up a rooftop hive. Working in tight, crowded spaces demands a certain ingenuity. Recently Andrew had to lower a 240-pound hive by rope down the rusty old fire escape of a four-story tenement after the building was sold and the new owner wanted no part of rooftop beekeeping.

Andrew pries the lid off of one box to reveal the bee society within. Thousands of little black and yellow insects crawl on top of one another to flee deeper into the hive, away from the smoke. Some of the bees glisten as though wet with nectar, and when they fly into my hair I feel them like drops of rain. There's an unsteady, dizzying buzz as they move in and out of my auditory range. A healthy hive at its peak in midsummer can sustain 40,000 to 80,000 bees with many different vocations. The queen lays up to two thousand eggs a day, creating all the new bees the hive needs, Andrew tells me. Drones are the only males in the hive, and their sole function is to mate with the queen. Their sisters are the worker bees, who serve as foragers for water, nectar, and pollen, and also act as guards and masons and nurses and undertakers and cooks. A forager flies up to two miles to extract nectar and pollen from flowers for food. Back at the hive, she passes it to the mouths of her fellow workers, who process it, removing most of the water, transforming sucrose into glucose and fructose and injecting a preservative enzyme. The bees deposit this new substance in a hexagonal cell of the honeycomb. When the cell is full, they cap it with whitish wax, protecting dark honey beneath—the bees' version of canning for the winter, since honey is bee food when no flower blooms.

Thrifty bees often produce more honey than they need to survive, and a good beekeeper can encourage them to overproduce very profitably. "Like human beings, they work themselves literally to death to gather wealth they have no need for," noted a

Brooklyn Heights beekeeper of the 1960s, who worked at a Wall Street firm.

Andrew judges his hives not only by their productivity but also by their prettiness. Of his many hives in three boroughs, Andrew's favorites are located beside the Brooklyn Bridge in Manhattan on the roof of the Bridge Cafe, the oldest wood-frame building in the city and the longest constantly running tavern (since 1794). The top stories once served as a whorehouse, but are now full of graffiti and old furniture. In the world of hive real estate, the roof is in a fabulous location, with iconic views. "Under the Brooklyn Bridge! In the shadow of the Municipal Building!" Andrew will gloat, as he reaches bare-handed into one of the six hives, bees stinging up and down his arms. "Ouch!" he says, grimacing, but not slowing down.

His second-favorite hives are on top of a luxury apartment building at Second Avenue and Fourteenth Street, where the bees zoom down toward bodegas and street traffic. Maybe they head east to the clover flowers of Tompkins Square Park, where the blossoms are muddled by the sleeping bodies of spiky-haired kids. Or perhaps they fly south to the flowers of Chinatown's window gardens, steeped in the scent of the fish market. This is the strange fact of urban beekeeping: You don't know exactly where your honey comes from. Single-varietal honey doesn't exist in the city because there are no enormous fields of heather or giant orange groves that would satisfy the hunger of a whole hive.

One of Andrew's assistants today is Kimberly White, a Baruch College student with a radiant face and gold-painted, stubby fingernails. She's originally from Saint Vincent and met Andrew one day at the Rockefeller Center farmers' market after her math class. From behind his jars and piles of sample spoons in the stand, Andrew said, "Try some honey?" "I tried it and I loved it," says Kimberly. "I had two more spoonfuls." As is his wont, Andrew urged her to buy.

"I can't buy the honey," she said.

"Don't you have a job?" Andrew asked.

Soon Kimberly found herself working for Andrew, selling honey from that very stand. She's interested in learning more about bees, she says, as a first step in her real mission: to figure out how to repair the environment. "I'm interning at Sustainable Flatbush," she says. "I'm supposed to be building solar panels."

Andrew's other assistant, Cecilia Lee, an NYU student from Argentina, has been excused from active duty because of her inappropriate attire. She ignored Andrew's emailed instructions to wear a long-sleeved shirt and full-length pants, and showed up for honey harvesting wearing a wild turkey feather in her long hair, a sleeveless shirt, and a short tulle skirt, exposing arms and legs most stingable. She says she wants to someday grow all her own food and live off the grid. Today, however, she just goes to fetch extra garbage bags. Then she sits on a step, holding a ball of beeswax, sucking on the ends of it, rolling it in her palm, releasing its perfume into the hot air.

Residents of this building have apparently complained of finding twenty-one dead bees on the front steps. "First of all, what kind of an asshole stands there and counts them?" Andrew had asked as he walked up the steps. And then he looked down. Disturbingly, there were indeed many tiny bodies of expired bees. He frowned. "Secondly, they shouldn't be there."

Once on the roof, Andrew has two tasks to execute quickly:

First, to figure out why so many bees are littering the steps and irritating the neighbors with their corpses. Then, to rob them of their honey.

"It's a strong queen," Andrew says now, admiring the hive. "Good proximity to the nectar source." He pulls up frame after frame bursting with honey. In some frames, the honey is dark, in some it's light, depending on what combination of flowers the bees visited. Not every frame is perfect. One is laced with white boils of brood, or bee eggs. Wherever the queen goes, she lays, so you have to keep her away from the honey. Andrew must have been late this year installing his queen excluder—a metal screen with openings large enough for worker bees to pass through but too small for the queen. "This guy is not well," Andrew says, pointing to a small round ball of a bee hobbling along as though without wings or legs. "The way he's walking—" It's not good, but Andrew sees no other telltale signs of mites or illness. After an inconclusive examination of two hives, he shifts his attention to the honey.

If the harvest is good, Andrew might find the comb on every frame covered in neat caps of wax, a full forty pounds in every box of maybe six hives in a row, totaling 240 pounds of honey in one trip. "Gorgeous!" he will say, grinning at the brilliance of his bees and all but doing a tap dance. "The babies are going to eat tonight! I can buy the kids shoes!" At a troubled hive, he might pull out only ten pounds of honey, and he'll be upset enough to slam the frames back into place and turn away. "But you're training people," someone will say encouragingly, noting his good work with apprentices. "I'll just tell the bank that," Andrew will reply darkly. Forty pounds of city-made honey, a respectable biannual harvest from one hive, is worth $1,600 at market. Andrew, who is single and has no kids, does have mortgages to pay—on his studio apartment in the Lower East Side and also on two properties in Connecticut—and he toys with the idea of buying a building in Brooklyn to fix up. Andrew needs honey.

Here on the roof on Second Avenue, the harvest is neither thrilling nor deplorable. Only two hives have honey, but they hold a good forty pounds per. Andrew tries to pull the full frames of honey out quickly, but he's spent too much time with his inspections and now the bees know what's coming. "The bees are a lot angrier now," says Andrew. "It's usually better as a stealth mission than a snatch-and-grab mission."

Their noise has intensified, thousands of tiny bodies helicoptering through space, wings flapping as though propelled by engines and, at close range, just as loud. I try to track one single bee: Is she spinning, dancing, darting? But they all move too fast, too closely together to differentiate. Scientifically, too, they are not individuals, I read later. Biologists call a colony of bees a superorganism—an organism consisting of many organisms, in which the division of labor is highly specialized and individuals may not survive by themselves. The noise they make all together sounds like a low-temperature sizzle.

"I'm already spilling honey all over, so they know I'm robbing them," says Andrew. The bees have embedded themselves in the honey, nosing into it, swarming over it. It's difficult to pry out any particular one without injuring her. And they're also crashing into all of us.

"They're going to get you!" Andrew yells to Kimberly, urging her to move. "They're going to sting you right through your clothes!" As the bees get more agitated, they crawl up Ceci's skirt and attach to each other in a chain between two layers of filmy tulle. In a jerky ballet, she wiggles and waves her skirt to get them out, still holding a ball of their beeswax in one hand.

After advance and retreat for more than an hour, the hives on this roof are finally emptied of honey. Andrew and the girls quickly wrap the supers full of honey frames in garbage bags. They pack all the equipment away, drop the wax, lid the hives, kill the smoke. Andrew and Kimberly each heave to their shoulders a sticky, plastic-wrapped forty-pound super, and we all clomp downstairs. "Shhh!" Andrew says. He doesn't want to annoy the neighbors and lose roof access.

Back on the street, the truck is still buzzing from the last stop, and a man slows and stares in disgust. "Are those *bees?*" he asks. Andrew jumps into the driver's seat to make a break for it before the man has time to call the city's 311 hotline and complain. Though keeping bees is legal, there's no need to attract official interest by driving through the city tailed by thousands of them.

With three hive stops, carrying hive tools and supers up and down stairs and fighting angry bees for their honey wealth in the blazing heat, the day has been exhausting, stressful, and only moderately productive. "You can see why I'm irritated when people come to the stand at the market and complain about the price of honey," Andrew says.

As he drives home, Andrew outlines his biography. He's a kind of renaissance man, who got the idea of keeping city hives while working as an assistant professor of English at Housatonic Community College in Bridgeport, Connecticut. He speaks a half dozen languages, studied Japanese lit, got a Fulbright in Moldova, and worked as a writer in India—but came back to his hometown of Norwalk when his mother was diagnosed with cancer. There, he started Silvermine Apiary, which sells wholesale honey to supermarkets. He also began a PhD at Yale in Middle East studies, and raised funds for the nonprofit Bees Without Borders he and his father launched to teach beekeeping in impoverished countries. Norm, a retired fire lieutenant, runs his own beekeeping business, Norm's Other Honey. Andrew's older brother, a police officer, also keeps a handful of hives. Andrew eventually abandoned his PhD—"I was more interested in spending time with my father and the bees." Andrew is dating a woman he met while selling honey at the market.

Aristotle and Virgil commented on honeybees, notes Andrew as he drives. As a gift between two betrothed, honey has been a symbol of love. But Andrew is more interested in the use of bees in war. In ancient Iraq, he says, fighters would catapult a hive at their enemies, "so the hive would burst, and you'd have a lot of unhappy people." Consequently, perhaps, there's a hadith, or saying of the Prophet Muhammad: Do not scatter bees in wartime. Medieval Europeans would pitch an angry hive off the castle ramparts into the thick of advancing troops. More recently, during the Vietnam War, guerrillas booby-trapped the roads so passing American soldiers would disturb a beehive and unleash a buzzing, stinging fury. "Clever," Andrew says.

He talks about his own confrontations with clouds of buzzing bees on the occasions when he's been called to a swarm. During a swarm, half the bees in a healthy hive fortify themselves with honey and fly off in a group with the queen in search of a new home. It is a perfectly normal method of hive reproduction, and not particularly dangerous—swarming bees are actually at their most docile, as they're just looking for a safe place to stay and don't yet have a nest to protect.

The trouble is that while swarming bees wait for their scouts to come back and reach consensus on the most advantageous bit of real estate, they will hover in a cluster for hours or even days. They want ideally to be in a tree branch about thirty feet high—but in a city, they will settle for anything roughly that height. Tens of thousands of bees might attach to a traffic light and one another, creating a dangling accretion of insects. Once Andrew flagged down a Heineken truck and paid the driver fifty dollars to let him clamber onto the truck's roof to reach bees. Store owners and street-corner observers emerged to offer the kind of advice they would give to someone parallel parking. "You gotta get higher!" "You gotta grab the bees with a plastic bag!"

Hot and tired, Andrew quotes from honey-related texts while navigating traffic. The bees have abandoned the back of the truck, so it is no longer identifiable as a honeymobile. The girls are quiet. The sheen of the day has worn off, but Andrew's still going.

"Who says the only reason for bees to exist is for me to eat honey?" Andrew asks. "Winnie-the-Pooh," he answers himself, "the bear has no pants, I'm telling you. 'Where the bee sucks, there suck I'?—*The Tempest*."

He could happily continue, but at Tenth Street, a woman wanders into the crosswalk in front of the truck.

"Hey, sweetheart, I have a green light and you have a red light—are you fucking color blind?" Andrew yells out the window.

"Yes, I am!" the woman calls back.

He scowls.

· · ·

BAFFLEMENT is part of tending bees. Often you don't know something is wrong until they die, and when they die it can be hard to figure out why.

When David Selig found his red-light bees producing scarlet honey, he was concerned enough to call Andrew. "Interesting," Andrew said. He'd never heard of anything like it.

So David consulted other hobbyist beekeepers in his Red Hook neighborhood of Brooklyn to find out if they had similar experiences. He was surprised to learn that every single one of them had recently found bees flying back to the hive aglow. And like his, their honey was a sickly, shiny red. At least a dozen hives in Red Hook and nearby Governors Island were affected. "I was dejected," Yeshwant Chitalkar, a first-time beekeeper, later told a reporter. "The bees looked like vampires."

Were the bees ill? Were their hives infested? Or—and this seemed most likely, given that you could see the red stuff through the transparent membrane of their honey stomachs as they flew back to the hive—had they imbibed something other than nectar? David knew his bees could be voracious. Once, he left a single frame of honey in his car, without noticing that the window was open. On his return, "I realized that the car was filled with bees. They were darting at me," he said. "I opened the trunk. It was like it exhaled bees. They were really just dive-bombing at me to get me away. So I drove around with my beekeeping hood and gloves for a few minutes, just to get them out of the car."

David had chosen to move to the Red Hook neighborhood of Brooklyn a few years prior because it was a forgotten peninsula, a rare New York City neighborhood where he could own a two-story redbrick row house with a rooftop view of water within a hundred feet in three directions. Here, the air smells cleaner, the temperatures are moderate, and the dead-end waterfront streets give the sense of a sleepy village. Once Red Hook had been the mouth of the great port city, and then it became one of the most industrialized areas of a working industrial city. The thick concrete ribbon of the Brooklyn-Queens Expressway and a giant block of public housing projects had functioned as a preservative, dividing the neighborhood from developments in mainland Brooklyn and freezing it in time. The offspring of generations of stevedores remain on the strip closest to the water, joined by arty newcomers like David and Cecilia.

Such a land contains myriad red nectars that could fool bees with flowerlike sweetness. Was the bees' sweet source a tree resin, or perhaps sumac? David found that mentioned in a nineteenth-century beekeepers' manual on Google Books. Dyed sugar syrup from a hummingbird feeder? Maybe even antifreeze from the school bus yard up the street? Ethylene glycol is sweet and often dyed. But as soon as it occurred to him, David knew this must be the answer: the maraschino cherry factory on Dikeman Street.

The unnaturally red honey in the Red Hook hives didn't taste like cherries, but neither do maraschino cherries, really, and the honey did taste supersweet.

To be positive, a slight, pale young beekeeper named Tim O'Neal sent a sample of the red substance in the hives to the state apiculturalist for testing. He also went to the monthly meeting of the New York City Beekeepers Association to find out if others had the same problem.

The meeting takes place in an upstairs room at the Seafarers & International House on Fifteenth Street in Manhattan. Afterward, Andrew Coté, the head of the association, fields a bedlam of queries. A girl selling T-shirts for the association asks Andrew for change, and he pulls out a billfold of hundred-dollar bills held together by a rubber band. Two Albanian men in suits introduce themselves as beekeepers recently relocated to Staten Island who want to become members. "We got to registrate, or what we got to do?" And then there's Tim. "So about the red syrup I collected," he begins. "I'm worried. But what I wanted to ask—if you hear of anyone else who has this red honey—"

"Okay, okay." Andrew nods dismissively.

While waiting for test results, David Selig does some legwork of his own. The maraschino cherry factory is a block and a half from his place, and when he walks by, he can see workers wearing long-sleeved hoodies with the hoods on, despite the heat, and swatting at the bees around their heads as they hose down big plastic cherry syrup vessels. Just as David has a red honey problem, it seems the cherry factory has a bee problem.

And then the results of tests on the sample come back from the state lab: The honey contained Red Dye No. 40, a defining ingredient in maraschino cherries.

HONEY is seen as something pure and natural, but bees are foragers whose guiding principle is: the sweeter the better. One beekeeper in Long Island who lived next to a candy factory saw his bees make their hive a rainbow of high-fructose corn syrup in red, blue, and green. According to apiarist lore, another beekeeper who lived near a chewing gum factory in Syracuse found that his bees produced a lovely, delicate spearmint- and winter mint– flavored honey—which he sold as mint flower honey until he realized its origin.

Rural beekeepers across the country say they have seen their charges sip from a leaking valve at a sugar refinery, or feast on liquid used to make cotton candy, or drink from melted snow cones, or suck up Coca-Cola for deposit in the honeycomb. Instead of pollen, bees have been known to gather fine yellow wood shavings from lumberyards, cornmeal from animal feed, and grain dust from mills. Yet most foreign substances, salubrious or not, do not have a telltale neon color to flag them in the hive. Who will be the wiser if they simply blend with the honey?

It turns out that New York City bees have long caused problems for sweets manufacturers. In 1905, a beekeeping supply store was keeping twenty-eight hives on its roof on Vesey Street in Manhattan, near two big candy factories. The bees flew into the boiling room of one of the factories through windows kept open "on account of the great heat within," wrote the *New York Times*. They sucked up what sustaining sugary liquids they could find, stinging workers who stood in the way, as well as a Board of Health inspector conducting too assiduous an investigation. The *Times* reported that the factory owner had "lost a lot of sleep lately figuring up how much sugar he has been robbed of to keep a colony of 3,000,000 bees."

Bees at City College in 1911 produced honey as green as pistachio ice cream. "Who outside of a nature-faker's book ever heard of green honey?" asked the president of the college, John Huston Finley. For a time, he suspected the bees of robbing chemicals from a biology laboratory, but then identified their more likely source as a candy kitchen on Amsterdam Avenue. Finley hatched a complicated scheme to get to the bottom of the matter: He would brand each bee in the college hive with red marks on its breast and its belly, and have his students, along with boys from the nearby Hebrew Orphan Asylum and girls from the neigh-boring Convent of the Sacred Heart, track the bees and race to the biology department to report each sighting. What could go wrong? The results of the survey are lost to history, and no one seems to have extended the inquiry to the cooks of the candy kitchen, who might have noticed bees in their recipes.

Still, at that time, people valued city honey. In an era with little regulation and much concern about doctored foods, people feared that distant rural beekeepers might stretch the honey by adding glucose and yellow coloring. Eaters of city-made honey, on the other hand, could "see it taken from the combs and go home satisfied that they are getting the genuine bees' product," wrote the *New-York Tribune* in 1900. Besides, beekeeping was the kind of homely project that could be as useful for city-dwellers as any-one else. Orphanages around town harvested their own honey to make cheap sweets for the children. As late as the 1950s, hospitals and private medical practices in Manhattan sometimes kept hives on the roof to use bee stings for arthritis therapy, until cortisone was discovered.

Yet 1920s Manhattan, filled with early, exhaust-spewing cars and coal-fueled engines, began to present particular hazards for bees. The manager of a beekeeping supply store on Chambers Street set up a hive in the store's window, but his bees produced a muddy honey from the city's sooty flowers. Decades later, the secretary of the City's Department of Air Pollution Control asked the same man to set up hives once again, in order to prove levels of soot had diminished. But the apiaries gradually disappeared as the city got fuller and dirtier, leaving few beekeepers to protest when eventually their practice was banned.

. . .

IN 1999, the administration of Mayor Rudy Giuliani added honeybees to a list of over one hundred wild animals, including hyenas, pit vipers, and dingoes, considered too dangerous for urban life. Article 161 of the health code thereafter prohibited the "possession, keeping, harboring and selling" of bees. It's not clear why the City suddenly outlawed honeybees after a long history in which the insects and their keepers had not been mentioned in the rules and were bound only by state regulations. It could have been part of the mayor's crackdown on all things people fear. When people think of bees they don't envision the gentle forager collecting nectar for her sisters, but an angry swarm buzzing after a frantic victim who jumps into a pond.

The outlaw status of the urban hive helped impart commercial cachet. A man named David Graves was the first to realize he could charge more money at the farmers' market for his clandestine urban honey. Tending hives throughout the city was a logistical challenge, so David took on a helpful apprentice, a New York City taxi driver from Haiti who agreed to drive him around in exchange for training. By the time Andrew Coté came into the business, David had established the rules of underground pro urban beekeeping: Never reveal the location of a city hive. Supplement your sales of the rare urban honey with quantity from hundreds of hives in the suburban and rural outskirts of town. Charge more for honey from the city.

Some risk was involved, as the City continued to issue fines. In 2009, officials carried out fifty-three inspections in response to calls related to harboring bees and wasps, and issued thirteen notices of violation and fines of two hundred to two thousand dollars.

A New York nonprofit called Just Food, which helps city people produce and access fresh food, organized to reverse the ban. Minneapolis, Denver, and Helena, Montana, were legalizing bee-keeping: Why not New York? Soon hundreds of people dressed as bees were dancing at a fund-raising Beekeepers' Ball. Restaurants and bars added to their menus special cocktails, desserts, and en-trées using local honey. People rallied on the steps of City Hall carrying signs that read "BEE FABULOUS!" and "THERE IS NO EXISTENCE WITHOUT BEEing."

Andrew, for his part, had doubts. He worried that in a tightly packed city such as New York, clueless amateurs—"yahoo cowboy and cowgirl beekeepers"—could create serious problems and give all of beekeeping a bad name. Yet as talks progressed, Andrew and other beekeeping advocates sat in on several closed meetings in drab downtown buildings with Department of Health person-nel. Together, they hammered out the details: Should the number of hives on a block be restricted? What sort of training should be available for beekeepers? Would registration be required?

In a dim, wood-paneled city hearing room in February 2010, gardeners, arborists, community activists, and beekeepers, includ-ing Andrew, testified in favor of lifting the ban. No one spoke in opposition. One speaker gave worldwide examples of beekeeping cities—membership is spiking in the London Beekeeping Asso-ciation; in Paris, there is a *rucher école,* or hive school, in the Lux-embourg Gardens, and hives atop both the Opéra Bastille and the Palais Garnier; the White House that year produced a bum-per crop of honey. "Well-tended colonies of pollinators can bring back devastated areas," said Andrew after the hearing, dressed in a brown blazer and yellow, honey-colored tie. "There are two hundred and fifty types of bees in New York City. I don't see why it would be so wrong to allow this one type here."

What Andrew likes to call "the Bitter Ages" ended on March 16, 2010, when the Department of Health repealed the ban.

ANDREW Coté high-jumps up onto the back of the truck bed—no hands. He tosses out five-gallon plastic buckets of pollen and propolis and crates of honey jars. He unloads and reforms a geometry of boxes and fold-out tables and signs that eventually make up his stand at the farmers' market, where he sells the products of his city-bred bees. It's seven a.m. and he's in a good mood; events of the day have not yet annoyed him.

"Your honey right here!" he likes to offer, agilely thrusting a plastic sample spoon toward every person—truth be told, every woman—walking by, a spoon dribbling a thick, sweet yellow that she is forced to catch with her tongue.

"Are you whipped honey?" Andrew will ask a blonde, who turns, initially suspicious, to his sparkling eyes, devilish grin, and sweet offering. She will slowly smile. "You will love it—you will *fall in love*," he says, holding her eyes as she puts the spoon in her mouth.

"It's a polarizing honey," Andrew will say, presenting buckwheat honey to a woman in a ruffled black skirt. "Some people don't like it. Wars have been fought and won, fortunes made and squandered, over buckwheat."

A woman with long black hair wearing frilly peach-colored shorts will approach the table. Where's she from? Andrew will ask. Singapore, she will say.

"You speak Mandarin?" Andrew will ask. "*Fong mi*." He knows the word for "honey" in dozens of languages.

Giggles and honey-buying ensue.

The pollen has to be scooped from a bucket into bottles for sale as an energy booster. Bees collect the high-protein pollen—a coarse powder on the stamen in the center of a flower that contains the plant's sperm cells—on their legs to feed their young. When they fly from flower to flower, they inadvertently drop bits of it at each stop, fertilizing some of the plants. Back at the hive, Andrew steals it from his bees with a trap that scrapes pollen off their legs. It's a grainy golden color, each bit of it a different hue, the texture of pet food pellets. It smells faintly of honey but not as sweet. And it smells of something else, deeper and more pungent, the sex of the flower.

The propolis, too, must be transferred to bottles, for sale as an antifungal and antibacterial. Almost crystallized, the color of flames, propolis is a mixture of saps and resins that bees collect from plants and use to seal up their hive—or even to seal up foreign objects that might putrefy in the hive, such as the carcass of a mouse that expires in their midst.

Andrew has everything he needs, down to a spray bottle of water to clean up honey spills. There's the honey—rural and suburban wildflower, blueberry, buckwheat, linden, whipped, whipped with cinnamon, and New York City honeys sold by the borough where they were harvested. Squares of honeycomb are kept in little clear plastic boxes in a cooler to preserve the wax, so when you bite into it, it's cold and light, and chewing releases bubbles of honey. Andrew lays down a blue line of painter's tape on the wood table to make a clean surface on which to set sample honey spoons. He puts out a macabre jar of hundreds of dead bees—Ukrainians buy them to make medicine, he says, though these already look gummy, like decay. He unloads a cash register tray stocked only with two-dollar bills—he likes two-dollar bills. He pulls out a tin smoker for effect, and props up a Winnie-the-Pooh stuffed bear. It's showtime. A good day at the farmers' market can easily bring in a thousand dollars in cash.

"Can I answer any honey-related questions?" Andrew asks of a twenty-something woman with a wave of dark hair who is frowning at his display.

She asks what you can do with beeswax and Andrew responds in a single breath: "Chew it like gum cut it up and put it on a cheese platter bake it with salmon serve it with any kind of ice cream."

As she gets out her wallet, Andrew says, "I'll give you a two-dollar bill for change because you're special."

She laughs. He smiles.

"I told her she's special," he says grimly, as she leaves.

"Personally, I'm a huge fan of the New York City rooftop medley," Andrew will tell people who ask his advice on what to buy. "We have such a bouquet—a plethora of nectar." But once at a honey tasting, Andrew confessed, "I don't have such a refined palate for honey. I enjoy them all, but I can't really tell them apart."

Soon comes a woman in her fifties with black-rimmed glasses, a streak of white in her black hair, and one of those raspy, seen-everything New York voices.

She says she wants a big container of honey, pointing to the sixteen-ounce bottle, but she doesn't want to carry it around all day. Andrew suggests the even larger thirty-two-ounce bottle.

"Does it spoil?" the woman asks, peering up anxiously at Andrew.

"Like a mother's love . . ." he begins.

"Eternal," she finishes, blinking her eyes and looking moved, as though she could be thinking of her own deep connection with her children. She promises to come back for the thirty-two-ouncer. "It's really eternal," she says again as she walks away.

"Different pitches for different demographics," Andrew says.

WHEN the ban was lifted just before bee season, Andrew had to teach his basic beekeeping class three times over to meet demand. Honey lust consumed the unlikeliest people. Rania Abu-Eid, a lingerie designer at Victoria's Secret, expected her honey to be light and yellow. "I fantasized about it, and said, 'Oh, it'll be like sunshine, that'll be just like me,'" she says. "But it actually came out all dark and complex, which is actually more like me." Maxine Friedman, a fifty-eight-year-old electrical estimator in sensible lace-up shoes, does not come across as one taken with flights of fancy, but she ordered bees on a whim. "I thought it was a good idea, but when I saw the live insects, I thought, '*Holy shit.*'" Vivian Wang, a lawyer, installed three hives on the roof of her twelve-story office building and hung a beekeeping jacket with an attached hood and veil on the inside of her office door. "What case are you billing to?" her boss would joke, as she trooped up the stairs to the roof in her beekeeping suit.

The principal of the elite York Preparatory School on the Upper West Side was inspired by Sherlock Holmes, who retired from solving crimes to keep bees. Five hives were on the roof within a week, and the school suited up, purchasing thirty beekeepers' outfits with different-size hoods to be small enough for sixth-graders and big enough for seniors. The school custodian, who once kept bees in his native Dominican Republic, watered the bees on weekends. When a twelve-year-old got stung on the ankle, the principal knelt and peeled back the boy's sock to remove a stinger caught in the thick white cotton. "I've only been stung once," said the student, explaining away his tears. "I'm not completely used to it yet."

Some beekeepers talked about the sacredness of honey across cultures. Roger Repohl is a longtime beekeeper who lives in the rectory of St. Augustine's Church in the Bronx, with old china, a cherrywood armoire, and an aging pastor and nuns. Roger, who has almost lashless eyes and parchment-like pale skin, gives talks at the Cloisters on medieval beekeeping. He appreciates the medieval English folk tradition of "telling the bees" about important events, like a death, birth, or marriage, so the bees don't get affronted and stop producing honey. Once, he found a child's leather jacket and a child's pair of shoes draped over the beehive he keeps in a community garden in the rectory's backyard. "Maybe the child is sick or something and they want to tell the bees," says Roger. He left the items there for a while, in case the owners came back to retrieve them—but eventually he picked them up off the hive and gave them to Sister Dorothy to dispense to the needy.

Now Roger shows new beekeepers how to extract honey in the rectory's dark, dank basement licked by flickering fluorescent light. He uses a metal comb to break the wax caps of the honeycomb, like popping bubble wrap. He places the thick white wax sheets in a centrifuge machine that looks like a big metal pot on stilts with a handle and an internal rack for three beeswax frames. He stirs his arm in a circle, faster, faster, until the whirring has its own momentum and he can barely keep up with the motion he began. A dark liquid whips onto the inside of the canister in iridescent streaks and pools in the bottom as the warm scent of honey rises in the room, giving the sense of sunshine bursting underground. Roger ties a ladies' stocking around the spigot at the bottom of the centrifuge to filter out debris as the honey pours into a white bucket below. And as the stocking fills, it takes the shape it was sewn to take—the shape of a foot—dribbling honey.

When his bees swarmed, Roger thought it a beautiful sight, thousands of them flying off in a cloud. "I think that 'beekeeping' is something of a misnomer," he says. "You can't keep the bees. If they want to go, they're going to go."

More swarms appeared in the city as more amateurs kept bees. One attached to a tree outside a discount clothing store in the Bed-Stuy neighborhood of Brooklyn. Wearing a T-shirt and no special protection, Andrew stood in his truck bed, at eye level with a quivering-multiorganism two-foot cone of bees dangling body-to-body. Yellow POLICE LINE—DO NOT CROSS tape attached to nearby trees cordoned off Andrew's entire vehicle. Calm, silent, before a gathering crowd and the crackle of police radios, he worked methodically with two other beekeepers to spray the insects with sticky sugar water to impede their movement, to the bewilderment of onlookers—"It's poison!" some of them yelled. Then he donned a protective hood, lifted a plastic garbage bin toward the bees, and shook the branch into the dark receptacle.

"Oh, shit, son," said one man, as thousands of bees dropped into the bin and hewed to the sides of the plastic, coating it with their bodies, making a lining of living bees. And then, with the application of a lid, the bee problem was gone.

"Damn!" said the observer. "They G's at this, man, they know what they doing."

As a siren shrieked from a departing squad car, Andrew shook the hand of the lead police officer and drove away, tens of thousands of bees the richer.

Andrew was not the only one on call to corral vagabonds. Anthony "Tony Bees" Planakis, an experienced beekeeper who happens to work for the Building and Maintenance section of the New York Police Department, was often summoned to the scene. When he worked with Andrew, Anthony contributed rigging skills learned in the army, NYPD vans with bucket trucks, and Fire Department tower ladders. Jim Fischer, who runs a separate, rival beekeeping Meetup group in the city, also responded to swarm calls.

Once, a tropical storm ripped off a hollowed-out branch of an enormous tree in Fort Greene, Brooklyn, exposing a honeybee hive. Appeals went out to beekeepers to save tens of thousands of bees. Jim and Andrew arrived with different tactics. Andrew took the aggressive approach, securing the police van and crane. Jim told the *New York Times* that he tried to abort the operation— which involved hoisting a beekeeper holding a chain saw thirty feet into the air—because high winds after the storm made it unsafe. He left when his advice was not heeded. "There was a lot more testosterone floating around than common sense," he said. Andrew stayed on to supervise. "I was happy to be a bystander if someone else could handle the situation," he told the *Times*. "I only moved ahead with my methods when no one else could manage the job."

Despite such turf battles, beekeepers have fostered community. Calling each other "beeks" for short, they greet each other saying, "How are you? How are your bees?" After the ban was lifted, they began to gather together at candlelit honey tastings in Brooklyn bars, or to extract honey en masse as a social event. They played Jeoparbee, featuring a host wearing a bee-print tie, and a Vanna White–style Queen Bee, in a Statue of Liberty crown, a black balaclava, and a yellow short-sleeved hoodie with black duct tape stripes, holding a honey dripper as a wand.

Monthly meetings of the New York City Beekeepers Association started routinely drawing more than a hundred people to listen to lectures about beekeeping around the world: In Yemen, a CIA report accused two honey companies of laundering money to Al Qaeda, and beekeeping is so associated with insurgency that if you're a honey seller, people assume you've probably served with the mujahideen in Afghanistan. In Borneo, people climb a tree and cut the hive to squeeze the honey out and then strain it with cloth. In Russia, the Mafia may well control the honey market.

They also discussed colony collapse disorder, in which worker bees disappear, though the queen, and often young bees, remain alive in the hive. Beekeepers in other parts of the country have reported losing almost all of their bees. Colonies can be expanded by dividing existing hives and breeding new queens—but it's expensive, and the gains barely hold against the losses. The problem mainly seems to affect commercial beekeepers, who move their hives from crop to crop in eighteen-wheelers, exposing bees to new pesticides across whole regions.

The new energy for beekeeping has focused media attention on Andrew. Early in the summer of 2010, producers for a reality TV show start to follow him with cameras. They watch him catch a swarm, lower a beehive from a roof, and conduct routine hive inspections. For one episode, the producers hire an actress to play a distressed woman with bees in her wall on a rented set in a car garage, and Andrew acts out coming to the rescue, four handheld digicams following his every move.

The *New York Times*, *Time* magazine, *Bon Appétit*, NBC, ABC, PBS, CBS, CNN, the BBC, WNYC, and Japanese, Korean, Swedish, and Australian television, among many others, have all featured Andrew. He basks in the attention but brooks little patience for journalists' dullness. "This is so unique," says a reporter for the NY1 news channel while interviewing him about rooftop hives. "It's either unique or it's not unique, but it's not *so* unique," Andrew retorts. "It's a very *sweet* reward," Andrew supplies a minute later, facing the camera and offering his sparkling grin. "Uh, literally sweet," says the reporter, smiling nervously as she repeats his double entendre. Andrew rolls his eyes.

He has other opportunities to court celebrity. Andrew appears on *The Martha Stewart Show* in an episode that also features the chef Mario Batali. Soon Andrew is talking about the role of the queen in the hive. "She mates only once in her life with fifteen to twenty drones in one, some would call it *shameful*, afternoon," he says, eyeing the camera and fighting a smile.

"They don't know how hard it is for us gals," Martha says, joshing in that prim way of hers. "We have to put up with fifteen drones, my God."

"Actually, it's not such a picnic for the drone," says Andrew, "because he dies in a spectacular way. . . . After he does his thing, his *thing* is barbed, and it remains with the queen, and he falls— presumably with mixed emotions—dead to the ground."

There's a second's pause before Martha retorts: "He doesn't have any feeling."

"I'm sure it meant something to him," says Andrew.

Martha scratches her nose and changes the topic: "So, eating local honey, by the way, tell us about that."

That same fall, Sotheby's opens its spare, minimalist halls to a charity auction of local vegetables, and also of Andrew—who promises to give the winning bidder a guided rooftop hive tour. In a well-lit gallery, among paintings by Julian Schnabel and Kenny Scharf, Andrew, whose salt-and-pepper hair was trimmed that morning, makes the rounds, carrying a whiskey spiked with scotch. "I'm Lot Number One," Andrew says by way of introduction to the perfumed and bejeweled tuxedoes and gowns. "I promise I'll bid for you," says a blond woman in a sleek black dress, sidling up to him. After the auctioneer introduces Andrew as "hot-tempered and bloody-minded," the blond woman starts the bidding at $500, but another woman counters. They keep topping each other as the price climbs to $700, $800, $1,000, $1,200. Finally, the auctioneer double-sells Andrew to both of them, raising $2,400, and assuring Andrew he can deliver his tour to the two bidders at once. Twenty-four hundred dollars. In a lucrative season, it is Andrew's highest hourly rate yet.

IN the offices of Arthur Mondella, the owner of Dell's Maraschino Cherries Company, cherry jars adorn every desk, fat globes of fruit floating in syrup in alarming shades of jade and Play-Skool hues of blue and orange. But mostly they're red, that shrieking, tropical sunset red that tops Manhattans and old-fashioned Cherry Cokes. Red Dye No. 40 is key to the recipe, along with vats of intensely sweet high-fructose corn syrup—Mondella goes through eight million pounds of the stuff a year.

There were always bees, said Mondella, probably since his

father and grandfather founded the business in 1948. In the past, he said, small numbers of them would show up to sip some cherry juice in the fall, when few flowers bloom with nectar. Mondella would throw shrink-wrap over the cherry bins as they moved outside among the five factory buildings, and the insects would disappear.

But this year, the bees came in the middle of the summer and didn't go away. They would crawl under the edges of the wrap, or go for tiny drops of syrup on the plastic. Mondella won't talk about whether any perished in his syrup—but bees are not swimmers. And Mondella complains that he had to throw away whole vats of cherries. To add insult to injury, he got stung. "I was outside, and we were getting swarms, hundreds of bees," said Mondella. "Well, it's not like Alfred Hitchcock's *The Birds*. But you'd see a bee. And then there'd be two. And then there'd be three. And then a dozen."

Soon Mondella learned that new local beekeepers were harvesting red honey. "When a beekeeper opens a bee factory next door, what can you do?" Mondella asked. Fearing that a few big shipments of insect-contaminated cherries could spell the end of his $20 million business, he contacted the Health Department and received only an unhelpful letter. "Talk about aggravating!" He met with officials at the Brooklyn Borough President's Office, then called a contact in a South Brooklyn business development network, who wrote to Andrew Coté: "The factory is at the end of its rope, losing money, and is looking for a solution short of becoming litigious." A few days later, Andrew showed up to troubleshoot with Mondella and Steven Leffler, the company vice president.

Nobody around Dell's cherry factory is unsympathetic to bees in general. Bees are necessary to pollinate cherries, after all. "If you have no bees, you have no pollination, you have no vegetables, you have no wheat, we have no trees, we have no flowers, and we have no world, okay?" says Leffler. The question is, what will make them stop slurping cherry syrup?

Bees are more likely to collect artificial substances when they can't find the blossoms they depend on, even for a short week or two before the next flowers of the season come into bloom. Could it be that during that particularly scorching July, their natural source of nectar burned out, and they discovered a taste for high-fructose corn syrup that they could not shake? Could it be that after beekeeping was legalized and various new parties took it up, there were too many new bees in a neighborhood with too little forage? Or were Dell's cherries simply too lusciously sweet to pass up?

Andrew suggests building screens and covering the cherry bins in sheets soaked in water and vinegar—bees hate vinegar.

Mondella particularly likes his own idea of selling the beekeepers feeders of high-fructose corn syrup to set up back at the hives so the bees don't even venture out toward the factory. "I can sell them as much cherry juice as they want. I'll give it to them at cost," says Mondella.

"They wouldn't want it," interjects Leffler, guessing the beekeepers won't approve of corn syrup. "They want natural."

Okay, then how about planting more nectar flowers, Mondella suggests.

A possibility, muses Leffler. "You have to have vegetation for these bees to feed on," Leffler says. If you have no flowers for the bees to work, all you get is trouble, he says. "It's like people who don't work. You have fifty people standing on the corner, hanging out, what's going to happen?" he asks, looking around the room. "Trouble," he answers.

Over a couple weeks, Mondella paid Andrew $250 an hour to examine the Red Hook factory and create a plan to deter bees, as well as to meet with beekeepers, prepare press releases, and field calls from reporters. Andrew was concerned that if the problem was not carefully managed, beekeeping would get a bad name and the ban would be reinstated. The factory had been there for more than sixty years and employed thirty people; the beekeepers were the newcomers. Andrew met the Red Hook beekeepers in a café to hash through solutions. He encouraged them to rein in their charges.

To calculate the ideal number of hives for the neighborhood, you would need to know the number of plants flowering throughout the season, their nectar-producing capacities, when they bloom, the variation in blooms, the weather, the soil sweetness and composition, the numbers and kinds of honeybees, as well as the numbers and kinds of wild bees . . . Impossible. Still, fewer bees could only help, Andrew reasoned, and he urged the beekeepers to reduce their hives by half, which they agreed to do.

The next summer, there would be fewer bees at the cherry factory, and Red Hook's honey would be more gold than red.

TRUTH is, we live in a world of easy sugar. You can swelter and sweat tending bees in a head-to-toe heavy cotton-polyester blend, a mask on your face, a hat slipping off your head, yellow netting and smoke in your eyes, even as you hear, tinkling at close range, the melody of the Mister Softee truck peddling swirls of refined and processed cane juice and high-fructose corn syrup. You can fight to extract sweetness from thousands of insects in a wooden box, in sight of a bodega where you can get Mr. Goodbar and Milk Duds, Swedish Fish, Sour Patch Kids, Coke, Minute Maid and Snapple, Pepperidge Farm cookies, and Betty Crocker cake and brownie mix. It's hard to imagine a time when honey was the only sweet going. When people would go to extraordinary lengths to extract it from natural beehives because they craved that sensation on the tongue.

These days, it seems bees can show us the mystery of urban living: We are so tightly packed, yet we often don't understand how much of an impact we have on one another. We often don't know what is down the street or upstairs from us. Some of the Red Hook beekeepers who worried about the bright red substance in their bees and in their hives lived or worked right around the corner from the cherry factory, but didn't even know it was there. The bees knew.

What else do they know that we have not been able to figure out? Bees find all kinds of things. They can be trained to identify environmental hazards, and have been used to sniff out radio-active materials, explosives, cocaine, and various pollutants, and also to detect land mines. Colony collapse disorder itself may be the symptom of an environmental imbalance we don't want to ac-knowledge but that the bees can't help but confront. "Beekeepers are knowledgeable through their bees," says David Selig.

But Andrew Coté doesn't think much about that. He looks forward to the next summer, when his bees will do what bees do, and fly out of the hive every morning in search of nectar from a flower. They will zoom past hot tar and stinking asphalt and, he hopes, resist the sweet temptations of spilled Cokes, splatted ice creams, spoiled milk shakes. All over the city, his bees will find the growing things, the blossoming things, the places where sweet, wet nectar awaits their collection drive. And Andrew, in turn, will collect, and sell, and profit.

VEGETABLES

THE TOMATOES ARE SMALL, hard baubles dangling off the vine: pale, early, orange veined with green. The corn grows six, seven feet tall, with leaves that rake your skin when you squeeze past. There are slender, fuzzy okra plants, two kinds of leafy, spreading collards, and puffy, purpled eggplants. It's ten o'clock in Harlem on a Saturday night in June. A steady hip-hop beat thumps from a BMW parked outside the garden gate. Inside the garden, moving from the Miracle-Gro tubs to the plant beds to the toolshed and back, with a slight limp and a single-minded deftness, Willie Morgan slips bright young collard plants into the soil.

"You can't plant in the middle of the day," he says. "It'll wither."

Willie first began growing a fruit and vegetable garden as a front for his gambling operation. That was back in 1969, when he ran an illegal numbers joint in a storefront on 118th Street between Fifth and Madison, and the long stalks of corn and curling vines of tomatoes seemed like good cover. He was lithe, with an easy smile and snappy clothes: custom-made suede pants and cashmere coats he also sold at a separate boutique. Back then, almost every block of Harlem had a numbers spot where people played the illicit local lottery. An enterprising numbers man—controller was the job title—had to devise ways to appear generous to the customers and legitimate to the cops. Vegetables, Willie thought, could be the answer. He went to the city's Department of Consumer Affairs and got a license to operate a greengrocer. He bought a scale and set up tables in his storefront to look just like a vegetable stand where he could give out free produce as a bonus to customers. Trouble was, he didn't have any vegetables. Then he came upon the idea of growing his own.

Forty years later, Willie has a slightly shy, slightly sly smile, warm eyes the same brown as his skin, a good-natured affability, and a black suede applejack cap. He will remember your phone number and birthday the first time you tell him—which makes sense, given his career memorizing bets to avoid a paper trail. Then, as now, his business depends on customer relations. In his current community garden on city-owned land, he's always glancing toward the gate and jumping up to meet someone calling, "Willie! I want some eggplants! I want 'em soft!" "Your corn tastes like sugar. You got some to sell to me?" "You got any herbs for carpal tunnel or for pain?"

Over four decades, Willie has refined his agricultural techniques in skinny, shady strips of land between tenements all over Harlem. He rotates his crops with a professional's precision to take advantage of every inch of soil and every minute of sun. "I'm on my third crop of turnips!" he says one day when I visit. In the southwest corner of his current 28-by-76-foot lot, as the growing season progresses, turnips follow turnips follow turnips. In the northeast corner, after the corn, collards. Because tomatoes are his best seller, he starts in at the beginning of the season, planting Early Girls in the southwest patch as the first of a succession of tomato varieties that will produce a steady crop all summer long. His soil yields zucchinis, cabbages and carrots, spicy and sweet peppers, stevia and basil, parsley, mint, and sage. He sells his produce to neighbors for cheap, because seeds and soil cost little and he doesn't need to worry about marketing, storage, refrigeration, or transportation. "Fresh okra is two ninety-nine a pound in the store," he says, raising his eyebrows at the scandal of it. "I sell it for one fifty," he assures, and even at this discount, the farm earns him a nice supplement to his Social Security check.

Willie's mind's eye holds maps of Harlem's past, and he likes to recount the landscape of a healthy economy of vice. Walking down 120th Street past graceful brownstones, he points out his own very first numbers joint, which thrived at Number 317, where he paid a lady to let him work out of her living room. Another numbers spot operated at 304, and the Bolivar and Tulsa bars on the corner gave Willie a place to step in for a vodka cognac or vodka with orange juice. In those early days, he said, most people he knew were still working some kind of a job, and there was plenty of money to be had feeding people's proclivities for risk and reward.

He would go out in the evenings, either to the club or the garden, to meet friends, take bets, and maybe put a trowel in the earth, and by day, he would give away almost all that he harvested. While his customers got addicted to betting, Willie got hooked on the seeds and the soil.

He would dust the earth with lime to "sweeten" it—though New York's rubbled dirt already had high pH, unlike the red, acid Georgia earth he knew in childhood. Eager to offer something special and rare, he would seek out hard-to-find seeds not listed in the catalogs, such as red okra, violet potatoes, purple string beans, and collards with dark, bluish crumpled leaves—"I always want to give people something they couldn't buy in the store," he notes. Friends of friends would send their favorites from their gardens and little local seed shops in Georgia and the Carolinas. He would fertilize with horse manure, when he could get it from the NYPD stables. He would build himself a spot of southern farmland in the teeming city.

Never a simple farmer, Willie was more of an agronomist-about-town. He would strut the streets dressed in a suede jacket and pants, fondly showing off "rhinestones, shiny stuff, anything flashy." He hit the numbers big in 1974 and opened Bodacious Unlimited, where he sold custom-designed clothing manufactured under the supervision of his seamstress mother. He has photos of himself drinking with Harlem aristocrats including the legendary boxing promoter Don King, also a one-time numbers man—"Sugar, he's the biggest promoter there is!"—and the musician Count Basie, celebrating at an after-fight party for Muhammad Ali.

Since those days many have followed Willie's path. Now it seems as though someone is angling to farm most every flat, open surface in the city. Beyond New York, across the country, new businesses will plant your yard for free and share the harvest, or home-deliver hoes and seeds and help you use them, or build a boxed farm fitted to your fire escape, or engineer your roof to bear heavy crops. Seed stores are sold out. Community gardens have wait lists a hundred names long. Despite this sudden interest, urban farming is no passing fancy; its history is as old as the consolidated New York City.

As late as 1880, Brooklyn and Queens were the two biggest vegetable-producing counties in the entire country. "The finest farmlands in America," one observer wrote, "in full view of the Atlantic Ocean." Outer-borough farmers trundled their peppers and corn and apples to the Manhattan market by boat and used the copious manure of city horses to fertilize their crops. Local farmers avoided cheap, durable crops such as wheat—which could be planted at a distance—and concentrated on expensive, fragile, and perishable fruits and vegetables that had to be produced near a market, setting up a model for what is harvested around cities to this day.

As New York developed and its land steadily filled with buildings, growing vegetables became a marker of crisis, during wars, recessions, and depressions. Over more than a century, land for agriculture has expanded and rolled back again and again in a dizzying reformat of the cityscape. Tens of thousands of people and thousands of lots have turned to agriculture as a way to deal with unused land and food shortages at every new nadir in the city's ragged cycle of boom and bust.

The idea of the urban garden first caught on just as local farms were disappearing, during a recession in the 1890s, when a group purchased vacant lots for the hungry to till. In 1917, as war ravaged Europe and its farmland, President Woodrow Wilson appealed to every man, woman, and child with access to ground to plant. "So far as possible," added the president of the National War Garden Commission, "all food should be grown in the immediate neighborhood of its place of ultimate use." Dutiful Manhattanites planted "all higgledy-piggledy"—in truth, their efforts were amateurish. People dumped seeds into the earth at all the wrong times, and so close together that few plants could survive.

After the stock market crash of 1929, the city got organized. Gardens were set up at sites throughout New York, each staffed by two expert gardeners issuing seeds and rigid planting schedules to men who rolled up their shirtsleeves and women who hiked up their gingham dresses. By the mid-1930s, they had planted five thousand gardens producing more than a million pounds of food.

During World War II, regular Americans all over the country grew more than 40 percent of the nation's fresh vegetables in Victory Gardens. Cabbages and corn poked out of the plaza of Rockefeller Center, bushy greens took over Manhattan backyards, and some people even commuted to other boroughs to plant and weed and harvest. The Jacob Ruppert Brewery on the Upper East Side ran advertisements urging, "Remember, 'V' stands for Vegetables . . . and for Victory."

Unknown to federal administrators, and even to many chroniclers of the times, an underground culture of gardening continued long past the various government mandates, as immigrants in skinny, humid tenements turned rusting tomato cans and wooden soap and cheese boxes into planters for tomatoes, eggplants, beans, and corn.

Vegetables sprout in the city when food prices suddenly soar, when incomes drop, and when buildings fall down and fail to be built back up, leaving behind that rarest of urban commodities: space. They grow when influxes of people come from the country, think to raise food, and know how to goad it into maturity. All of these factors converged in Willie Morgan's late 1960s Harlem. And there was also a new scourge destroying the fabric of a neighborhood, even as it created new possibilities for agriculture. Fire was sweeping Harlem and beyond, creating a city of vacant lots. In 1978, in a measure against blight, the city launched Operation GreenThumb, to make vacant lots available to gardeners. Willie signed up.

Over the years, Willie has moved from plot to plot at the whim of city administrators who decide to develop land he has cultivated but who always seem to consent to finding him a replacement. When the city founders, he gets more space for vegetables; when the city booms, he gives it up. His current garden, on 122nd Street near Eighth Avenue, is a verdant wonder in a neighborhood that has been urban-renewed, burned out, abandoned, rebuilt, and halfway redeveloped. Over decades, brownstones have been renovated; new condominiums have risen. Still, for years, the only nearby places to get provisions at night are a Popeye's Chicken, a Dunkin' Donuts, a few delis that reek of cat pee, a liquor store. And Willie's.

YOU might say that Willie's bit of Harlem has returned to its roots. For hundreds of years, Harlem was a farming village. Lenape Native Americans cultivated the fertile terrain spreading from an inlet off what is now 125th Street, near Willie Morgan's garden. Their specialty crops were squash, beans, and corn, which they sowed together so the tall corn stalks would support the growing bean vines and the low, prickly squash roots would deter predators and moisten the soil. They also ate from wild orchards of sweet apples and pears, picked strawberries, blueberries, mulberries, huckleberries, raspberries, blackberries, and cranberries, and gathered barley, chestnuts, hickory nuts, and acorns, as well as herbs such as purslane, white borage, agrimony, pennyroyal, elecampane, and sarsaparilla.

The first Dutch farmers found the land they called Nieuw Haarlem easy to farm, as it had already been cleared, but they worked with their muskets at the ready, in case of attacks from the people whose fields they had usurped. The rich, dark earth yielded more than the soil of lower Manhattan, and canoes and wagons filled with uptown vegetables, meat, butter, and tobacco helped make New Netherland self-sufficient.

As time passed, the great families of the settlement planted vegetable fields, fruit orchards, and greenhouses full of delicate crops at their uptown estates. Their names are familiar to us now mostly through street names: the Delanceys, Beekmans, Bleeckers, and Hamiltons. On the edges of their manors, squatters erected shacks from wood, twigs, and barrel staves, and raised livestock and produce to sell downtown at market. A goat grazing on a rocky outcrop became the emblematic image of Harlem. Finally, by the mid-eighteenth century, after years of hard use, farms simply refused to yield. Wealthy owners deserted their estates. In the first round of a cycle that would later repeat many times over, the city acquired many abandoned properties for resale.

By the early nineteenth century, Harlem, like all of Manhattan, was transforming. In 1808, John Randel Jr. had begun to survey the land, mapping out a grid of streets. The construction of this grid would eventually flatten the island's topographical irregularities—hills and valleys, streams and swamps, and bursts of marble and schist—turning wild and cultivated lands into even blocks suitable for dense, high development. Not everyone considered this progress. Unhappy landowners pelted Randel and his colleagues with artichokes and cabbages, sicced their dogs on him, had him arrested by the sheriff for trespassing, and sued him for damages after he pruned their trees. But as waves of immigrants from Europe continued to arrive, housing grew short, and many people saw the solution in the dense promise of the grid.

In Harlem in the mid-1800s, political bosses out to enrich

themselves purchased choice lots and then arranged for the city to build macadamized streets and install hollow-log pipes to bring in clean water from upstate reservoirs. Elm trees were planted, gaslights and sewer lines installed, and the value of the real estate increased instantly and exponentially. Land became far more valuable for its potential than for its current use; it only had to be drained, filled, divided, parceled, and auctioned. Its fecundity was forgotten as investors focused on its remarkable ability to support an undreamed density of high-end housing. By the time they were done, around the turn of the nineteenth century, block after block of modern, overpriced row houses went unrented. Speculators were foreclosed. It seemed Harlem had overdeveloped.

Soon black Realtors stepped in to fill vacant apartments with black tenants. From the earliest days of European settlement on Manhattan, people of color had kept one step ahead of trouble with whites by settling on the city's periphery, which as the city grew, moved northward: from the notorious Five Points slum, which spilled over the edges of today's Chinatown, to Little Africa, around the current Sullivan, Thompson, and MacDougal streets, to the coldwater flats of the Tenderloin in Midtown West. Racial violence flared in the hot summer of 1900, when thousands of whites rioted in the Tenderloin, using lead pipes and their fists to beat blacks, who soon after, fled for the safety of half-empty Harlem.

Black dentists and doctors, nurses and pharmacists, lawyers and hotel owners moved into grand, speculator-built brownstones made of Harlem's own underground schist, ornamented with dragons and lions and suns with tongues. Black photographers and printers, undertakers and barbers, cooks and barkeeps and dancers followed to narrow brick row houses. Rents were high—

landlords charged blacks about 50 percent more than whites for the privilege of decent housing. Those who couldn't afford whole apartments rented floor space, bathtubs, coal bins, and basements. Some even "hot bedded," sharing a single mattress with a stranger who worked opposite hours and left the sheets still warm. The institutions followed the people to Harlem—the churches, the Odd Fellows, Masons, Pythians, Elks, the Music School Settlement, the *New York Age* newspaper, the White Rose Working Girls' Home, Banks's Club, a raunchy honky-tonk place, Barron's Little Savoy, where Jelly Roll Morton performed, the Douglass Club, with its one-legged pianist—as though the fabric of a whole neighborhood could simply be dropped down like a mantle to dress brand-new buildings.

In the waves of migration that followed World War I, the South, too, seemed to empty itself into high-rent Harlem. A new culture was taking shape. Just as writers came north to tell the tales of the southern plantations, and musicians came north to remake juke joints and Saturday-night stomps into blues clubs and jazz parties, ordinary people who came north would also re-create southern cooking, and eventually help improvise a new kind of agriculture in American cities.

EVERY human being is a museum piece. Along with DNA, we inherit the language, knowledge, and values of the people who raised us, and those who raised them. Among the most profound and unshakable parts of our inheritance is food. Recipes from the Old Country often last generations, longer than language, sometimes longer even than ritual and religion. In fact, brain researchers now believe that our tastes in food are formed at a very young age—before four or five—and they tend to stick for life. When you look at bits of land where people plant vegetables in the city, as often as not, you're looking at a story of the past.

Willie Morgan was growing produce long before he started doling it out to Harlem gamblers. He spent his earliest years in southern Georgia, in the wood home of his grandparents, who farmed cotton and peanuts on a plantation and taught him to raise, trap, fish, and shoot all kinds of edibles. They were sharecroppers who knew that whatever the outputs, whatever the inputs, the owner's arithmetic would leave them broke. So they grew their own vegetables, kept curly-tailed, grunting pigs, and hung their own fatty pork and sausages in the smokehouse. Willlie learned that okra was itchy on the skin. He found out how to fertilize with ashes and manure, and he investigated the particularities of nurturing sweet potatoes and sugarcane. He drew drinking water from a well filled with fish.

Willie was the first child of young parents—his mother was only seventeen when he was born—who soon moved to New York City seeking higher-paying factory jobs, leaving him in his grandparents' care. His parents would come down to Georgia to visit two or three times a year, bearing northern gifts, like clothes in the up-to-date city styles, and a real baseball uniform, with a glove and high socks. But Willie didn't really know his mother and father, and he was dismayed when they "snatched" him away to live with them in the city when he was nine. There had been no time for Willie to harvest his own small plot of land before leaving, so his grandmother gathered his produce, canned it, and mailed the Mason jars north to Harlem. That December of 1947, Willie, who had never seen snow, encountered a sudden twenty-five inches of it, the biggest snowstorm in New York history. In that first bewildering, frigid, impossibly snowy winter, he ate the products of his own faraway fertile land. That was the beginning.

UNDER slavery, black people were deprived of control over almost all aspects of their lives—but they had to eat. On any little spot of naked dirt—provision grounds, they were called—people managed to raise their own okra, black-eyed peas, watermelons, and certain beans and yams, all of which had traveled with their ancestors on slave ships from Africa. That food created a new southern cuisine. And that cuisine migrated, along with the people, to Harlem.

"Dear Charlie," the southern leader Booker T. Washington wrote to a New York friend in 1907, "the chitterlings went forward to you last week." By the 1930s, a trucker would drive up from Georgia or North Carolina to his particular corner in Harlem, open the back doors, and turn his truck into a storefront that sold watermelon, pecans, hog's head cheese, chow-chow, cane patch syrup, and smoked hams—before turning around and heading south to restock. One Grady C. Houston built his business up to nine food trucks, shuttled by nephews, cousins, and brothers. Some of Harlem's greatest success stories involved southern food, like that of Pig Foot Mary, née Lillian Harris, a teenager from the Mississippi Delta who bought a three-dollar washbasin, an old baby carriage, and two dollars' worth of pigs' feet, and set up a business selling chitterlings on wheels. She eventually saved enough to open a Harlem shop and invest in local real estate, becoming one of the wealthiest women of color in the city.

Some onetime farmers simply continued to plant. Plenty of sharecroppers found themselves scrubbing or assembling or sweeping or serving, coming home at night to a Harlem tenement whose air shaft windows showed only slats of sky. Of course they craved country food, and some grew their own fresh collards to wilt with salt pork, tomatoes and tender okra to simmer in stew, and new potatoes to mash with cream.

A woman named Nora Mair saved cheese and butter buckets, filled them with earth, and set them on the fire escape full of potato plants, which her sister would fertilize with horse manure she swept up in the street. Caledonia Jones's family planted beans and black-eyed peas in long wooden cheese boxes on the windowsills of their third-floor apartment—level with the Eighth Avenue elevated train that passed by the open window. Cal and his cousins would tear out neat little peas from their pods and pelt the passengers on the El. In fact, all over the city, the El trains were level with windowbox gardens, and the *New York Times* observed that passengers passed by close enough to "snare a carrot."

WILLIE lived with his parents and his younger sister and brother in a four-bedroom apartment with a breeze from Morningside Park. From his third-floor window, Willie would watch girls amble along the park's pathways, and then run downstairs to chase the one he liked. In winter, he would jump his aluminum sled down the steep, rocky hill of the park till his ten-o'clock curfew. Nearby, the Chaplains, the Royal Knights, the Mutineers, and the Commanches fought with daggers, ice picks, and zip guns. There were reefer pads and card sharks, gangsters, crapshooters and numbers runners, and white storeowners who were rude and overcharged. Yet there was security, too. Willie's father, Leroy, worked in a belt factory, and his mother, Mary, was a seamstress in a garment factory, and both kept the same jobs for decades. Willie's family knew neighbors for blocks around whose stories echoed theirs.

Harlem, circa 1947: People fleeing southern racism and low wages would show up hauling suitcases filled with fresh peaches and snap peas, fig preserves, and country hams that they had packed in southern kitchens to bolster their new lives. You could follow the smell of Saturday-afternoon cooking to nighttime rent parties, where the guests would make cash contributions toward rent and the hosts would offer music, dancing, homemade gin, and southern victuals. "Music too tight. Refreshments just right," promised one old announcement. "There'll be plenty of pig feet/ An lots of gin/Jus ring the bell/An come on in," read another.

One block in Harlem, 138th and 139th streets between Lenox and Eighth avenues, was said to be the most densely populated in the country. Still, a Harlem man might travel out of the city to the woods to hunt possum or venison or wild duck. A woman might wander her way through the local park, picking mint and leafy greens, cherries, blackberries, little nuts, and wild onions. Southern food made in Harlem came to symbolize both a fondness for and a triumph over the past. Thelonious Monk wore southern food like a badge, playing New York clubs with a collard in his lapel.

But by the 1950s, old, ill-maintained buildings were crumbling, and banks refused to lend money to Harlem landlords for repairs. Uptown manufacturing jobs were evaporating—two-thirds were lost in the 1960s. In that same decade, heroin coursed through the neighborhood, and about 14 percent of Harlem residents used the drug. Desegregation was skimming the top off Harlem society, as black people with means moved to the previously all-white suburbs. Racism was alive and well in Harlem's white-owned companies, where a white candidate could beat a black candidate for most any job.

The *Times* estimated that more than half of Harlem's economy hinged on the policy numbers, the illegal lottery that employed about 100,000 people and used its cash flow to bankroll local bars, restaurants, corner groceries, and apartment houses, as well as any political campaign that had a hope of winning. You put in your numbers on the way to work, and in an area with few legitimate banks, you turned to the numbers man if you needed a loan or wanted a partner for your business. The game was simple. Victories at the local horse races generated three numbers. Pick the winning three and you could make six hundred dollars for every one dollar you put in. Hitting the numbers big could mean making rent, or even, in one sweep, enough money to buy an apartment. All of Harlem seemed to live by dream books, privately published guides to lucky betting that listed events, activities, and even words that might appear in dreams, with corresponding three-digit numbers.

After high school, Willie became a singer. His R&B band traveled to North Carolina, Virginia, and Washington, D.C. Soon he also took a night job labeling packages at UPS. People told him, "Be smart, keep your job." But it was a short leap from singing to hanging out in bars and clubs—and from there to the numbers.

"I saw these guys were making all this money," said Willie. "I got me a couple good people, and said, I can do this thing." While his little sister worked in the child welfare department and his younger brother became an architect, Willie started as a runner, the person to take the bets for a small commission. Then he decided to chance it as a controller, the middle manager who runs the operation but is still subservient to an Italian mobster banker from the East Side.

Running a numbers spot meant hearing about Bumpy Johnson, an early numbers lord who branched out into other enterprises. Bumpy was the kind of gentleman pimp, or philanthropist thief, who would buy thousands of dollars of Christmas presents for needy children even as he introduced the heroin that might someday addict them. Willie rubbed shoulders with the likes of Frank Lucas, the heroin dealer who subverted the Mob by importing the raw product direct from Southeast Asia, and then having his staff of women wearing nothing but surgical masks process it in Harlem. Willie and his Italian bankers would drink Courvoisier at Thursday-night meetings in a private room at the legendary Patsy's Pizzeria, the place Francis Ford Coppola visited to find models for the mobsters of *The Godfather*.

But Willie's great innovation was his own. Other numbers men gave their customers a dozen eggs, or a chicken for the weekend. Willie cleared a rubble-filled lot next to his new ninety-dollar-a-month storefront on 118th Street with an eye to growing a vegetable garden. It was not voluptuous land, not the sweet and fertile red soil of his Georgia childhood—but flat, dry, and cracked, with broken glass and bricks he had to clear out. For three hundred dollars, he brought two dump truck loads of soil from Long Island and shoveled them over the yard. Then he slipped corn, collard, and tomato seeds under the earth. It felt good to work the dirt—"I was a kid again," he said. In midsummer, as his harvest began, he drove up to the Hunts Point market in the Bronx to bulk buy wholesale treats he couldn't grow, such as oranges and green bananas. After that, his yield was steady. Once a week, to sweeten the bets, he could offer his customers a brown paper bag full of groceries.

Early on, he understood the importance of marketing to women. Many of his first customers were mothers playing the numbers to put food on the table. A bit of fresh, free produce could certainly make the difference when such a woman decided where to gamble. With the guys, Willie would pull up the vegetables and someone else would bring some meat. The men would place their bets, fire up the barbecue in the yard, eat together, and take home leftovers.

So it came to pass that Willie Morgan fed his bit of gambling Harlem. His heavily fertilized, rapidly grown, unusually large vegetables filled people's stews and soups and sides, their dinners and lunch bags and party spreads, as their bets filled his pockets.

FOR decades, as the national economy boomed, Harlem foundered. The neighborhood became known less for its jazz clubs and home cooking than for its vacant lots. These started multiplying in the 1950s, as abandoned buildings were demolished. Empty lots became dumping grounds, and neighbors would "air-mail" their garbage down from upper-floor apartments. Some people began cleaning up the lots and transforming them into gardens, but the scale was small and the efforts spotty.

Things changed when riots erupted in Harlem in 1964 after a white cop killed a black fifteen-year-old boy. Suddenly government viewed poor neighborhoods and their vacant lots as breeding grounds for discontent. A few weeks after his inauguration, Mayor John Lindsay and his wife, Mary, shoveled refuse out of a Bronx lot he had designated as a "vest-pocket park," or mini-park. Soon, the people of Harlem adapted his idea to clean up lots to grow vegetables, and civic groups presented a course called Rubble to Roses, with tips on urban agriculture. "I hope," a Harlem resident wrote to the *Amsterdam News*, "that this sense of not owning anything of our own here in the city might be overcome in the actual getting together and digging."

Because if one thing was becoming plentiful, it was land. In the past, prissiness had ruled the city's open spaces like a bulwark against chaos. Men were not allowed to take their shirts off in parks; children were upbraided for playing on the grass—it would "bruise"—and community groups that dared to plant flowers on city properties watched maintenance workers uproot them. All that was changing. The overbuilding that had created Harlem was rolling back. Housing was coming down, at first building by building—a fire here, a demolition there. Soon, there was open space everywhere. On Willie's block in 1969, there had been a liquor store and a car shop and a drugstore, along with a row of narrow-windowed, small-roomed nineteenth-century brick tenement buildings packed with Willie's customers. Over the next decade, while he busied himself in the garden, something astonishing happened. The whole row of tenements came down, one by one, until on the south side of the street not a single building was left on the entire block.

It turns out that neglect starts fires. Where a landlord failed to fix the boiler, or pay the gas bill, or repair the electricity, a space heater or a jerry-rigged outlet or a pot of bathwater warming on a failing gas stove could lead to a conflagration. "Milkers" would buy a building for cheap only to cut maintenance and even heat and hot water to maximize rental profits. They might hire a professional "finisher" to come in with wrenches and screwdrivers to strip whatever copper wiring and brass and lead pipes could be sold. They might even hire someone to torch the place, for insurance money. The fire department no longer had the manpower to inspect buildings and enforce codes, and its hydrants and trucks often broke down. In poor, packed neighborhoods, firehouses closed, and, predictably, fires spread. People will tell you about going up to their rooftops in the 1970s to see two or three fires burning at once. They would avoid making evening phone calls because of the screaming sirens at that time of day. They would smell the burning every time they went outside. They would watch their neighborhoods literally turn to ash. Harlem, the Lower East Side, the South Bronx, Central Brooklyn, Williamsburg, Bushwick, Washington Heights, Brownsville, East New York—they all burned. FDNY veterans still call the 1970s "The War Years."

It wasn't just fire. From 1970 to 1980, the city's economic output fell by 20 percent; average income dropped by 35 percent; and a million jobs were lost. Heroin flooded the streets, muggings, burglaries, and armed robbery spiked, and the murder rate almost quadrupled. In a few years in the 1970s, central Harlem lost almost a third of its total population, and other neighborhoods across the city emptied too. "Something happened," one elderly man told the *Times* in 1975, as he sat on the Coney Island boardwalk near a stretch of vacant lots, staring at the sea. "Everything is changed now."

The housing commissioner, Roger Starr, thought the city was just renewing itself. "Planned shrinkage" was his proposal to encourage hundreds of thousands of poor people to move away so their land could be renovated. "Stretches of empty blocks may then be knocked down, services can be stopped, subway stations closed, and the land left to lie fallow until a change in economic and demographic assumptions makes the land useful once again," Starr wrote in an article in the *New York Times Magazine*. His controversial proposal cost him his job, but people continued to debate to what extent the city's ongoing shrinkage of services was in fact part of a deliberate plan.

Beginning in 1974, budgets were stripped bare as the city teetered on the edge of bankruptcy. In some neighborhoods, the Sanitation Department stopped picking up curbside garbage—never mind cleaning the multiplying charred vacant lots that were becoming a symbol of urban failure. The Parks Department held off on fixing benches, painting pools, and installing new seats on swings, and there was talk of jettisoning parks that could not be maintained—not of making vacant lots into parkland. People in poor neighborhoods began to think the City was intentionally targeting them for service cuts as the closing of police and fire stations only assisted the frenzy of arson and accident that produced more vacant lots. In 1975, with the city more than $12 billion in debt, President Gerald Ford refused to help with a federal bailout. "Ford to City: Drop Dead," the *Daily News* headlined.

Meanwhile, city lots filled with detritus. A building would burn down or be wrecked, and its remains would not be removed. Bricks and beams and mortar would crumple and crumble, disintegrating into litter, attracting more of the same. Businesses quit paying licensed carters to haul their refuse to the costly city dump. Whole neighborhoods became dumping grounds. Cars, fridges, stoves, sofas, tires. Red bags of medical waste, Glad bags of office papers. Even Sanitation Department trucks were found dumping in city-owned lots. Dumping begat litter. Box springs and pop cans, a single roller skate, butane lighters and hamburger boxes,

Polaroids and Budweiser bottles, syringes, chicken bones, baby clothes. Vacant lots became an ashy catalog of all the city didn't want, including the lots themselves.

A tough, vigilant neighborhood advocate could sometimes stop vacant lots from taking over. Mildred Gittens, for instance, made it her business to ensure that her bit of West 136th Street did not sink into decline. She joined the police council and routinely called the cops to eject squatters from empty buildings. She knew the local urban renewal rules forbade demolitions, so when she found a demolitions man at work on a brownstone a few doors away, she threatened to sit on site until he stopped. "The minute you put a hole in the street on the block, you get garbage and everything will be thrown in there. It would look like H-E-L-L," Mildred spelled out genteelly. "No empty lot," she said. "No, darling. No empty lot is going to be there."

But elsewhere, kids played ball on fields of glimmering, multicolored shards of glass. They made trampolines of ripped, rotted mattresses with coils like rusted talons. They swung from the ends of thick, oxidized wires dangling from upper-floor fire escapes. They hid in abandoned refrigerators, pulling the door shut and playing with that stickiness that made it hard to reopen. They tripped over used syringes piled in prickly mounds like poisonous, low-lying urban cacti. They played with matches, watching as the flames spread, double-scorching already burned places. They went digging and turned up knives and guns. People died on those lots. Worse than worthless, the areas were liabilities.

A new Vacant Lot Task Force in the Sanitation Department experimented with barricades, bollards, and berms to stop dumping. Deploying a fleet of heavy-duty dump trucks, hydraulic lifts, and front-end loaders, the force cleared about 22,000 tons of debris a year—only to see new garbage appear in the same places, said Ginny Gliedman, the task force director at the time. Besides, the goal was never to keep every vacant lot in the city clean—but rather, in the way of the shrunken ambition of bureaucracies in crisis, to spend federal grants.

In another attempt to expend minimal effort for maximal return, the city seeded 150 junked-out acres with clover, rye, fescue, and wildflowers, a mixture farmers use to replenish the soil in fallow fields. The result was sometimes "quite peculiar," acknowledged Gliedman, as the seeds took root in some places and not others, giving the effect of a bald junky patch scattered with a scruffy stubble of growth—and some residents complained. They wanted manicured lawns and garden beds, they wanted evidence of concern and protection, they wanted their neighborhoods not to be burning and vacant and look like a war zone subject to odd, desperate horticultural experiments.

All over the city, people began to clean and plant and seed and hoe. They grew cotton for Q-tips and tobacco for cigarettes, but as often as not, they planted to eat. Peanuts, beans, and black-eyed peas, cherries, figs, and peaches, potatoes, tomatoes, peppers, and squash. It was as though people were summoning the resources of their country childhoods to get them through city hardships.

Their plants thrived in the abandoned lots in cut-off milk containers, half-gallon ice cream boxes, and even ancient tea kettles. People grew seedlings in tires and rusted boilers and funerary urns, old work boots (one seedling per shoe), and the giant wooden spools Con Edison used for cable wire. Greens shot out of sinks, porcelain bathtubs, and plumbing fixtures, as though someone had dropped whole bathrooms outdoors to be seized by the forces of nature. Old Colt 45 malt liquor bottles served as watering cans, and broken eggshells and coffee grounds as fertilizer. To stymie rats, they turned hamster cages over young seedlings. They locked their hoes and spades and trowels into dead, old cars parked on the lots like four-door toolsheds.

Discarded bits of cars had piled up in a lot on Maggie Burnett's block of West 149th Street. "I was in shock," Ms. Maggie said, when she realized that drug dealers had also taken over apartments in the cream-colored tenements across the street. One day, a thug threw a pistol into her basement, she said, and afterward, she accompanied the cops to another building, where they found two bodies perforated by gunshots. Finally, sick of the chaos, she decided to clear out the junk-filled lot. The dealers didn't want it clear, she said, they didn't want do-gooders out on the street watching their business. "They threatened me," she said. Yet she and a few defiant others planted cabbages, cucumbers, squash, onions, and tomatoes. Mr. Walton—"God rest his soul"—served as sentry, day after day, sitting in his chair by the garden fence. For Ms. Maggie, digging into the earth recalled a South Carolina girlhood, walking in her father's tracks while he sowed seeds with the mule. But in New York, she often had to break to call the police. The dealers were raided, and raided again, and then, after many years, they were gone. "People like that, you can't let them tantalize you, get on your nerve," says Ms. Maggie today, clear-eyed, straight-backed, relaxing in her shady, carefully landscaped garden near her fruiting pepper plants. "You got to fight."

A quest for agricultural land was turning into a citywide movement. Downtown, a woman named Liz Christy hurled balloon "bombs" filled with water, peat moss fertilizer, and wildflower seeds over chain-link fences onto city-owned vacant land. After a year of bombings in 1973, her Green Guerrillas group gained the imprimatur of legitimacy when the city offered its first "community garden" lease in 1974: a lot for one dollar a month.

The City developed a new policy of permitting residents to plant on urban renewal sites when financing was still years away. Effectively, officials were contracting out their own mandate to keep city-owned properties clean and safe. There was no longer any pretense that government was up to the task.

Yet the lots were multiplying faster than they could be planted. By 1978, the city owned 32,000 unused lots, most filled with rubble and urban detritus. "Parts of New York City seem to belong neither to man nor to nature," wrote the *Times*. "The former's work [buildings] has been demolished, the latter's [vegetation] erased by rubble. What's left are *wastelands*."

IN Harlem, love of the land was fraught. Early on, conservative black intellectuals had argued that African Americans would always be bound to southern agriculture. Booker T. Washington described the farm as the "Negro's best chance," maintaining that only a country life "working on the soil" could "uplift," and he founded the Tuskegee Institute in Alabama as an agricultural college. Some of the great literary figures of the Harlem Renaissance came from a farming background, including Jean Toomer, who had majored in agriculture at the University of Wisconsin, and Claude McKay, who attended both Tuskegee and an agricultural college in Kansas. Yet African American notions of agriculture were tainted with memories of the hard labor and brutal force of enslavement.

Eldridge Cleaver noted in the 1960s that during slavery "black people learned to hate the land" and for this reason, "even today, one of the most provocative insults that can be tossed at a black is to call him a farm boy, to infer that he is from a rural area or in any way attached to an agrarian situation." He wrote that blacks "have come to measure their own value according to the number of degrees they are away from the soil." Even nowadays, says Karen Washington, an African American advocate for gardens in New York City, it can be hard to combat the sense that farming is the kind of demeaning labor that people left the South to avoid.

But for Willie Morgan it was simple: Growing things was part of his past. No one ever meant to abandon agriculture, he insists. People came north for jobs, hoping all the while to retire to the farm. In any case, in his generation, African Americans who started their lives on the farms of the South would stamp their history on the geography of New York City.

IN Washington, on the roof of the Longworth House Office Building, the Brooklyn congressman Fred Richmond planted a vegetable garden. He installed four-by-eight raised beds of squash and tomatoes, radishes and lettuce, in dark earth mixed with manure and sludge furnished by the USDA. Richmond was the only urban member of the House Agricultural Committee. He liked to explain that New Yorkers ate the combined output of forty-two million acres of farmland, and a million people in the city used food stamps, whose terms were set in the Farm Bill. His position also made sense because Richmond was considering a run for statewide office and ag could win over upstate voters. In the meantime, the millionaire industrialist entreated colleagues to clamber awkwardly out his office window and visit his garden. "You'd have to flop one leg out and climb out, and women with skirts would grumble, 'How am I going to do this?' and they'd get up on a chair and swing their legs out," said Glenn Van Bramer, Richmond's legislative assistant.

During a visit to a steam bath, Richmond convinced Jamie Whitten, the powerful southern congressman in charge of the appropriations subcommittee for agriculture, to fund a $1.5 million pilot program for food gardens in New York, Chicago, Los Angeles, Detroit, and Houston. Others barely noticed that a section on urban gardening had been included in the 1976 agricultural appropriations bill. "This is a step to improve urban blight," said Richmond, who had taken to reading magazines such as *National Hog Farmer* on the commuter flight from Washington to New York. An arrest over soliciting sex from a sixteen-year-old boy ended Richmond's political career—but his gardens were just taking off.

Soil holds the history of a place. In New York, it's a tale of boom and bust, as almost all city soil has at one time or another had a building on it—and then, when the building came down, *in* it. John Ameroso, who was hired to implement Fred Richmond's federal urban agriculture program in Brooklyn, found his staff knew plenty about crop rotations but had much to learn about this brick-riddled earth. "Rubbled soil" is the term Ameroso began to use, as he figured out that bricks—composed of lime, clay, and sand—combined with organic matter to make ideal growing material. "They kept pulling bricks out. I said, 'Use the bricks as part of your growing medium,'" said Ameroso. His Cornell University Cooperative Extension Program hauled horse manure from police department stables to hundreds of sites, and in 1978 alone produced 540,000 pounds of vegetables and fruits worth $400,000.

All of urban agriculture was experiment and improvisation.

Soil in many lots was saturated with lead used in gasoline and cadmium used in diesel fuels, as well as other dangerous heavy metals. To investigate their effects on plants, Cornell grew crops in tainted soil and fed them to guinea pigs, and examined both the plants and the guinea pigs' livers. Ameroso soon found that keeping the pH of the soil near neutral tied up the metals so the plants did not take them in, and any trace amounts concentrated in the leaves, not the fruit. Adding organic compost could help reduce the concentration. There were ways to make polluted land produce wholesome food.

Urban gardening was one of those brilliant ideas that worked like a Rorschach test to reflect whatever the beholder wished to see. It would provide food for the hungry, nutrition for the ailing, therapy for the distressed, and expression for the creative. It would educate children, employ the elderly, and help fix the environment. It would reclaim neighborhoods from blight, build community, and reform and redeem the city.

Around 1978, Peter P. Smith III, commissioner of the Department of General Services, the agency in charge of all city-owned property, dreamed up Operation GreenThumb. He had been struck by the utility of gardening while gazing at roses in bloom on the site of the old Women's House of Detention near his Greenwich Village home. In his plywood-paneled office in the Municipal Building, smoking cigarillos and sipping from a coffee cup labeled PETER, he outlined his strategy to *The New Yorker:* "The fact of the matter is that a vacant and unprotected lot can result in many more injuries and lawsuits against the city than a lot used and protected by a group of gardeners," Smith said. "If we're just lucky enough, a community group will come in and clear it," he said. "When a group has a lot and farms it, the members stop thinking, That's the *city's* land over there, and start thinking, That's *ours*. And of course, it is, too. If the city owns it, they own it."

A coatroom at General Services was converted into an office for Frank Silano, the silk-tie-and-shades-wearing bureaucrat charged with managing the program at its inception. Flooded with fifty applications a week, almost all of which were requests to grow food, he developed the grand ambition of renting out 10,000 lots to gardeners for a dollar per year per lot, furthering the process of turning green a good portion of the most ravaged land in urban America. Some twenty-one agencies offered horticultural advice, seeds, topsoil, and tools. Would-be lessees crowded into the converted coatroom to sign the agreement. *The New Yorker* related a jovial transaction:

"Sign right by the X," says Commissioner Smith to one applicant, the last in a line. "Good luck."

"Did you get the three dollars?" the commissioner asks Frank Silano.

"Sure did," says Silano.

"We just made six dollars for the city!" says the commissioner.

Soon the city was also in the business of manufacturing soil for gardens, using compost from truckloads of grass cuttings, tree trimmings, and leaves to produce two hundred tons of topsoil a month.

"The ultimate use would be to build housing. But we didn't have the money," said Mayor Ed Koch, years later. "If you have the money, you can do anything, and if you don't have money, you do the best you can," he said. The job the city did was, in his estimation, "terrific."

"It was a bit of a sop," said Ken Davies, who was another of the program's early managers. At twenty-eight years old, just out of ag school, he would drive an old broken-down, city-owned car to the far corners of the boroughs to check in on hundreds of lots under his jurisdiction. "It was a way of giving a little something to communities. You could say it was awfully little."

The view from Harlem was more critical. Mildred Gittens had worked to keep her piece of West 136th Street free of vacant lots, but as far as she was concerned, the city should have long before found ways to provide the full retinue of services—mortgages and loans, building code enforcement, firefighters, police officers, slumlord courts, housing rehabilitation—to prevent the dangerous vacant lots from ever existing. Gardening was irrelevant, she said—"I thought it was ridiculous."

Willie Morgan also believed that government should have kept housing viable. "I was mad," he said. "I felt that the politicians could have done something to get the buildings for people. Build them up. Let people have them cheaply."

But people who had retreated behind triple-locked doors, ceding their streets to dealers, came back outside. Their plants needed watering, pruning, and weeding, even amid drug deals and shootings. These people made their blocks safer by their very presence. In that sense, it was the most basic form of community development.

The gardeners also actively battled local forces of destruction. One group on the Lower East Side wielded hoes to chase away junkies and pushers. Others schemed to take so many photos at weekly barbecues that the heroin traders would flee. With grim energy, another group quietly re-requested streetlight repairs every time their neighbors tore them out from their bases to cloak themselves in darkness. There were more prosaic struggles too:

theft, vandalism, attrition. Birds ate the baby lettuce, and squirrels, the corn.

Another problem lay in wait. From the city's perspective, the
gardeners were temporary custodians until land could be improved or sold. But everyone knows a loan can be hard to recall.
From the beginning, some bureaucrats "were scared about where
it would lead," said one of them. At private meetings, the question
kept coming up: "How are we ever going to get it back?" "We put
in bold red letters on our Green Thumb leases that this is a temporary use," said Terrence Moan, the deputy commissioner of the
Department of General Services in the 1980s. "To create a force
that would oppose the development—that would make no sense."

Some community groups had the foresight and resources to
form land trusts to purchase the gardens outright. Some lost the
gardens when the city's Division of Real Properties deemed a site
"prime" for development. Most kept renewing their leases. By
the 1980s, the most quintessentially urban city in America had
sprouted as many as 1,000 gardens and 10,000 gardeners.

EVENTUALLY, in the 1970s, when buildings all around Willie's garden had come down, there was no reason to stay on 118th Street.
"My customers were gone," he said. He stopped paying rent, let
his small farm lie fallow, and moved on.

In the decades that followed, he opened a new numbers spot
and tended another garden—a little lot on 123rd Street owned by
another numbers man. He bought a new business, a bar called
Top Club, as Harlem settled into a new low of violence and deso-
lation. When the state-run Lottery considered running a daily
game to compete with the local numbers joints, the Harlem num-

bers barons sent a telegram: "Mr. Governor, if you have this taken away from us we will all have to apply for welfare, which you say you don't have a budget for. We do not intend for anyone to take numbers away from us because we invented it." The Lottery launched anyway, undermining an active, if illegal, spot in the Harlem economy. Tiny rocks of concentrated crack cocaine hit in one last, all-encompassing wave of destruction. Kids would hold a gun to you for nothing. Bulletproof Plexiglas appeared in every corner store. Top Club and other bars failed, said Willie, "because people were afraid to go out."

Yet Willie joined a fellow retiree from the nightlife—and two others retired from union jobs at Ford and General Motors—in a new garden. This particular terrain had once been occupied by 2197 Frederick Douglass Boulevard. Long ago, Willie recalled visiting a high school friend who lived there to rehearse R&B in the living room. Neglect had made that living room an open field, under hoe and rake for more than a decade by the time Willie arrived. By the early nineties, his colleagues wanted more to relax than to produce, and they offered industrious Willie ever-larger pieces of rubble to turn. Keeping nightclub hours for farmers' tasks, soon he was sowing half the lot, which took up a quarter of the block. Early in the season, he sometimes worked until two a.m. with a few friends for company, his hands rhythmically patting seeds into the cool earth. He set up an informal business selling what he grew from the ground. This time there was no gambling involved; Willie was dedicated to vegetables alone.

By the late 1990s, a new Harlem was emerging yet again. Although many brownstones had been destroyed, neglect had preserved others—original marble vestibules, stained-glass windows, oak and cherry floors and stairs, brilliant tile fireplaces, and twelve-foot ceilings were shabby but intact. As real estate values rose citywide, Harlem residents began to find handwritten notes taped to their windows and slid under their doors: "Want to sell?" In 2005, the Corcoran real estate company opened an office just a block from Willie's garden, where seventeen full-time agents pushed uptown properties.

Downtown, the dot-matrix printers of the city's Integrated Property Information System spat out green-lined reports on Harlem gardens, saying, "QUERY DISPO REQUESTS," which in city jargon meant to check for potential for disposition: development or sale. Representatives of various agencies would meet and trade properties: "I've got three lots on DeKalb Avenue, and you've got two lots. I need to build a school. What do you want me to give you for your two lots?" Letters went out to Green-Thumb gardeners: "Please be advised that your organization's agreement with GreenThumb is CANCELED, effective immediately." A neat checkmark would fill the box by a handwritten fill-in-the-blank explanation: "Site has been sold to private owner for development."

Pleased with the incoming funds, Mayor Rudy Giuliani set about selling off the city's surplus land in earnest. A fax dozens of pages long spilled onto the floor in the downtown offices of GreenThumb, notifying directors that all the gardens under their jurisdiction—more than seven hundred—were to be transferred to the city's housing department to be developed. Soon, more than a hundred gardens were put on the auction block. Vegetable plots were bulldozed, protests were organized, and gardeners arrested. "This is a free market economy," Giuliani told protesters, with his inexorable tendency toward confrontation. Welcome, he said, "to the era after communism."

His obtuseness helped turn a tribe of peaceable, solitary gardeners into activists. "No gardens, no peas!" yelled Haja Worley, a tall, soft-spoken Harlem construction worker who was incensed when a bulldozer mowed down his forsythia, Rose of Sharon plants, and several rare mulberry trees. Eventually Haja got his own talk radio show on WHCR, *Harlem 411*, which he used as a forum for eviscerating local politicians. He called Harlem gardeners together to strategize. Even apolitical Willie took the A train down to City Hall to save his tomatoes.

The gardeners argued that time had changed the deal. A few decades prior, no one would have guessed that ephemeral vegetable beds could have the concrete physical power of bricks and mortar to change a neighborhood. But the gardens had become community institutions, where people organized birthday parties and Mother's Day picnics. They were places that confronted problems—where neighbors would enforce a drug ban, and where juvenile offenders were sometimes sentenced to work rather than detention or a fine. While cleaning and clearing and planting and harvesting, people had preserved and protected their small spots of land. "We consider ourselves grassroots developers," said Haja Worley.

It's a tricky thing to figure out when to sell a property in a neighborhood coming out of its nadir. A 1999 study by the Brooklyn borough president found that 96 percent of 440 sites sold at public auction in previous years had remained vacant, often used for illegal dumping or car storage. When the direction of the neighborhood is still uncertain, developers may be willing to stockpile properties but not actually build. Sometimes gardens were torn down for no particular reason.

For renters who garden in a tough neighborhood in

recovery, development brings the feeling of watching something slip through your fingers. Several NYU researchers proved the intuitive claim that community gardens increase sales prices of nearby properties, most noticeably in the poorest neighborhoods. So gardens can have an ironic effect: They improve the neighborhood enough that real estate values pick up and someone wants to develop—and eradicate—the gardens. And rental prices can rise high enough to force out the gardeners.

It turned out that the gardens were the city's soft underbelly, vulnerable to every kind of change. They had been the landscape of the city's lowest point—places to shoot up and turn tricks and deal drugs. Zucchini and corn and tomatoes had risen from the ashes, in a kind of interim claim for the collective spirit. And now these same lots bore early witness to the real estate recovery, as the first shiny condo buildings appeared on them like a mirage in the char.

In 2002, the city finally settled a lawsuit brought by the state attorney general on behalf of the gardeners. The agreement allowed some gardens to be sold or developed, but offered hundreds of others permanent protected status and stipulated that in future, displaced gardeners must be offered alternate space nearby. A few years later, when the city moved to develop housing on his garden, Willie accepted relocation. He went shopping for a new garden, surveying the few remaining city-owned vacant lots in his corner of Harlem. He found a place on 122nd Street that seemed perfect: small, but bordered on one side by another vacant lot and on the other by a park, allowing for plenty of sunlight. "When I saw this—bam! That's it!" said Willie. "People said, 'They ain't going to let you put no garden there! You dreaming!'" It was just a few blocks away from the busy commercial strip of 125th Street, where street vendors hawked bangles, bags, baubles, holy books and self-published novels, and enough scented oils to keep all of Harlem smelling like Rivers of Honey and China Rain. It's a good neighborhood for growing things, Willie thought.

In fact, it had been done before. More than a decade prior, Haja and Cindy Worley had cleared out piles of axles, bumpers, fenders, needles, and a half dozen abandoned cars and delivery vans to garden those lots and several adjacent ones. In the mid-nineties, the city had closed the garden in order to develop part of the site. Now Willie's garden could be built on the remainder.

GreenThumb director Edie Stone wrote Willie a formal letter offering a choice of three plots, including the one he wanted on 122nd Street and Eighth Avenue. It was Block 1928 Lots 104 and 105, a pile of garbage and concrete slabs Willie dreamed into his future farm. He moved in with new soil and seeds in June 2005, and that very first summer he planted a full and profitable harvest.

"**WILLIE!**" calls Belkys Diaz, who lives just around the corner on St. Nicholas Avenue, as she opens up the latch on the fence at the front of the garden. Her hair is pulled back tight in a ponytail, she is wearing a cross and a low-cut white tank top, and she is pacing, impatient. "I want some tomatoes," she calls. "I want 'em half ripe!" Willie, ever amiable, goes wandering between the second and third rows of tomatoes, looking for some yellow ones. It's okay if they have faint stripes of green unripeness or red readiness, but he knows what she wants, the in-betweens. "I'm a tomato eater. I eat 'em in the morning and at night," Belkys confesses to me. "It's the third day in a row she's bought tomatoes," affirms Willie.

I once asked Willie if he'd thought about planting organically.

"I thought about it . . ." he said, and faded out. That didn't even merit a real answer. What Willie wants is yield. If his corn stalks are seven or eight feet tall, and if Miracle-Gro helps them along, well, so much the better, and he'll keep a row of gallon water bottles filled with a greenish chemical stew ready to bathe the crops. Willie believes the fertilizer helps compensate for a soil laced with bits of 275 West 122nd Street, the tenement building that once stood on this lot and long ago crumbled into the earth, and now also 273 West 122nd Street, the new building taking shape next door, shedding bits of cement and brick as it grows taller. Willie's pest control system, however, is chemical-free: a pile of stones he stockpiles to lob at birds and squirrels.

Vegetables are Willie's currency. He carries them to the doctor's office to give out to receptionists and nurses. "I never have to wait for an appointment," he says. He takes them to the guys at the corner deli and can always count on a cheese sandwich stuffed with his own tomatoes. When his neighbors throw a party while Willie's still out working the turnips, they come by to pick up stevia and mint to make mojitos and invite him to join them. Willie used to bring vegetables to the 101-year-old doyenne of his Harlem neighborhood, who wrote him a letter of support when the garden was threatened with development. "She's a lady," he said.

Willie delivers to his mother, his sister, his banker son, his hotel manager daughter. His brother drives up from Raleigh, North Carolina, each summer and takes home three dozen half-ripe Harlem tomatoes packed in tissue paper, swearing that they're sweeter than the ones down south.

Preparing for a special delivery, Willie gets out a pocketknife and slashes great stalks of mint to stuff into a clean, clear plastic bag, and ties a fistful of basil with a rubber band. He chops some stevia, twist ties the stems, and puts the bouquet in a plastic water bottle filled with greenish Miracle-Gro-infused water—"a preservative," he says—as though it's something from the florist. He keeps handwritten customer lists on scraps of paper, with cell phone numbers to call so people come to the garden when the vegetables are ripe.

One day, a man comes walking by with a top hat, sunglasses, and greased-back long, wavy hair, sipping from a brown bag imperfectly concealing a can of beer. "I ran the bar," says George Walker, introducing himself as a colleague of Willie's from Top Club. "I helped him plant, too. We're Geminis together. We spread the soil together."

Another time, a friend who went to the same elementary school as Willie comes by to lay down seeds. "He's a good singer," says Willie. Turns out the man used to sing with James Brown, before he went on to a career as a restaurant cook. "I don't want to leave him to work alone," says Kenny Fox, as he follows Willie's instructions precisely for dropping down seedlings weighted by the surrounding clumps of soil, piling on the fertilizer, and pouring in water.

Many afternoons, Bubie Rizzo, an American Neapolitan with one bluish eye and one brown one, comes by the garden. Bubie will sit back in the chair, sprawl out in his white linen pants, squint up at the sky, and intone, "Weather's changing." In truth, he is less interested in growing vegetables than in accounts in the *New York Post* of the imprisonment of various mob bosses, as he talks with Willie about their mutual friends "from the East Side," their code for their former Mafia associates.

Willie's past here is as alive as the vegetables he grows.

But Harlem is different now. It starts with the kinds of

condominiums recently constructed next door to Willie, sleek, serene dwellings finished with milled oak, zebra wood, and stone, with such amenities as a roof terrace with an outdoor fireplace—overlooking Willie's garden, which has become an asset that real estate agents mention to sell new apartments. Middle-class and well-off people of all races have moved into sandblasted and refurbished brownstones. Less obvious is who is not on the street: in the past decade, the city has experienced an exodus of working-class African Americans, who can no longer afford to live in the place where they grew up. All over the city, people are missing. It's now possible to pass whole densely built Harlem blocks where it's hard to imagine the devastated city that not so long ago supplied plenty of room for southern migrants to grow vegetables.

DOWNTOWN, in the high-ceilinged offices of GreenThumb, decorated with mismatched 1970s officeware and posters from garden campaigns, rows of filing cabinets are filled with notes on gardens now defunct, and labeled: "MANHATTAN CANCELED." "BRONX CANCELED." "BROOKLYN CANCELED." The gardens have left reams of paper in the city bureaucracy, as well as neighborhoods transformed.

When Willie first moved into his current garden, there was room for the sun to shine in. There were vacant lots to the east and the south, and to the west, a short building and a tiny park. He named the place Our Little Green Acre, in homage to the actual acre he'd tilled before—which became a housing development with a ground-floor Chase bank and a Starbucks. But a few years ago, construction began on three sides of Willie's new garden all at once. As each new floor rose up, it blocked more sunlight and splattered Willie's parsley, eggplants, and collards with cement. Willie was undismayed. His garden had official Parks status, so the developer would have to offer something in exchange for a permit to drive a crane over the tomato plants to carry steel beams to the upper floors. Maybe that season you could taste in his vegetables the building materials, the insufficient light—the rise, again, of real estate.

Willie bargained hard, and two of the developers ended up contributing to an iron fence at the front, a toolshed at the back, a little patio paved with interlocking bricks, a sprinkler system, and a setup for a barbecue. The next season, after the housing crash, as all the construction around him halted, Willie simply planted again.

"Nobody figured I could do this," says Willie of his ability to keep plants alive in the city over so many years. He's seventy-three years old now; he's been gardening in the city for more than half his life. He pauses, and surveys his land. His eyes move from eggplants and tomatoes to the new twelve-story building, and the strip of shade it made on his collards. "I'll be able to grow something, I know that," says Willie. By now, he knows that the most desolate of urban landscapes can be made into fertile ground.

MEAT

AS LIGHT BREAKS over a dark line of trees in the distant reaches of Queens and the heat of the day begins its rise, Tom Mylan reaches into the back of a red Sierra GMC pickup, heaves out a dead pig, and throws it over his shoulder. Struggling under its 220-pound weight, he pitches it forward onto a plastic-covered plywood banquet table, where it lands with an unnerving thud. The pig is a Tamworth-Saddleback cross, long and lean, descendant of the native pig stock of northern Europe, but raised right here in Queens, on the grounds of New York City's largest working farm. Tom Mylan is a Brooklyn butcher with blue eyes and a white apron, who has been hailed as a "rock star butcher" by the *New York Times* since he began cutting up whole animals for a Williamsburg shop.

Tom had first encountered the animal he is about to roast as a piglet right here at the forty-seven-acre Queens County Farm Museum. He toured the rocky, woodsy edge of the farm where the piglet was fenced in, and the animal smelled the meat on his butcher's boots and burrowed in with its hard snout. Tom slapped its side as you would a dog's and felt its rough, bristly, orange and black coat as the hog bit his toes and then followed him around the property, nipping at him. Here where the pig nibbled Tom, now Tom will eat the pig.

Surrounded by corn stalks and grapevines, Tom builds an aboveground fire pit, seven-by-four-foot square with cinderblocks for walls. In the center of the pit, he starts a fire with charcoal briquettes supplemented by hardwood logs. The barbecue heating, Tom tends the pig curled fetally on the table. He scores its thick skin with a box cutter so the fat can render and the meat can absorb his marinade of guajillo chiles, garlic, olive oil, lime juice, salt, pepper, and cumin. With a cleaver and a little hand saw, he cracks the chine bone—so the animal can splay out butterflied, fore and hind legs extended, empty, eviscerated belly exposed. With chicken wire and the help of a farmhand, Tom attaches the pig to a custom-made steel rack, and balances the whole rack-with-pig on the cinderblock walls over the fire.

A scroll of smoke blows across the hot, blue sky and Tom stands under it, smoking an American Spirit yellow and sipping a Brooklyn Brewery beer. The by-product of this beer, its leftover mash, had once helped nourish this growing pig, when it was trucked over from Williamsburg as feed. Tom flattens the spread of wood and charcoal on the fire. The pig has to cook both slowly and evenly so the muscle fibers don't contract and dry out, and so the collagen converts to gelatin, keeping the meat juicy. Clearly this cooking technique was developed by people with lots of firewood and spare time.

By dusk, the hog is hissing and crackling, its skin mostly an orangey fake-tan color, with highlights of red and charred black.

It takes four men to lift the hot rack and sizzling animal back to the table, where Tom cuts the pig loose and leaves it to cool. An intense, porky perfume summons people—casual farm visitors, Tom's restaurant friends and fellow butchers, and guests who had officially signed up for the farm's 2009 Fourth of July pig roast campout.

People reach out to peel off roasted skin, burning their fingers as juices drip out of the meat, but they don't stop. They reach for the skin of the back, the meat of the cheeks, they dig with their fingers into the cheekbone. "I want pig!" kids start to call.

Tom draws his knife through the flesh of the pig's shoulder and its thigh, extracting more rich, wobbly pieces of fat-infused white meat. Soon the animal is a slash of intense, savory flavor in barbecued pork sandwiches. Wetting and oiling the flimsy paper plates, the meat is a fragrant and intoxicating cut of intensely smoked pork, with fugitive heat from the chiles and a special kind of tenderness from the richness of its marbled fat.

After dinner, Tom hotwires the farm's E-Z-GO golf cart. He and the other butchers grab their ladies and their bottles and race around the farm grounds—right past the empty pigpen—only to come back and dance by the bonfire to Ace Frehley's "Back in the New York Groove," spraying each other with booze. Tom, Ben Turley, and Brent Young have just quit their jobs and are about to start their own butcher shop. Hard work is ahead, but at the moment, they feel free and happy to be alive.

"The three of us remember it as the best night ever," Tom would say years later. Late that night, Tom falls asleep in a half-collapsed blue tent he is too drunk to completely set up, in a field of dozens of similar tents. All around him, people are drinking and dancing and now sleeping under the stars, bellies and hearts full of this meat they consumed on the very spot where it was raised.

It's become an extreme-locavore standard: Catch your own meat. Eat it on site. Revel with the hipstavores, the gastronauts, the local fooderati, around an open fire. Find a more primal connection to the land where you are, even if that land is New York City. Still, there's something arresting and implausible about this bygone open landscape on the edge of Queens, where the pig ate nuts and roots and brewery mash and, in turn, offered up its flavorful meat to be consumed. Roasting a whole pig is drama and spectacle, like edible storytelling, Tom says. The moral of the story is that meat tastes better when it's well-raised, carefully cooked, and eaten in an atmosphere where strangers might become friends. "The whole point of doing this, for me, anyway, is to really get people's undivided attention and make them think about where their food comes from," Tom says.

The very name of the butcher shop that Tom and his partners are preparing to open—The Meat Hook—harks back to an earlier time, when whole animals were delivered to New York butchers and their carcasses moved on hooks on ceiling tracks. Now, sirloin and strip steaks and pork chops are mostly vacuum-packed, boxed in enormous plants and shipped directly to supermarkets. But Tom is nostalgic for that earlier era, when people knew their butchers and understood their meat.

"I like to call it regressive, before boxed beef, before feedlots," he says. "The Meat Hook is an act of nostalgia, but is also trying to move everything forward."

"In my secret heart, I wish we could go back to the America of my grandfather. He could tell you what any cut was on the steak."

. . .

NOTHING is so antithetical to the urban, the urbane—the sophisticated city—as keeping and killing livestock. A European visitor to New York in 1830 was appalled that slaughterhouses were "scattered over many populous districts of the city," filling the air with "the most noxious effluvia." Blood saturated absorbent wooden slaughterhouse floors, where it rotted and gave off "offensive odors," complained the New York Board of Health. Offal piled in the sewers produced horrible fumes, and draped across the sewer openings was a pretty white mold feeding on animal decay, which people called "lace curtains."

The miasma theory of disease postulated that illnesses such as diphtheria, scarlet fever, smallpox, cholera, and typhoid arose from noxious odors. People were outraged by the prospect that animal smells were not only unsavory, but also unsafe. In a meeting with the city's sanitary inspector, one reporter unrolled a map of recent diphtheria and typhoid cases, showing that they coincided with the slaughterhouse districts—gotcha!

Yet in an era before refrigeration, animals had to be marched into the city "on the hoof," to be killed near where they would be eaten. Steak, it turns out, is a city meal. The American myth of the cowboy on the open plain had its terminus in a crowded, dark city restaurant where people ate their steaks standing up, dispatching the cows the cowboys corralled. Beef eaters were simply more common in cities, whose sheer numbers of people could support a steady demand for large animals.

Changing the system to remove the animals, contain the slaughterhouses, and find other ways of delivering fresh meat to cities took hundreds of years. As recently as the late 1950s, cows, pigs, and sheep were still walking through Midtown Manhattan streets en route to massive slaughterhouses. Even now, some of the eighty local live poultry houses also dispatch goats, lambs, and even cows, serving immigrants who expect to look into a living animal's eyes, feel its flesh, and know it's fresh before killing it to eat. An uncountable number of animals are still raised for food in backyards, basements, community gardens, and city streets.

FROM the very start, newcomers remarked on the plentiful meat they found in this wild land. The Dutch in Manhattan ate buffalo, raccoon, beaver, wild rabbit, turkey, and deer. A traveler from Holland visiting Nieuw Amsterdam supped on a roasted haunch of venison, bought from Indian hunters. "The meat was exceedingly tender and good, and also quite fat," he wrote, and the turkey and goose were also tasty. The remarkable thing, the traveler wrote, was that "everything we had was the natural production of the country."

Soon after the Dutch settlers arrived in 1624, so did three ships called the *Horse*, the *Sheep*, and the *Cow*, named for their cargo. On the journey across the ocean, each animal had its own stall with three feet of sand on the floor, and an attendant who received a bonus if the beast arrived alive. The imported livestock, generally left free to roam, trampled the fields of the native Lenape people, who retaliated. The massacre of swine belonging to a major landowner on Staten Island launched what became known as the Pig War. Cows, horses, oxen, and hogs were eventually exiled to winter on Coney Island, back when it was actually an island. Its watery borders served to pen in the animals, who grazed the wild grasses with nowhere to go except to their own eventual slaughter.

Yet a century and a half later, New York was a blooming, fetid city of animals, where market shoppers had to navigate "the heads of sheep, lambs &c., the hoofs of Cattle, blood and offal strewed in the gutters and sometimes on the pavement, dead dogs, cats, rats, and hogs." Poor women kept their goats tethered to posts and allowed their pigs to forage in the streets. Rich ladies and dandies were disgusted. As New York continued its ascent to national pre-eminence, concerns mounted about the animals in the streets. The city's health inspectors struggled to edge species by species out of public view and establish a clean, modern city.

The world of meat was full of old-fashioned ritual that re-sisted change. Herders moved cattle along the streets of today's Lower East Side to the slaughterhouses on the banks of the Col-lect Pond. Alongside the pond, the legendary Bull's Head Tavern on the Bowery became a literal stock market, where drovers and butchers negotiated for animals over beers, taking breaks to watch dogfights and bearbaiting outside. Most days, the butchers would wheelbarrow their meat back to their simple stalls before dawn. Butchers wore white aprons over their elegant black suits with bowties and top hats. On days when especially fine cattle came in, the butchers would parade the animals with a marching band past the homes of wealthy customers, to lure them outside to order particular cuts of beef.

"Sounds like a very efficient advertising campaign," says Tom Mylan.

ON a sunny day in June 2006, in a dim restaurant in back of a general store, Tom Mylan is sitting on a barstool. He has steel-blue eyes, a square jaw, and Clark Kent glasses, and only his heavy build and reluctance to make eye contact save him from being a classic pretty boy. At this moment, he is the manager and buyer for Marlow & Sons, a Brooklyn restaurant that is also a little so-old-fashioned-it's-hip one-room general store. He is wry, funny, and also obsessed.

No one yet associates Tom Mylan with meat or sees him as the conquering hero of hipstavore Brooklyn. For now, Tom is fascinated with local cheeses, and also curating what he doesn't mind saying is the largest selection of honeys in town. That means chestnut, lime, wild strawberry, and dandelion Italian honeys; starthistle and fireweed honeys from California; thick, opalescent Hawaiian honey from a single grove of kiawe trees, so light that it tingles on the tongue; and city-produced local honeys from the South Bronx and Fort Greene, Brooklyn—some thirty honeys in all. Tom took the train to fetch the Bronx honey himself, taping cases of little jars together so he could carry them on his shoulder on the subway.

Tom spent his earliest years in Reno, Nevada. His parents divorced, and Tom's mom worked the swing shift as a cashier in a hotel casino. Tom would often come home alone after school and make pizza bagels for dinner while he watched Julia Child and Jeff Smith on TV. Cooking meant company. For years of Christmases, Tom gave his mom the latest version of Jeff Smith's *Frugal Gourmet* cookbook. Watching food TV was Tom's first indication that there was a world beyond what he knew, a place that tasted different.

He went to art school then moved to New York with no clear plan, carrying a roll of canvas and an easel, in order to paint, and a laptop so he could write a novel. Soon he found a job at the famous Murray's Cheese Shop in the West Village. Chefs would come by the store and invite the cheesemongers back to their restaurants for a little tasting on the house. Tom and his friends ate food they couldn't afford: "It made us aspirational," Tom said. On a lunch break, one would buy some pork from the old-style butcher Otto-manelli, another would pick up rare figs at the farmers' market. In the evening, they'd all end up at someone's apartment, drinking wine and stuffing figs into a butterflied pork loin.

Creative people like Tom were glutting the boroughs. Many took jobs as waiters and busboys and hostesses and line cooks. Some had artistic success. ("The guy who had the big afro in TV on the Radio was the world's worst barista at Verb," says Tom. "The drummer from Here We Go Magic was one of the best bartenders that Diner ever had.") But most found the econ-omy could not support their creative production. Many of Tom's friends with English degrees and BFAs in photography and sculp-ture began to invest their creative energies in the food jobs that paid, instead of in the creative work that didn't. Maybe that's the point, Tom says: Food is an art the economy will sustain. "Food *is* culture," he says.

At his new job sourcing food at Marlow & Sons, Tom can-celed orders for European cheeses and sought out blues, bloomy rinds, and hard cheeses from farms in Vermont, Connecticut, and New York State. He also started making his own foods for the restaurant and store. He roasted end-of-the-season local chiles, soaked them in vinegar, and pureed them for a house hot sauce. He made peach bitters out of peach stones and grenadine out of the seeds of fresh pomegranates. Using milk from Evans Farm-house Creamery, he figured out how to make yogurt after visiting online forums. "Most of the people who make yogurt are hippies," he warned. "They're not very technical or precise."

"There are not that many people who get what's in this shop.

Either they eat out all the time or they're artist types who subsist on beer and cocaine," Tom told me matter-of-factly in 2006. "I'm interested in what is most special, most interesting, closest geographically, and closest with that thing in our heart."

In the months that followed, Tom continued to ramp up his quest to master the fine arts of food. He made ricotta and ricotta salata cheese. He bought a still and began to produce delicate apple brandy from fruit picked nearby, and absinthe using home-grown herbs. He started a food blog under the name Tom Murda Murda Marcyville, after the Jay-Z song set in the Marcy Projects across from Tom's place. "To get a proper crust on the steak you need to get the surface of that fucker dry and salty," he wrote. "Anything less and you'll be steaming it on that weak-sister, cut-rate, bullshitty stovetop in your apartment. Trust me. If you live in an average NYC apartment you have the same lame $270 gas stove I have and those bitches put out exactly jack and shit for BTUs (those are heat units)."

He came late to curing meat. There is something violent about tampering with the flesh of an animal, and for a guy into extreme-homemade foods it was the last frontier. Tom experimented with curing soft salted duck breasts and pork pancetta. Then he moved on to a whole prosciutto he hung in a drafty corner of the living room in the loft apartment he shared with his girlfriend, Anna-liese Griffin, a writer. The meat had a profound perfume that at first filled the entire loft space, and then, after time, as the pork sealed itself in its hermetic preserve, could only be detected at close range. At night Tom and Annaliese would sit on a little couch by the window, smoking cigarettes, inhaling the cool air from outside along with the deep, pungent smell of curing meat. Tom worried that its core had gone rancid and maggoty, but a year and a half after he had strung up the pork, Tom cut into it and found a delicious, full-flavored, dry prosciutto, which he served to friends at Easter.

Tom proceeded to produce most every meat he could think of—pancetta, guanciale, sausages, bacon, pastrami. It was fun, but otherwise he felt stuck. He wasn't getting traction selling his writing, and he'd quit painting. He toyed with moving upstate or to the West Coast to become a farmer. "While I haven't made it big time or lucked into my true calling I do, however, cook up a couple nice grass-fed steaks from time to time to grease the wheels of love and affection at casa T and A," he wrote on his blog.

Then in 2007, Marlow & Sons decided to start sourcing its meat from small nearby farms, which could deliver only whole, unbutchered animals straight from the slaughterhouse. The restaurant needed a house butcher. Soon Tom found himself apprenticing at Fleisher's Grassfed and Organic Meats, in Kingston, New York. At first he cut himself, often, to the bone. "Sorry I bled everywhere. Pig roast 4 Eva," he wrote on Facebook. Then he spent a year working in back of Marlow & Sons, in a portable space he described as "a 6x8 box, outdoors with a locker full of dead animals."

It was something like a mythical chrysalis period, because by the time he emerged, his fortunes had changed. His fingers had developed so much new muscle that his hands were discernibly larger. The *Times* anointed him a sexy "rock star butcher" possessed of mighty forearms, familiarity with flesh, and a certain kind of local fame. In time, the very publications that had rejected Tom's writing accepted his musings on meat. He began to get ten calls a week from people seeking butchering training. His skill and passion for meat increased in tandem, until he began plotting to open his own butcher shop.

Around the time Tom began dabbling in meat, pop culture had a meat moment. The *New York Times* ran an article about women who reveled in ordering bone-in sirloins and cowboy-cut rib steaks to impress their dates. Cookbooks appeared with names such as *Charcuterie: The Craft of Salting, Smoking and Curing* and *The Whole Beast: Nose to Tail Eating. Meatpaper,* a new magazine in the Bay Area ("news and views from the *fleischgeist*"), was publishing articles about meat and culture, as in a story on the consumption of lamb, bull, and goat testicles, which some Middle Eastern and Asian cultures believe can boost men's sexual prowess. "These are mostly masculine fantasies," the article quoted the New York University professor Krishnendu Ray as saying. "Rarely do people eat breasts to get bigger breasts."

It was part of a cultural shift, the return of old-fashioned, unprocessed, richly flavored foods—as opposed to low-fat, chemically enhanced, supposedly healthful ones. The trend also seemed to reflect a desire to discover more moral ways of being a carnivore, by rejecting the industrial meat pumped full of antibiotics and hormones and produced on feedlots, in favor of animals raised carefully on small farms.

It looked like a moment to remember that New York has long been an enthusiastically carnivorous city.

IN 1818, when keeping swine in the street was standard, New York's mayor had a butcher indicted for the practice. A few years later, when officials began rounding up pigs, crowds of hundreds of women freed the animals. Hog riots broke out in 1825, 1826, 1830, and 1832, all with the same resolution: the women saved their bacon. Despite officials' best efforts, by 1842, roughly 10,000 stray pigs wandered city streets, and before a decade had passed, the number had doubled.

Snorting and squealing, copulating and defecating, the pigs offended the leaders of the bustling new metropolis, as historians have noted: "Our wives and daughters cannot walk abroad through the streets of the city without encountering the most disgusting spectacles of these animals indulging the propensities of nature," declared the mayor in 1818.

Even Charles Dickens, that expert on urban squalor, remarked on the pigs he encountered on Broadway, New York's most glamorous avenue. "Here is a solitary swine, lounging homeward by himself," he wrote. "He has only one ear, having parted with the other to vagrant-dogs in the course of his city rambles. But he gets on very well without it; and leads a roving, gentlemanly, vagabond kind of life . . . turning up the news and small-talk of the city in the shape of cabbage-stalks and offal."

"Sometimes, indeed," the English writer continued, "you may see his small eye twinkling on a slaughtered friend, whose carcase garnishes a butcher's door-post, but he grunts out 'Such is life: all flesh is pork!' buries his nose in the mire again, and waddles down the gutter: comforting himself with the reflection that there is one snout the less to anticipate stray cabbage-stalks, at any rate."

Finally an armed squad stepped in to subdue the swine. A team of health wardens, policemen, scavengers, meat and street inspectors, and night and dock watchmen, carrying pistols, clubs, daggers, pickaxes, and crowbars, waged war on pigs in the summer of 1859. In the battlefields of Hog Town, the West Side district between Fiftieth and Fifty-Eighth streets known for its shanties and pig pens, police turned up hogs under beds and behind stairs, in cellars and garrets. They eventually drove some 20,000 swine north to the upper reaches of Manhattan. By the 1860s, no living pig was welcome below Eighty-Sixth Street. Those who hoped to remake New York as a nonanimal kingdom turned their attentions to other species.

Cows suffered their own dismal fate. As Manhattan's pastures turned into buildings in the 1820s, they had lost grazing grounds. The unfortunate solution was to set up dairies adjacent to distilleries so cattle could nourish themselves on the hot slop—the by-product of making liquor—pouring out of the stills. Two thousand cows survived on this diet at Johnson & Sons, a distillery between Fifteenth and Sixteenth streets on the West Side, where the slop traveled to the animal pens in a tunnel under Tenth Avenue.

The system produced ulcerous, ailing cows whose milk—perhaps three-quarters of the city's supply—often sickened those who drank it. When the cows stopped producing milk, they were slaughtered and sold as meat. This beef had unusual qualities, observers noted. It reeked, and had to be sold quickly or it would "putrefy on the dealer's hands," wrote an incensed reformer, Robert Hartley, who added that the meat was so bloated that cooking it would cause it to "shrivel up to the bone, or be reduced, perhaps, to one half its original dimensions." The move to pasteurize milk came as a reaction to the products of these diseased cows, but the poor continued to consume their cheap meat.

Healthier cattle also walked to the city from distant farms. The drovers were thought to be scoundrels, classic middlemen moving between city and country, telling a thousand lies as they haggled and teased the farmer out of his beef and the butcher out of his cash. At farmhouses and drovers' taverns with names like the Bull's Head and the Drovers' Holm, men and beasts would be liquored and fed, watered and grazed, according to their respective needs. Swimming their animals across streams and sleeping with them under the stars, drovers moved 200,000 head of cattle on the hoof each year as late as 1825—escorted by a menagerie of pigs, horses, and lambs from the Bronx down through Manhattan.

Yet whenever a maddened bull escaped from a cattle drive to gore bystanders, someone suggested that drovers should be restricted to nighttime marches. Whenever a new round of cholera or yellow fever broke out, people remarked that maybe slaughterhouses should be moved out of residential neighborhoods. In 1866, the city empowered a new Metropolitan Board of Health, the country's first permanent public health agency, and one of its early orders of business was to regulate meat. The board quickly imposed strict new rules on butchers, stopped animals from ranging free, and banished slaughterhouses to a few blocks around Fortieth Street on the East and West sides. Portending the future, enormous modern slaughterhouses opened up across the Hudson in Bergen, New Jersey.

The status of the city's butchers was changing. Once, they had been masters of life and death at the top of the food chain, the bosses of the markets. The last of the wild land had passed through their hands, as they broke down such increasingly rare creatures as buffalo, white hares, bears, deer, moose (the snout was a delicacy), otters, swans, and grouse. They had marched in civic parades, proudly bearing signs that read, "We Preserve by Destroying," and "To all we divide a part." But when the butchers launched a lawsuit against the slaughterhouse restrictions, they lost.

By the 1870s, Tom Mylan's predecessors still cut up the 320,500 cattle, 1.2 million hogs, 1 million sheep, and 100,000 calves slaughtered annually within Manhattan. "The lowing and moaning of the cattle, the clatter of their hoofs upon the stones, the noises, not loud, but suggestive, connected with the act of killing," offended the ear, requiring segregated districts for slaughterhouses, wrote the public health experts. Yet it was hard to imagine banning cattle altogether in a city largely lacking refrigeration. "Slaughtering establishments are just as essential to a large city as dry goods houses," wrote one supporter to the newspaper in 1899.

The presence of animals had inspired the creation of health codes and agencies, and enlisted armies of enforcers, but the city would continue to house cows, pigs, and sheep, alive and dead.

IN the months before opening the Meat Hook, his spare, minimalist butcher shop in the Williamsburg neighborhood of Brooklyn, Tom Mylan donned safety goggles and old jeans to renovate his 1,000-square-foot space. The Meat Hook would be part of the Brooklyn Kitchen, a "food dork megaplex" including a cooking supplies shop, a food bookstore, a grocery store, a homebrew shop, and a lab with classes on food and drink. Tom mounted wall panels, set up display cases, and assembled butcher tables. He looked into installing a meat hook system to hang the meat, but the ceilings were too low. He was so excited to get a used band saw that he blogged about its delivery at 11:30 on a Sunday night, and promised to buff and polish it to shine like chrome. "Please tune in for the next episode of *Pimp my Band Saw*."

The Meat Hook, Tom's new-style homage to old-school butchering, opened in the fall of 2009. The well-lit main room has a wooden table for cutting meat and a glass counter for displaying it. On the counter is a framed photograph of a guy eating sausage, with the handwritten message, "Tom, that's your motherfucking sausage in my motherfucking mouth. –Adam." A sign on the wall reads MOTHERFUCKING MEAT, MOTHERFUCKER! Nearby are books such as *Raising Beef Cattle*, *Pocketful of Poultry*, *Basic Butchering of Livestock and Game*. Another counter is piled with scabbards—holsters for butchers' knives—and iPods; while the one iPod in use in the dock shuffles through Cypress Hill, Lynyrd Skynyrd, and Soulja Boy. Most important, though, is the meat, which comes exclusively from small farms nearby and is appetizingly arrayed in stainless-steel refrigerators with green-lined shelves that highlight the red flesh and perfect lines of white fat. If something dead can be glowing with health, it's the meat at the Meat Hook.

Here, Tom and his partners, Brent Young and Ben Turley, and their staff of two more "born-again meat cutters," receive whole animals from nearby farms and turn them into cuts of meat. Each week, they get an average of two cows, three pigs, two lambs, a hundred and fifty chickens, ten ducks, a few rabbits, and, seasonally, turkeys—thousands of pounds to sell. They cut hams specially for their friends. They produce dozens of kinds of sausages. They make country pâté. They sell leaf lard, duck fat, suet, and old-fashioned schmaltz. On the butcher's table in the middle of the room, in sight of their customers, like some kind of performance, they cube bits of pork shoulder and pull cheeks of lambs to make sausages. They visit all the family farms that supply them to see that the animals continue to be sustainably raised with wholesome diets and care. Tom married his girlfriend, Annaliese, just before the butcher shop opened, but he has had barely any time with his bride. He spends about seventy hours a week at the Meat Hook. "Everything that's in these cases," Tom says, gesturing at the surrounding meat, "it's like our heart and soul." He told a visitor once, "I spend every waking moment doing it. It's nuts. *I'm* nuts."

"We're doing things the old way," says Tom, long after the shop has closed for the day, sitting at the counter with a gin and tonic—a position clearly familiar to him. "To be quite honest, we're in over our heads." They're not old guys, he says—they don't even know old guys. So they have to figure out for themselves the best, most efficient old way—that is, often, a new way.

Beyond the butcher shop, the Brooklyn Kitchen store sells nearly limitless variations on standard kitchen gadgets. There are basters, dual basters, bulb basters, half a dozen kinds of timers, four kinds of popsicle molds, a cherry pitter, apple and tomato corers, five kinds of fruit peelers, and three kinds of fruit slicers. This is a temple to a particular vision of the good life for young, urban America, and you get the sense that you can buy this good life with Tom's skirt steaks and pork rounds and chicken livers.

Once upon a time, the fantasy of the rock star meant sex and debauchery—the reckless freedom a generation wanted to taste. Now, apparently, rock star status includes the domestic fantasy of a married butcher in a flannel shirt who works in a store full of kitchen gadgets and likes to talk about environmental issues while he cuts meat for dinner.

. . .

IN the 1870s, the Chicago clearinghouses shipping beef and pork to East Coast cities realized it would be cheaper to send dead meat than live steers. They built massive stockyards and slaughterhouses where they could "disassemble" cows and pack the carcasses to travel efficiently. In a leap of technology, they harvested ice from the Great Lakes and stored it in stations along the train routes to cool the meat they sent in rail cars all the way to eastern cities. Prices went down, and *Harper's Weekly* heralded a new "era of cheap beef."

Yet in New York, local demand for kosher meat sustained independent slaughterhouses, meatpackers, and butchers, and the city remained the largest meat processing center on the East Coast until World War II. Between 1880 and 1920, more than 17 million immigrants landed at the port of New York. Many had lost family farms or had seen their artisanal trades disappear. *They were hungry.* In the old countries, they had barely enough food to survive, and if meat was available, it was the animal's least appealing and cheapest parts, used to flavor broths and stews.

In New York, they found a rich, meaty city where the easy access to beef and pork and mutton symbolized achievement. In America, the higher the salary, the more meat people ate—a fleshly standard of success. One man recalled that his grandfather would put a toothpick in his mouth as he left home "to give the impression that he had eaten meat."

Look at old records of the businesses along cobblestoned Fourteenth Street and you can see the fourteen-block wholesale meat market take shape, soon to dominate the northeast. The Centennial Brewery converted to meat in 1901; the Merchants' Print

Works turned over to poultry distributors in 1911; a row of stores became a cold storage warehouse for meat in 1921. A big brick building on Thirteenth Street became a vocational high school for food trades, including butchery, complete with a walk-in cooler, a sawdust floor, and deliveries of whole animals for students to break down.

Freight trains sped down Tenth Avenue to deliver meat to the Fourteenth Street Market. Men known as West Side cowboys would wave a red flag or swing a lantern at the head of the train to clear the way. There were still so many train accidents that the street became known as Death Avenue. The High Line, an elevated freight line, had to be constructed from Thirty-Fourth Street down to Spring Street, cutting right inside of warehouses to make second-story meat deliveries. The butchers moved the animal carcasses from hooks in railcars to overhead meat tracks, shedding fat and blood.

You could walk into any cooler and see men hacking away in syncopation, fat flying, their bosses looking down on them from squinty-windowed upstairs loft offices. Other wholesale meat markets operated in the Bronx on Brook Avenue and in Fort Greene in Brooklyn, with smaller centers in Queens and in Harlem. Kosher sausage factories, including the Hebrew National hot dogs company on East Broadway, grew up all over the Lower East Side, making bologna, frankfurters, wienerwursts, corned beef, corned tongue, and kosher cooking fat for the new delicatessens. As late as 1929, a full third of the city's beef was still slaughtered locally for Jewish customers. The West Side of Manhattan developed into a vast complex of stockyards and stables, which filled the city with a perfume of shit and death when the wind came east from New Jersey. The city, eager to retain the fresh meat and the jobs, subsidized the industry throughout the early twentieth century.

ONE morning at the Meat Hook, Tom is slicing bacon while looking toward the door. He's expecting a delivery of two new city-raised, freshly slaughtered pigs from the Queens County Farm Museum. Everyone's excited. Ben Turley, a tall butcher with pink cheeks like rosy tattoos, came in early to be present for the delivery. But so far, no pigs.

It's easy to find time-filling tasks. Ben uses a cleaver to turn chunks of bacon into wide, fatty white strips. Sara Bigelow, a lean, black-banged butcher who works for the Meat Hook, snips the links between sausages. Another new butcher, the handlebar-mustachioed Matt Greene, slices ham. Tom uses his iPhone to photograph Canadian bacon—he often texts pretty meat pics to the restaurateurs he supplies and the farmers who supply him—until the phone interrupts him by vibrating. "The girl delivering the pigs was stopped because she was in the carpool lane," he says as he hangs up. "Apparently she thought the pigs in the back counted as passengers."

During Tom's first visit to the Queens County Farm Museum, the head farmer had wanted to talk about marketing his pork. The place had long been a kind of petting zoo for school groups and families around the quiet Glen Oaks neighborhood, but the new farmer, Michael Grady Robertson, had broader ambitions. He hoped to build a working farm that would raise and sell pork, chicken, beef, mutton, and goat. He saw it as an opportunity to teach New Yorkers about small-scale, humane meat production, in contrast with large-scale industrial techniques.

He also saw it as more moral to keep the animals to nourish and educate people, rather than as living toys for children to pet. He wanted advice from Tom about how to solicit meat orders from restaurants, what they might pay per pound, when the pigs should be slaughtered, nuts-and-bolts sorts of things.

Soon, in the fall and spring, the Queens farm was getting new piglets from a breeder and allowing them to root about the grounds in movable pens. Pigs are such efficient foragers that some farmers rent them out to clear land. These pigs were rotated in and out of different blocks of woodland to clear poison ivy and garlic mustard and make room for healthy tree and plant growth. From fall to spring, or spring to fall, the Queens pigs foraged and ate feed, farm scraps, and leftover mash from the brewery, until they were heavier than most grown men. They were slaughtered in a job-training program for prisoners on Long Island and sent to Tom for butchering.

The ultimate flavor of the pork is unique to these pigs, raised on the peculiar fruits of the boroughs. "Awesome" is the word Tom uses to describe the taste. Richer, fuller, inordinately better than industrially raised pork, the meat of the Queens pigs is also chemically different, Tom says. Industrial pork rots quickly when exposed to light and air and produces a fat that feels slightly prickly, something like Velcro on the tongue. The pork from Queens has a more intense flavor and a smoother, lighter texture.

At the Meat Hook, the bell on the door keeps ringing and the flow of customers is steady. "Hey, you! Want to play video games with me tonight?" Ben calls from behind the counter to a stranger.

"I brought this for you," says a different man, bearded and flannel-shirted, tenderly placing a plastic container on the counter. "It's the last of my chicken stock. I wanted you to try it." A guy who works at the wine tasting room of Brooklyn Oenology stops in, an editor of local *Edible* magazines buys merguez sausages, and the founders of a new distillery show up and ask Tom's advice on stills. "We're trying to build a human community around something cool that we do," says Tom.

Finally, while Tom's out front smoking, the red pickup truck from the Queens farm pulls up, and a sweet-faced farm girl, as Tom calls her, smilingly introduces her dead pigs. "This one has a nineteen-and-a-half-pound head," she says, patting it affectionately.

Tom hugs her warmly with his thick butcher's arms, squeezing her hard and picking her up off the ground. Then he takes the first pink pig in a similar embrace, heaving it over his shoulder and walking inside, the knives of his scabbard clanking together while the pig's curly tail wags on his back. He deposits the first pig in the walk-in cooler, and comes back for the next, which he flops onto the butchering table in the center of the shop.

The pig is pink-skinned and mostly plucked, but has short bristles on its nose and its chin, like an old man no longer grooming himself with much attention. Tom plans to sell the shoulders and hams in the shop but to return the chops and sausages to Queens to serve at a dinner on the farm.

"Mmmm," he says, tapping each fingertip, making eeny meeny miney moe fingers as he decides which end to butcher first. Sometimes he'll toss a coin: If it's heads, he'll start from the snout; if it's tails, he'll start from the hindquarters. This time, he picks up a rear leg and lights into it with a five-inch Forschner boning knife from Switzerland.

He works his knife along the animal's tendons and muscles, freeing each piece from its confines in the binding fat. There are two butchering techniques, he explains. In one, you cut alongside the muscle and bone, and in the other, you cut through them at cross angles. Tom does both. He makes a kind of fist over the knife to give him leverage to draw it back toward himself in the pig. "It has double the usual fat," he says, assessing the white gel, three inches thick. "The meat is this amazing dark red color because the pigs have just been eating fresh vegetables from the farm," he says, holding the carcass steady. "Muscles that do a lot of work have more flavor. Muscles that do less work have less flavor."

This is a beautiful specimen, but Tom plans to make future pigs even tastier. Hogs that eat acorns near the end of their lives taste intensely porky, he says; the rich, tannic nuts amplify the flavor of their meat, making it as different from regular heritage-breed pork as most heritage-breed hogs are from industrially produced pigs. Tom had an idea for a promotion in the store: If you bring in five-gallon buckets of acorns to feed the pigs in Queens, you get a discount on meat. He likes the thought of building the pigs' flavor.

Tom returns to the animal to peel its skin, which comes off in neat strips, as if he were peeling a fruit. Somehow it looks appetizing, even raw. "If it's killed badly, you'll see little blood spots, showing the animal was stressed," he says. "This one doesn't have that." He digs his knife in, jerks it around, and pulls out a pig drumstick, then a pig hoof. He has a sureness of hand and he leans into the cut, using his weight to drive effortlessly through the flesh. He went to art school for sculpture, and it's easy to imagine him carving clay with the same careful motions. At times, Tom lays his palm down flat, moving across the animal with unexpected intimacy, extending his hands-on physicality to the pork.

I remember that Tom told *Nerve,* the online literary sex magazine, that becoming a butcher had changed his perception of human beings. "I definitely look at everyone and everything like I'm judging a steer on the hoof. Remember that you want an animal that has a shiny coat, has good conformation and isn't too skinny," he said. "Skinny animals have bad genetics and taste gamey." He's confident and sure of his touch and his impact on the meat, and if there's something sexy about butchering, it's that—it shows a man who's comfortable with flesh.

SHEEP and cattle scampered to their deaths on Fortieth Street at the East River, an area spotted with gas tanks, tenements, and junkyards, until the place was slated as the headquarters of the newly chartered United Nations. As planners articulated a new vision for a city scrubbed of industry, the East Side slaughterhouses cleared out to make way for a postwar icon of global power.

That left only the West Side slaughterhouses to supply the Fourteenth Street Market. As the streets clogged with chrome-trimmed Packards and Cadillacs with fins, it became more challenging to drive cattle through Midtown West. Back in the 1870s, a cow tunnel had been built under Thirty-Fourth Street so the cattle coming in from New Jersey by barge would not disrupt traffic, and in 1932, a second tunnel was constructed under Thirty-Eighth Street. By the 1950s, freight trains deposited animals directly in the Manhattan stockyards adjacent to most of the slaughterhouses.

A block away on Thirty-Ninth Street, only the New York Butchers Dressed Meat Company slaughterhouse, featuring six limestone heads of rams and steers on the façade, still had to move cattle through the streets. A "Judas steer"—an animal docile enough to lead the rest of the herd to the slaughter—would head off the procession through alleys and up the street to New York Butchers. Once when the Hudson River froze, a steer galloped across the thick sheet of ice toward New Jersey. Sometimes, animal handlers from the slaughterhouse had to chase a steer through Midtown streets with a tranquilizer gun. In one unsavory episode, they caught a steer by smashing into him with a truck, tying him to the vehicle, and dragging the moaning beast for blocks. The following year, workers finally built a fourteen-foot-high aluminum-covered bridge from the stockyards so animals could walk securely to the slaughterhouse.

At New York Butchers in the 1950s, two men would lift a steer into position as a third slit its throat so the beast's life would end in a single stroke, making a kosher kill. The "head man" would cut off the head, and the skinner would use long, graceful sweeps of his knife to peel the hide. A butcher would step in to drop the intestines in a corner, and place the lungs, heart, and lymph nodes in separate little trays. Inspectors would examine each tray, palpate the liver, and cut through the wet, warm heart—seeking any indication of tuberculosis, measles, or worms, recalled Enrico Sciorra, who then worked there as a USDA veterinarian. Men cut all night long, and then loaded meat into trucks packed with ice for delivery to Fourteenth Street plants.

But people complained. They wanted the slaughterhouses out.

It wasn't the stench of death or of meat—it was the rich, overpowering smell of life: the manure, the feed, the anxious, crowded animals. Slaughtering ceased by 1960 and the building was eventually judged unsafe and torn down in 1991.

THE staff of the Meat Hook offers classes on making sausage and charcuterie, on barbecue (either Texas or Carolinas style), on how to cook meat, on braising and roasting, on country hams, on meat and gin, on pig butchering, and even one they call date night butchering—"It's Saturday night, you can have a couple drinks," Tom Mylan once explained, "hang out, watch some butchering, and go out to eat afterwards." In a sense, Tom is teaching people how to eat meat the old-fashioned way. Most people are used to buying chicken breasts and strip steaks, not figuring out what to do with livers and knuckles and lesser cuts of loin.

Tom launches his pig butchering class while sipping a Genesee Cream Ale. He gestures toward the rows of Brooklyn Lager and the bottle opener attached to the wall: "Help yourself." Before class begins, there will be warnings about the three-horsepower Hobart grinder, which works through more than twenty pounds of meat a minute. "Your arm probably only weighs three or four pounds, so stay away from that," says Ben Turley. As the group assembles in the butchery, sipping on beers, Tom will carry in the pig: dead, plucked, gutted, pink.

He will explain that it was killed calmly, cleanly, without pain, electrodes like salad tongs on its head zapping it unconscious so its jugular vein might be quickly slashed. Next it was dunked in scalding water, scraped of bristles, gutted, relieved of heart and lungs, and finally sprayed with a mild dilution of white vinegar to kill bacteria. In Tom's telling, it sounds neat, careful, almost kind.

Tom will pick up the pig's head and point to the tasty bits. "The brain is edible," he will say, "though not one of my favorite things." Not as nice as lamb brains, for instance. "Young animals have better-tasting brains," says Tom, who traces the geography of the pig as he cuts into it. The neck, the shoulder, the top butt, the picnic ham, he says, naming each part as he separates it from its attachments.

Center-cut pork chops, the loin, the belly, spare ribs, baby back ribs, the sirloin, the tenderloin. The ham, the hock, the trotter. He explains the animal using a combination of technical butcher's terms and profanity, which gives the impression of speaking just between you and me, as though he has picked you personally to share his deep secrets of meat. He mentions amazing YouTube videos made by packing house workers with cell phone cameras: "It's almost like a crazy Samurai movie, where they'll sharpen their knives and they just go *whoooosh,* and you're like, 'Did they even touch the meat?'"

Parts of the animal embody taboos in food: raw things, slippery things, bits that are wobbly and jiggly and gristly, scrappy and shimmery and sinewy. This is what butchering is about, Tom says. "We add value to the undesirable parts of the animal." There's only one skirt steak on every cow, but the rest of the animal can't just be thrown away. When you receive a whole animal from a farm instead of boxes of identical, factory-produced parts, you have to figure out utility for everything.

Tom will suggest throwing in a dollop of mustard if you can't take the organy goodness of sautéed kidney. He will talk about uses for the Jell-O-like leaf lard from the animal's gastrointesti-nal tract. He will tell how he makes jerky sticks out of beef and pork hearts and tongues, chili containing pork skin, scrapple from the head meat, blood sausages and blood cakes. The shop boils bones and scraps into broths, including Chinese chicken broth, ramen broth, and beefy Vietnamese pho. "It might only take you six months to learn how to cut up animals anatomically," Tom likes to say. "It takes years to figure out how to sell every part of the animal. If I see anything in the trash, it's our failure."

Tom will show the class his ebony-handled knife with a carbon-steel blade and hand-hammered brass star-shaped rivets. Unlike plastic, the ebony does not get slippery with fat. The knife was a special sale from Tom's knife-sharpener, Robert Ambrosi, who is part of a clan of sharpeners who have served the city's meatpackers for generations. It was produced long ago by Robert's great-grandfather's upstate company. Tom will tell his students that he doesn't like to use his new band saw after all, because it lacks romance and manual labor—and because, well, he's scared of it. Tom is so enamored of the knife, on the other hand, that he posted its photograph on his Facebook page.

"You want meat that smells like meat and looks like meat—not pink, but bright red. It shouldn't smell like a refrigerator," says Tom to his meat and gin class, in which students learn to pair various kinds of meat with particular gin drinks. The resin-ous spices in gin work well with pâté and duck, Tom explains. To go with drinks including a Tom Collins and a gin martini, Tom has prepared country pâté, lamb, dry-aged steaks, and chorizo-stuffed duck hearts—looking moist and shaped just like the med-ical diagrams of human hearts, only tiny. "It's very sanguineous, like, sort of bloody," he says. "It tastes a lot like duck breast but more profound."

When Tom takes questions, his students are more curious about their teacher than his subject: Is there a kind of meat he doesn't like? ("I'm willing to try anything," he says, "so when I say beef liver is really gross, it's pretty fucking gross.") What's the weirdest meat he ever ate? ("I like escargot and whelks and all those sort of snail things. I've never eaten oxen. I've had really good venison.") "Ostrich?" asks a woman in the class seductively, tugging at her earlobe, tilting her head down and looking up into Tom's eyes. ("I don't know shit about ostrich," he says. "I haven't butchered ostrich. I haven't eaten ostrich.") Did he always want to be a butcher? ("I was vegetarian for two and a half years.")

At the end of the night, he sits on a stool at the meat counter in the empty shop. Tom runs through ideas for putting meat animals in cities and suburbs. You could raise a goat on an urban rooftop, he suggests. "There's a lot of people that have three- or four-acre backyards, or woodlots behind their house," he said, citing New Jersey, Westchester County, and the Bronx. "These people could own a cow," he proposes. "From one football field you can raise steers every two or three years that can feed the football team for a month."

THE butchers at the old Fourteenth Street Market had other concerns. Many among the older generation had trained in Europe and landed in New York as the flotsam of war. Some had completed old-fashioned apprenticeships, such as one man who had worked in a slaughterhouse in France, where tradition required the apprentice to drink the warm blood of the first lamb he killed.

Sam Solasz learned butchering as a Jewish child in Poland, and perhaps his experience with slaughter served him during the war, when he lost his parents and fought against the Nazis with the partisans in the forest. He arrived in New York in 1951 carrying his butcher knives and ten dollars that he had earned cutting meat on board the ship. On his first full day on American soil, he got a meat job, and when he opened his own meatpacking business, a *landsman,* or countryman, at the West Side slaughterhouse saved him the finest animals.

Sam would wake his sons Mark and Scott around three a.m. on the days they didn't have school, and pack them into the backseat of the gold Delta 88, where they slept on the way from Bayside, Queens, to the Fourteenth Street Market. Mark remembers that it was always dark—his whole experience of his father's work took place at night—and the locker room, with gray metal lockers, was lit with old bare lightbulbs.

The butchers' sons apprenticed under their fathers' tutelage, bouncing through the cobblestoned market trundling buckets of calf livers. The sons joined their fathers for lunch at Frank's steakhouse, where sawdust covered the tile floor, and men hung up their white coats on the wall and sat down, without bothering to remove their scabbards, to eat kidneys and sweetbreads, oxtails and calves' liver and tripe. When it was time for the sons to graduate to full-time work, companies would craft shareholders' agreements with two different classes of stock: fathers and sons (the sons couldn't vote).

There was no Pathmark, no Fine Fare, no Trader Joe's. The

city's butchers showed up before dawn at the meat market, moving from cooler to cooler, stopping at one for lamb, one for veal, one that only had briskets, another only flanks, poking, prodding, and, finally, stamping the meat they wanted so it would be delivered to their stores.

But that way of life was already disappearing. In 1961, a company called Iowa Beef Packers invented a new way to distribute meat. The goal had been to "take the skill out of every step of butchering," one of the owners candidly said. This way, IBP could "take boys right off the farm" and install them in jobs on the disassembly line. In enormous new rural plants, cutters broke down each carcass into forty-four primal cuts stripped of most bone and fat. The meat was packed in plastic Cryovac packets and piled into boxes for shipment. Supermarkets in poor neighborhoods could now choose to order only rumps. Shops in rich areas could order only steaks. Soon IBP cut and boxed 65,000 cattle in a week, and grew bigger than all of the previous generation's leading Chicago-based packers put together.

The rambling, crumbling, Mafia-infiltrated Fourteenth Street Market didn't stand a chance. Just as sending dead animals had once proved cheaper than shipping live ones, now moving consumer cuts clearly costs less than transporting forequarters and hindquarters. The small, aging multilevel shops around Fourteenth Street were struggling to renovate and keep up to code, as black mold bloomed on the ceilings of the coolers, flaking paint fell into fresh meat, narrow wood doorways became encrusted with fat left over from meat scraping off as it was carried in. The market was so congested that trailers making meat deliveries had to wait an average of an hour and a quarter to even enter the loading area. Deliveries took over the sidewalks, so that a passing pedestrian could be hit by a flying calf on its way from a truck into the building.

Until spring of 1970, IBP was unable to sell its prepackaged meat in New York City because labor unions refused to handle it. But as the Midwesterners learned New York ways, IBP offered bribes to meat buyers at the city's new supermarket chains. Neighborhood butcher shops disappeared. The new system reduced local meatpackers to unpackers of boxes, removers of specific cuts of meat, shippers.

Meanwhile, the city had acquired a hundred acres in Hunts Point, a dilapidated and remote section of the South Bronx, to build modern, contained wholesale meat and fish markets. The new meatpackers' cooperative built members spacious two-story plants, extensive loading docks, and meat rail systems tailor-made for their products (higher for beef, lower for mutton and pork). Slowly the Fourteenth Street plants began to move in, receding from public view.

In a larger shift, New York at midcentury, the country's biggest industrial center, was sloughing off industry. The idea had been discussed for decades, since the Regional Plan Association in 1929 had proposed moving industry out of the city to make room for pristine, modern office towers and housing developments. The "stench of slaughterhouses filled the air a few hundred feet from Times Square" the association wrote in its 1929 Master Plan. "Such a situation outrages one's sense of order. Everything seems misplaced. . . . One yearns to rearrange things to put things where they belong." Members of the association included leading property owners with family names such as Rockefeller, Morgan, and Roosevelt, as well as representatives of the New York and

Penn Central railroads and First National City Bank, who stood to profit from increased real estate values.

New York in 1947 had more manufacturing jobs than Philadelphia, Detroit, Los Angeles, and Boston put together, noted historian Joshua B. Freeman. As well as the meat market, Manhattan was a place of Districts: Fur, Printing, Flower, Leather, Diamond, Button, Electronics. There was still a queerness about the city's small semi-industrial concerns: importers of armadillo meat and ostrich-egg agents, dealers in medical leeches and medieval-style engravers.

But real estate owners and policymakers began to talk more and more about "the best and highest use of the land," that is, commercial and high-end residential real estate. In 1961, a new zoning law prohibited heavy manufacturing in large sections of the outer boroughs and in all but a few neighborhoods in Manhattan. From 1968 to 1977, as more rules changed, about 600,000 industrial jobs disappeared from the city, some of them in meat. The people who owned the newly zoned lands made a fortune.

The Fourteenth Street meat market was a holdout, where butchers in blood-spattered white coats built fires in oil cans on the sidewalks to warm their hands. The High Line moved its last three carloads of frozen turkeys in 1980, and then the elevated tracks fell out of use. Homeless kids who lived on the salt mountains by the West Side docks came by to scavenge cuts of meat. Transvestite prostitutes with blond wigs and pink chiffon pants scouted the cobblestone streets. "The sidewalks run with rivulets of greasy blood," wrote the *Times*, "and prostitutes pick their way around discarded chunks of fat."

Yet each year, more of the meatpackers sold out and retired to Florida, as their children made it clear they had no interest in the brutal, backbreaking nighttime world of meat. A single real estate investor had bought nearly a fifth of the market area from failing meatpacking plants and then sat on his holdings, thereby preserving the market. He died in 1999, leaving the area open to development.

THE remnants of the Fourteenth Street Market have now mostly moved to Hunts Point in the Bronx. At three a.m. on a Tuesday, a forty-four-foot refrigerated semi trailer pulls in from Chicago and backs into the loading docks of Master Purveyors, still run by Sam Solasz and his sons, Mark and Scott. The rear panel opens to reveal a pristine, preserved cold cargo: 42,000 pounds of forequarters and hindquarters of beef, all hanging by the leg from hooks attached to the ceiling of the truck. The truckful adds up to the carcasses of a hundred steers, worth more than $100,000. Stooped, laryngitic, wearing a hoodie that says CIRQUE DU SO-LASZ from his daughter's bat mitzvah (where real Cirque du Soleil contortionists performed a female-on-female act that shocked his Conservative Long Island synagogue), Mark Solasz yells out orders to the men preparing to unload the truck. "Why you smiling? Wipe that smile off your face!" he says.

Sam, Mark, and Scott quit the old meat market on Fourteenth Street in 2001, when they were facing lease negotiations on their rent of $6 a square foot at a time when neighborhood rents had shot up to $100 a square foot. Only about twenty-five meat companies remained at the Fourteenth Street Market, down from more than a hundred a decade prior.

Now at Hunts Point, they have designed their own low-slung

two-story facility with long rows of loading docks and plenty of parking. Mark manages clients and arranges meat deliveries. Scott supervises meat processing and the dry-aging room. Their father, Sam, now in his eighties, grinds meat. The business moves more than 300,000 pounds of meat a week, including dry-aged beef for legendary restaurants such as Peter Luger and Smith & Wollensky, and also boxed beef for grocery stores such as Fairway.

Prime meat—the top 2 percent of the country's cows—costs more than twice the price of choice and select meat, and has to hang. Laying the meat out flat crushes the muscle, stops the moisture from evaporating, and dissipates the flavor. But Mark Solasz's meat is not like Tom Mylan's meat. Mark's meat mostly comes from big, distant farms, few of them interested in organic practices or grass-fed ideals, and most of them using plenty of antibiotics and grain for feed.

A hanging-meat system requires specialized luggers to lift quarter steers that weigh more than 250 pounds. Big Ron Jennings, a giant of a man at six-five and a steely 260 pounds, works with his partner under the white light of a single bulb in the truck. The light illuminates thick yellow fat, red stripes of muscle and the men themselves, as they use their bodies like machine conveyors to transfer carcasses to the warehouse's system of ceiling hooks. It's about technique, Ron says. "A guy with mediocre-type power can still do the work because he knows how to *carry*, how to grab hold of it, how to hold onto it towards your body." Propelled by an even push, a cold quarter steer can swing out of the truck with frightening heft and force—shedding bits of fat and tissue as it jerks through the air and then slams into the other quarters of cattle that preceded it.

"Watch your back—*watch your back!*" screams Ron as a man crosses the path of a swinging forequarter, his boot leaving footprints in the fat on the ground. Despite the crushing weight, the luggers work methodically, in a kind of audible rhythm: quiet as they lift meat from the truck's hook; a ding as they hang it on the warehouse's hook; an ear-shattering *clang-clang-clang* as they slide the hook with its meat out of the truck and send it along the line on the loading dock; then a sudden dull silence after one quarter hits the rest of the meat and all swing wildly. "You ain't done yet?" Mark calls into the belly of the truck, where George and Ron have emptied a third of the beef. It takes hours to empty the load.

The meat swings into the fabrication room—more aptly, the defabrication room—where it is cut while still on the hook, shrinking in size and then waving more precipitously, emitting a tangy mineral smell. The workers hack with perfect choreography, burrowing their knives into the hunks of flesh that hang all around them, moving toward the deadline of morning, when the trucks pull out of the loading docks to make deliveries. The Spanish radio station La Mega occasionally raises its voice over the band saws, the thump of cuts of meat hitting the table, and the loud fans. In the permanent winter of refrigeration, the workers wear cheap work boots or sneakers, gloves, and hoodies with the hoods up under hardhats. They almost never slip on the floors greased with fat and as slippery as an ice rink. They almost never lose grip on the knife.

The workers don't talk to each other; instead, they communicate with their knives: as one man slices into an animal, those around him move away. Every so often each meat cutter sharpens his knife or dips it into boiling water to sterilize and heat it so the blade cuts cleanly through the cold fat. This is close work. Guys hug opposite sides of a quarter steer as they each cut in, their blades facing each other. They carry sharp steel hooks they use like hands to move the meat where they need. Like Tom Mylan's butchers, these men understand the arts of meat.

The aging room, with its rows of prime Angus hindquarters, is arranged something like a dry cleaner's, but with the thick funk of decay. These giant hunks of meat contain cowboy, rib, T-bone and porterhouse steaks, short loins and sirloins and chateaubriands, filet mignons, and tournedos, which need only to be carved out. Aged sirloin is gray, very dry, and looks hard, but is soft to the touch, like a very tender beef jerky. The meat stays in this room for four weeks before being sold and its contents at any given time are worth hundreds of thousands of dollars. "The best of the best," Sam says.

When Amy Rubinstein, part owner of the renowned Peter Luger Steak House, walks into the room to choose meat, Sam attends her. Amy moves slowly through the room, punching her brass stamp into the white fat and pink flesh of the hindquarters that strike her as sufficiently marbled, well shaped, and silky for her restaurant. "I'm looking to see what the true grain is like on it," she will say as she pokes the meat with her latex-gloved finger. "I think this is bloodshot," she will observe, massaging a $390 hunk of meat.

Her rejections irk Sam.

"Amy, nothing wrong with it," he will wheedle. "Amy, you missed two good pieces of meat on that hook," he will point out, but Amy will move on. Sam used to offer first pick of his meat to Amy's mother, famous for wearing a fur hat and pearls into the meat coolers, and now her daughter has taken over as his chief customer. By the end of her inspection, her white butcher's jacket purpled with ink from the stamp and pinked with blood, Amy might have claimed 130 hindquarters and 75 shells, and spent well over $40,000.

Mostly, though, Master Purveyors sells boxed meat. "Give me a boxful of tenders," says Mark on the phone. "Did he get mixed bones today? Did he get any leg bones? Femurs? Ten of those. Don't forget the top rounds."

Mark is swaying a bit as he leans one hand on his desk, out of breath. He's tired from being awake, this night and every night, and spending only four, five, six hours a day away from work; three, four, five hours sleeping. His desk is littered with Immodium, Pepcid, old paper espresso latte cups, and an imperially high pile of invoices, orders, uncashed checks, phones.

It's hard on the family, said Mark. This job is like saying, "Hey, honey, I'm not coming home tonight—for the next sixteen to twenty years. And I'm going to work twenty-hour days every day." Mark takes one phone call after another: "Can you get that off the truck? I need the weight on it! Quick, let's go!" "I got to go downstairs and chop up those rounds of veal!"

The sun doesn't so much as come up over the meat market as the blue-violet of the sky becomes less dense and a whiteness comes in from the east. Hundreds of pigeons and seagulls perch on the edge of the warehouses across the way as scraps, bones, and fat are carried outside. At the loading dock, workers move neat boxes of meat into the open mouths of trucks that bear the name MASTER PURVEYORS INC. PRIME CITY-DRESSED BEEF. A few hours after sunrise, Master Purveyors disgorges the last set of trucks into the South Bronx.

. . .

THE slaughterhouse districts of Manhattan, the *shochets* for hire among the tenements, the neighborhoods studded with butcher-shops, have all disappeared. Supermarkets, with their own meat supply, have obliterated much of the independent meat trade. But much remains.

A handful of old-fashioned butchers still work in every borough of the city today. A whole lamb, two goats, and a rabbit, all skinned and naked-looking, hang in the window alongside pillowy lengths of tripe at Biancardi Meats on Arthur Avenue in the Bronx. "You want juicy? Like the last time?" asks the owner, Sal Biancardi, as a woman walks in. The parents and grandparents of many of his customers shopped at this store, buying meat from his own parents and grandparents.

Snow falls softly out the window, as the radio keeps Moe Albanese company while he works alone. His shop, Albanese Meats & Poultry, founded by his father, Vincenzo, has been open for more than seventy-five years, longer than any nearby business on Elizabeth Street, where boutiques now sell chic shoes and two-hundred-dollar jeans. Inside the butcher shop, the very old man—he won't reveal his year of birth—moves slowly out from behind the room's main furniture, a refrigerator half full of odd cuts of meat, to greet a customer. Rent on his store has gone up, but Moe holds on. "I'm going to make chop meat out of that," he says as he slaps a thick round of beef onto a scale. "It's steak. And I'm going to make some chicken cutlets. We don't precut anything," he says with pride, noting that he still picks out beef forequarters and hindquarters on hooks from the Fourteenth Street wholesalers. "This is not a supermarket. You come in, you order it, we cut it fresh right in front of you."

In the Ozone Park section of Queens, Imran Uddin, a heavy-set, short, thirty-four-year-old man who favors fleece hoodies and a New York Knicks cap, runs the Madani Halal slaughter-house, which appeals to nearby South Asian immigrants (Imran's Pakistani father founded the place), and also to assorted others—Caribbeans, Central and South Americans, Europeans. Dominicans want brown chickens like the ones they kept in their yards back home. Imran's heritage breed chickens are chewier, more chickeny tasting, not soggy, without that "water texture" of those from the supermarket. South Asians often want goats with a reddish coat, Imran says, which they say reminds them of the wild goats in the mountains of the Himalayas. People come to Imran seeking lean sheep, or fat ones, and they walk into the pen to feel the flesh along the animals' spines. His customers want grass-fed, leaner meat, which they say smells like grass, like the earth itself.

Taking a chicken's head in one hand, Imran will quickly whisper, "In the name of God the most gracious and most compassionate," in Arabic, and in one swift movement use the other hand to cut the throat, often as the customers look on. "This is their sustenance, and they want to feel they have control over it," he says. He serves a poor, remote, immigrant neighborhood the fresh, heritage, humanely raised meat that people from many rich neighborhoods seek but can't find; he charges by weight, maybe seven dollars for a whole chicken. At Imran's slaughterhouse, you can look your chicken in its milky, cataracted dark eye, which seems to hold a wink as the eyelid falls half shut. You can guarantee its freshness by witnessing its death.

In 1980, the number of city slaughterhouses had dwindled to only six, but then came waves of immigrants who considered it common sense to examine an animal alive before eating it and today there are eighty. Al Noor Live Halal Poultry on the edge of Park Slope in Brooklyn has a restaurant attached, so you could theoretically pick out a live animal to kill and then have it cooked. At one place in Flushing, Queens, a cow occasionally chews its cud in the basement. At Cohn Live Poultry, whose phone tree gives instructions in Yiddish, slaughterers say the Hebrew prayer for the blood of the animal. Latino slaughterhouse owners hire halal slaughterers to attract Muslims. Halal places allow Jewish shochets to bring in their own knives for a kosher kill. Even the kosher and halal places are known as *viveros,* the Spanish word for live poultry houses, and raise the local beacon of their trade, the sign POLLO VIVO.

The blacklash was inevitable. Residents of an upscale apartment building in the Greenpoint section of Brooklyn complained in the *New York Times* of being awakened at dawn by "a collective cackle" as trucks from upstate farms each day unload six hundred chickens emitting that pungent, country-fair smell of animal concentrate. State legislators from Queens pushed through a law that for four years bars new slaughterhouses from opening within fifteen hundred feet of a residence—that is, most everywhere in New York City.

Yet some slaughter takes place without such niceties as an official license, governed only by the imperatives of hunger, tradition and thrift. If you go looking, you can find enough urban backwoodsmen raising meat in New York City to give you the sense that slaughter could lurk in any Queens estate or Bronx high-rise. Women and men in every borough still raise chickens, turkeys, ducks, or geese for meat. A forty-nine-year-old Argentine mechanic in the Jamaica section of Queens breeds dozens of rabbits in his backyard so he can slit their throats, slip off their skins, hang them on a tree branch, and make rich winter stews. A taxi driver in Brooklyn crams more than 400 Coturnix quails into his crowded basement, as part of his self-education program to retire to farm fowl in rural Haiti. A Pakistani family near Liberty Avenue in Queens holds a goat in the yard for sacrifice during the Eid al-Adha holiday. Italians keep capons for slaughtering at Christmas. A Parks Department official acknowledges that hunting groups in Highland Park in Queens and along the Harlem River in the Bronx train beagles to rouse rabbits from cover so they can be shot. People sometimes catch the turtles and ducks in the Central Park pond. Every so often rumors surface of a prowling pigeon hunter, bagging pigeons right off the street to cook for food.

AFTER a few pig roasts on the farm, neighbors of the Queens County Farm Museum began to agitate against keeping animals to raise for meat. They didn't want mouth-watering porky smells wafting out of a place they considered a petting zoo. In 2011, the pigs became the object of a campaign. Word had gotten out that the farmhands had culled ducks, roosters, and hens that had been destroying the vegetable beds and taken them home for food. People went to the farm "for a soothing experience," said a woman who started a petition drive against its raising meat animals. "They viewed the animals as pets, not as meat." A state senator who helped fund the farm added pressure. The farm backed down. After centuries of debate over the role of livestock in cities, the latest experiment failed to take hold. There would be no more pig roast bacchanals under the stars.

Tom Mylan is no longer talking about keeping meat animals

in the city. He now calls his fascination with locally produced meat "a brief period of whimsy." Tom's field of view has become larger, as he considers what it would take to overturn a national meat industry where the four largest beef companies control more than 80 percent of the market. "We're looking to make the biggest difference in the way people eat meat that we possibly can," he says.

Over the summer of 2011, the Meat Hook opened a hot dog and burger shack on the beach in the Rockaways, part of a surfer's eating complex organized in part by the Brooklyn restaurateur David Selig, who keeps beehives on his rooftop in Red Hook.

Tom started to think about how great it would be if he had a reliable source of the high-quality, carefully raised meat he sells in his butcher shop. He had learned some best practices from books and his favorite farmers. "Everything from feed to breed affects the quality of the meat," he wrote in an article. "Cattle born early in the year are better than those born in the fall. Too much nitrogen-rich clover or alfalfa before slaughter, and a whole beef carcass can be ruined by scatole, a microbial metabolite that makes the meat smell and taste like . . . scat." Soon he found himself caught up in books, PDFs, and YouTube videos on soil microbes, breeding, glandular function, trace mineral nutrition, and multispecies stacking. He subscribed to *Acres USA, Stockman Grass Farmer,* and local farming newsletters from Lancaster County, the Hudson Valley, Maine, and Virginia. He wrote an application for a grant to establish a breeding, research, and teaching farm.

He is in the process of developing a twenty-year plan that he hopes will contribute to changing the way Americans eat. It starts with his pasture-based husbandry and vocational school, right now just a vision in a grant proposal. Yet in four or five years, he hopes, he will have started a program to train new farmers to develop breeds of cows whose offspring thrive on grass, grow quickly and efficiently, and turn into remarkably delicious and well-marbled steaks.

What he wants is to develop animals that will be less than half the size of the typical American thousand-pound steer and do well on grass and forage. They would be the ponies of the bovine world, descended from compact British breeds—Devons, Scottish Highlands, belted Galloways—broad, short cattle that efficiently convert grass to protein. They would reach maturity for slaughter at as young as twenty months, seven months younger than when most steer are slaughtered now.

Maybe these new cattle will be the stock from which the world-changing herds of the future are bred. Maybe he can train a generation of farmers to produce high-quality, tasty, sustainably raised meat for a reasonable price. Maybe he can sell the meat to Walmart and grocery stores and fast food chains across the country. If he succeeds, it wouldn't be the first innovation in meat to come out of a city struggling for hundreds of years to find optimal ways to sate carnivorous appetites. "This is a mission for me," Tom says.

SUGAR

YOU CAN'T CATCH the sweet candy smell in the air anymore. You won't see the rivulets of sugar flowing in shades of brown and tan and old yellowed paper, and, finally, white. You don't smell the cinnamon where the girls in hairnets packed cinnamon sugar into baby doll bottles. You won't find Shade Man asleep on the night shift, wearing sunglasses so no one can catch him in the act. You won't see crane operators reaching down to the holds of the boats on the East River to grab sugar as though they're digging up earth, to dump on the warehouse floor in heaps, like mountains of snow.

Instead, at the Domino Sugar factory in the Williamsburg section of Brooklyn, paint peeling off the walls and ceilings flakes onto the floors. Unmatched swivel office chairs still huddle around an old TV. Forklifts have been abandoned in the middle of a room, their seats splitting and decaying; hoses are unspooled; doors are open. The disintegrating old factory feels like a place where workers just left for a cigarette break—and never returned. Little here suggests the centuries of labor and strife that brought this refinery to this spot on the Brooklyn waterfront.

There are coal cities and steel cities and car cities and gold cities. New York, in some ways, is a sugar city. Global geopolitics, circa 1620: Sugar, tobacco, spices, and salt move empires. Planters and mill owners on the sugar plantations of the Americas live in opulence, their homes furnished with gold, silk, and chintz, their meals accompanied by the music of private orchestras, slaves and prostitutes ready to serve at their pleasure. Far away, the Dutch have emerged as the world's most successful seafaring traders, and Holland in its golden age of art and science also reigns as Europe's dominant sugar refiner. The Dutch West India Company is founded in 1621 to make money for its shareholders in a new global economy increasingly tilting toward sugar. Three years later, the company's yachts, galliots, ketches, pinks, and pinnaces begin to set anchor on Manhattan Island.

The company's waterfront settlement was to be a modest trading post for furs and timber, as well as a transportation hub for ships on the Atlantic circuit from Europe to South America and the Caribbean. But as the company settled in Manhattan, it also captured a chunk of sugar-rich Brazil, making that sweet commodity a prime concern. And it was sugar, in the end, that lured the Dutch away from their Manhattan holdings. When the English took over their little trading colony, renaming it New York, the Dutch gave it willingly in exchange for the tropical country today known as Suriname, whose cane crops they considered more valuable.

Sugar was the industry that elevated old New York, helping transform it into a cosmopolitan, powerful financial center in the 1700s. By the mid-nineteenth century, refineries on the Brooklyn waterfront were processing most of the sugar in the country. New York sugar fortunes were invested in gaslight, cable lines, railroads, and distant colonial empires. Local banks—including one that would become Citibank—emerged to support the new wealth. All of this prosperity depended on plants grown and harvested far away, first by slaves, then by their underpaid descendants. Eventually, New York's sugar lust helped reshape islands including Puerto Rico, and the failures of the sugar crop helped drive those islanders to New York, following the path that sugar had laid for them.

THERE'S a standard way to organize a Puerto Rican community garden in New York. Build a small wooden brightly painted house—a *casita*—suitable for members to gather with friends, play dominoes, drink beers, and eat *arroz con gandules*. Out in front, place layers of carpets to form walkways so the feet don't muddy in the swept and raked front yard. Keep a few chickens, for eggs, maybe some ducks and rabbits, or, very rarely, a goat. Hang a poster-size map of the island and many Puerto Rican flags. Play music. One thing you will *not* do—nowhere, no way, according to gardeners throughout the city—is plant sugarcane. Except in Jorge Torres's community garden off 179th Street in the Bronx.

Watering his cane plant from a plastic Mountain Dew bottle filled with rainwater, Jorge wears a navy blue shirt with PUERTO RICO across the front, white sports socks, black wingtips, and dark nylon dress pants. He is only about five-two, but has a handsome face with chiseled features, mahogany skin, and large amber eyes. He works so fluently that at first I don't notice that his left hand is missing three fingers—a construction accident, he says. He is valued in the garden, where he serves as coordinator. Once there was a different coordinator, but she was accused of graft—

selling off soil and flowers that came free from the Parks Department. It turned ugly. Acrimonious meetings were held until Jorge took her place and worked to gain people's trust. "Mr. Torres," the local community planning board wrote, "has the overwhelming support and cooperation of the majority of his neighbors." He is similarly committed to his family—after raising their children, he and his wife, Margo, adopted more young relatives whose parents "had vices," as Jorge delicately puts it. His granddaughter stops by to hand off her own child for babysitting, and Jorge nuzzles his baby great-grandson cheek to cheek.

On party days in the garden, he arrives at six a.m. to line up a row of pig shoulders on a spit. As people appear, he fills plastic cups and circulates a tray of chips, popcorn, and Cheez Doodles. He cranks up the generator-powered bachata, salsa, merengue, bomba and plena loud enough to project a block away refrains about the enchantments of a bygone Puerto Rico. In the casita, his friend Socky, a grandmother in a silky purple halter and black kitten heels, twirls and waves her black skirt as she dances.

No one pays much attention to a blue plastic pot of seedlings that Jorge carefully tends, but each spring he plants a piece of sugarcane in the garden among the squash plants. When it's tall enough, he cuts it to eat, and plants another bit. The sugar waxes and wanes, a lone stalk of cane in the South Bronx.

Sugarcane is grown from cuttings from another cane plant— in Jorge's case, a piece his daughter brought home from a visit to Puerto Rico. She expected her father to eat it and taste the island. Instead, he stuck it in a planter in his three-bedroom apartment, propped it up on the windowsill, and hoped that glass-deflected light and lukewarm tap water would mimic the hot sun and rain of the tropics.

His friends and relatives were skeptical—New York City's climate is far from optimal for cane, which requires up to eighteen months to grow and cannot survive a sudden drop in temperature. The average winter temperature in the Bronx is near freezing, unlike the average of 80 degrees in Puerto Rico. But the cane quickly grew tall and strong enough for Jorge to take cuttings for new plants. "We would get annoyed—there was so much cane growing on the windowsill, we couldn't see outside," said his daughter Nydia.

The party guests in the garden understand Jorge's attachment to cane. They are people from Puerto Rico's sugar world—Glory, originally from the steaming southern coastal city of Guayama, so perfectly suited to growing cane that most of it was subsumed into a giant plantation; María, from the western city of San Germán, where her father's first job was to steer the oxen that pulled the sugar carts; Sylvia, from southern Salinas, where her brother knocked his teeth out while working in a cane field. Jorge himself comes from the northeastern coffee and tobacco highlands of Aguas Buenas, an area that converted to more profitable sugarcane before he was born. Sugar veterans like them turn up all over the city—Haitians in Crown Heights, Dominicans in Washington Heights, Jamaicans in the North Bronx come to escape the hardships of labor in the cane fields and cane-based economies that produced less and less cane and provided less and less sustenance.

"*Es un orgullo*," says María Torres, Jorge's friend, admiring his sugar plant—it's a point of pride. "We had sugar all over our island. And all that sugar came *here*," she says, with a sweeping gesture that reaches far beyond the nearby cabbages and pigeon peas, beyond the neighborhood of six-story buildings repeating themselves block after block, to take in all of New York.

The story of how Jorge came to plant this bit of cane from the southern coast of Puerto Rico in the borough of the Bronx is the story of New York City itself. But the forces that brought him to New York began to conspire long before the man or even the city existed.

MOST people don't think much about where sugar comes from. It tastes like pleasure and looks like purity. Surely it must be retrieved naked, bare, and white, as rock crystal from some natural recess. But no. In fact, it comes from the sap that fills a freakishly tall bamboo-like grass that was eaten in New Guinea at least 8,000 years ago. The plant made its way to India and was being processed into syrup by 327 B.C., when Nearchus, a general of Alexander the Great, marveled at "a reed" that "brings forth honey without the help of bees." The Arabs planted this reed in Sicily, Cyprus, Malta, and Rhodes, and in various parts of Spain, sometimes using slave labor—but no planter of sugar could ever harvest enough. The European voyagers of the fifteenth century who ended up, lost, in the New World, had been questing for, among other things, lands suitable for growing cane.

Christopher Columbus—who, it turns out, had once worked as a sugar buyer—was the first to bring cane to the Americas in 1493. The landscape sustained sugar better than any other place he knew. "The sugar canes, the few that were planted there, have taken," he wrote to Ferdinand and Isabella of Spain. *Saccharum officinarum* thrived in Spanish-occupied Santo Domingo, and its processed juice was shipped back to Europe as early as 1516.

"Our sugar islands," the Europeans fondly called the bits of land they claimed and crammed with cane plants on the Caribbean Sea. Soon Africans were shackled, forests were stripped, and Jamaica, Barbados, Saint-Domingue, Antigua, Montserrat, Saint Kitts, Saint Lucia, Saint Vincent, Nevis, Grenada, Guadeloupe, Martinique, Cuba, Puerto Rico, Trinidad and Tobago all grew sugar. In many cases, that single crop became the whole economy, and slaves became cogs in a relentless cutting and processing machine—the closest approximation to a factory yet invented.

Beginning in the 1500s, Europeans imported several million Africans to the Caribbean, at least a quarter of the total number brought to all of the Americas. The workers stooped in the fields using machetes to hack through the cane wood near the ground, to preserve the maximum amount of juice-filled stalk. Cane juice spoils quickly and has to be extracted and processed right away; in the mills, the cane was crushed and its sap reduced and dried. During the harvest, the mills worked twenty-four hours a day, leaving enslaved workers so tired that they would catch their fingers and hands in the giant grinding rollers. "A hatchet was kept in readiness to sever the arm," one historian wrote.

In this environment, a small-eyed, sharp-nosed bureaucrat named Peter Stuyvesant moved up the ranks of the Dutch West India Company. He had started his career in the rich Dutch sugar colony in Brazil in the 1630s. In the West Indies, he served as governor of Curaçao, Aruba, and Bonaire. He converted farmers to sugar crops, loaned them money, sold them slaves, and transported their sugar to market, turning an enormous profit for the company. He became known for his genius at translating sugar into wealth, without ever even planting cane. When he lost his right leg in a Caribbean battle, Stuyvesant was sent to govern New Amsterdam. Adapting his particular mercenary skill to Manhattan's prospects, the new director general began shipping food to the Dutch Caribbean and taking payment in "clever and strong" slaves who cleared land, hewed wood, and built the wall on Wall Street and the road to Harlem. Stuyvesant, meanwhile, kept attuned to the sugar markets, and when the English took Manhattan from the Dutch, he sent his son back to Curaçao and instructed officials to furnish him with the best plots of land for planting sugar.

Sweet sugar could be many things. The Dutch certainly had a weakness for cakes and custards, fruit compotes, cookies, from the Dutch *cookjes,* and a fried treat they called dough nuts. They used unrefined sugar and molasses as well as refined sugar, all of it cheaper and more freely available in the New World than in Europe. "The quantity of these articles used in families, otherwise plain and frugal, was astonishing," wrote an Englishwoman who had spent time with a Dutch family in New Netherland. Yet the company town of New Amsterdam also considered sugar to be a symbol of command over a global network of commerce: When a Dutch official visited New England, he arrived with "a noise of trumpets" and presented, among several gifts, "a chest of white sugar." As an item of trade, a little bag of sugar could buy scissors and thimbles and knives and needles; a ten-pound sack would buy a strand of Venetian pearls. Europeans had first discovered sugar in the apothecary, and continued to use it as a drug. One Dutch cookbook common in New Amsterdam kitchens suggested that a spoonful of red currant juice cooked with sugar could treat pestilence or cool a hot fever, and that a sugary black cherry sauce could strengthen the heart. (Boil black cherries in wine and sugar, add cloves, cinnamon, ginger, galangal, nutmeg, mace and grains of paradise.) Sugar was a delight, an elixir, a panacea, a currency, a symbol, a product of dark arts.

Down in Curaçao, Dutch West India Company officials would inventory the thousands of pounds of sugar in chests and barrels and load them onto galliots such as the *Nieuw Amstel*. On the months-long journey to North America, the men on board subsisted mainly on salted meat, as well as the fresh tuna, bonita, and shark they caught at sea. Salt water and salt air corroded shoe leather, so they went barefoot; their shirts and pants would stiffen with sweat and dirt and salt until they fell apart. It was a perilous journey as light vessels on the open seas could be tossed about in a storm, by "such an excessive Rain, that as we had one Sea under us, we feard another had been tumbling upon our heads," as one traveler of the time described.

It must have been a relief to dock in the freewheeling and boisterous international port of New Amsterdam. Records remain of testimony of a fight at the home of a Dutch wheelwright after an Englishman's wife, "notwithstanding her husband's presence, fumbled at the front of the breeches of most of all of those who were present." A woman who found her husband in a tap room asked in court, "what he was doing with another man's wife . . . touching her breasts and putting his mouth on them."

Licentiousness and abandon were furthered by another product of the cane plant: its distilled liquid form, rum. The Dutch built the first distillery in the North American colonies in 1664 on Staten Island. This distillery likely made the first local rum from West Indies molasses, the sticky brown liquid that oozed out of the bottom of a mold of drying sugar. The newly renamed city of New York increased molasses imports year after year, and by 1770 the city supported seventeen rum distilleries. Rum was served at home, in doctors' offices, and on board ships. In taverns, you could get a rum shrub (a pale pink, effervescent drink of rum mixed with a syrup of fruit boiled in vinegar and sugar), a flip (hot rum with beer, sugar, or dried pumpkin, topped with a "flip" of cream, egg, and sugar), a mimbo (rum with loaf sugar), a black-strap (rum and molasses with herbs). You could also drink a calibogus, a sling, a bombo, a syllabub, a punch, a bellowstop, a Sampson, or a stonewall. Strangers were well regarded if they were "bumper men" and "good toapers"—that is, drinkers—and alcohol consumption for white men added up to seven shots of rum per day.

In the rough port city, "bloods" lurked in the small, crooked streets to harass young ladies: "Dam'd fine girl, by G—d!" they would call. "Where do you lodge, my dear?" New York became a pirate haven, where there was a blurry line between business-man and buccaneer, as local merchants financed pirate voyages to capture goods they needed, including sugar and slaves. Captain Kidd lived at what is today 7 Hanover Square until he was con-tracted to go to sea to hunt pirates—and somewhere out on the deep blue, between Madagascar and the West Indies, he became one himself. Pirate ships would fire salutes as they set out to sea, and return to openly unload and sell their booty.

"White gold," sugar was called in the eighteenth century, when it became the world's leading commodity, to its era what steel and oil were for the nineteenth and twentieth centuries. It made no sense to plant tropical islands with anything else, the thinking went. By about 1720, half the ships passing through the port of New York were traveling to or from the sugar islands. To feed the booming Caribbean, New York farmers planted export-able crops such as barley, oats, and corn, but especially the blond wheat grown up along the Hudson River. Brewers and fisher-men, trappers and foresters, millers and distillers, all ratcheted up production to send south. In return, the port of New York took in minor tropical products—cotton, indigo, limes, salt, cocoa, pimento, ginger—and, most profitably for everyone involved, rum, molasses, and sugar. A growing shipbuilding industry provided vessels for the journey—requiring lumber, iron, tar, turpentine, pitch, and rope, and accelerating the local manufacture of each.

One in every four men was a sailor, and the New York seaport began to follow Caribbean seasonal rhythms. From November to January, the port bustled as captains and crew set off southward to off-load their products and claim fresh sugar; the pace slackened in the dead of winter, with everyone away trading on the islands; and it picked up again from April to June as ships returned ahead of the hurricanes and disease of the tropical summer. Profits from the West Indies trade supported new luxury businesses such as silversmiths, wig makers, and bespoke tailors. Yet for the most part, New York's sugar business was not sugar itself—chronicles mention only one sugarhouse in that early period, on Liberty Street. Instead, the port city supplied food and fuel to the distant, hungry sugar islands.

That changed. After a few years of operating a small sugarhouse, in 1730, Nicholas Bayard placed a "PUBLICK NOTICE" in the city's newspaper to announce that he had "erected a Refining House for Refining all sorts of Sugar and Sugar-candy," and had "procured from Europe an experienced artist in that Mystery." The chemistry of obtaining pure white sugar from brown was poorly understood, but it clearly involved elaborate ritual—boiling, brewing, cooling, heating, mixing, pouring—that seemed like magic or alchemy. Sugar was an exotic luxury whose many everyday uses had not yet been imagined; the wealthy would often simply break off clumps to hold between their teeth while drinking tea.

In the mills of the West Indies, the sap of the cane plant was extracted, reduced in massive cauldrons, and then dried, the minimal preparation to make unrefined sugar. Soon the arts of sugar refining were practiced in various sugarhouses in New York, where Muscovado, or unrefined, sugar was wetted, heated, and filtered, and eventually poured into conical molds. After the liquid drained, the top of the mold gave the whitest, driest sugar, the middle section was golden and moist, the bottom was brown and stickily wet, and a gooey ooze dripped out—denoting a gradated system of value: Single Sugar, Midling Sugar, Bastard Sugar, and Molasses; some of which could be refined again to produce Doubeld Sugar, or further treated to become Powder. The stuff could be sold in casks and hogsheads and as small lumps, lumps, and sugar candy. But most people bought blue-paper-wrapped conical loaves for the house, and they would use sugar nippers—strong, sharp-bladed iron pliers—to break off clumps to eat, and sugar hammers to pound out smaller portions. As well as the Bayards, other old families such as the Livingstons, the Cuylers, the Roosevelts, the Stewarts, the Van Cortlandts, and the Stuyvesants found themselves in the business of sugar refining.

Because slow ship-borne messaging created a delay of months between placing an order and receiving the goods, selling sugar was a futures trade, forecasting supply and demand. "We are of Opinion Good Bright Muscovado will be wanted here towards the fall of the year," wrote the merchants John and Henry Cruger. Ambitious young bankers monitored the sugar markets from their countinghouses. Newsmen at the *New-York Gazette*, the colony's first newspaper, published reports of West Indies harvests, shipping traffic, and hazards such as piracy and storms. Everyone was interested in the ebb and flow of sugar. Confectioners began to advertise "all kinds of sweet meats, sugar work, sugar plums, cordials," for the wealthy to serve at dinner parties and teas. Intense, giddy sweetness was moving within reach.

The problem with this enterprise was that it rested on the backs of African slaves. Because of the Caribbean trade in sugar, Manhattan became the most important slave port in North America. The *Witte Paert* sailed into the harbor in 1655, stinking from the waste of three hundred African women and men confined for months in the holds. Soon slavers docked regularly in the East River, and from 1700 to 1774 they unloaded as many as 7,400 slaves—more captive Africans than the total population of New York City at the start of the period. At first almost all were "seasoned" workers from the sugar islands of the West Indies who came on the return leg of New York–based merchant ships. Fully a fifth of the city's people were black—more than any other city in the North. Black women often worked in the home, and men assisted their owners in their trades. They served as butchers and farmers and shoemakers, but the city's highest concentration of slaves was in the Dock Ward neighborhood on the East River, where sugar traders lived and managed busy wharves and warehouses.

Leading New York sugarers already moving cargo through the Caribbean found it hard to pass up on the lucrative slave trade. John Van Cortlandt's sugarhouse, according to the looping, calligraphic handwriting in his leather-bound account books, might go a week without selling a thing, or fulfill five orders in a day; he usually sold ten to twenty loaves of sugar at a time, but could sell more than a hundred, or as few as two. So his small house also trafficked in guns, swords, pistols, and bags of lead, and to supplement these enterprises: slaves. Among other ventures, in

1764, Van Cortlandt bought the brigantine *Mattey* and instructed Captain Richard Mackey to bring slaves from Sierra Leone to sell in New York or in Barbados for "as much good sugar and rum as will freight the vessel."

Some combination of remorse and disgust about the slave origins of the city's sugar wealth surfaced in the 1780s, when proposals began circulating to replace the tainted juice of the cane plant with clean sugar from the good American maple. A 1790 letter to a city newspaper advocating a boycott of slave-produced sugar suggested the maple tree as a "boundless" source of physical and moral sweetness. William Cooper, a leading New York anti-cane campaigner, took out a land patent covering an enormous tract upstate, around Lake Oswego, and promoted it as a site for a maple tree sugar plantation. He envisioned an elaborate system of maple sugar sharecropping, in which landlords would provide tenant farmer families with tools, credit, and transportation to market, he told the Agricultural Society of the State of New-York. Maple sugar, he promised, did not require "the lash of cruelty on our fellow creatures." Yet the profitable cane sugar trade only grew, and before the end of the century, it had helped build the colonial backwater of New York into the new country's capital and largest city.

THIS was the city that would one day receive Jorge Torres from the cane fields. "I was around sugar from the time I was born," Jorge says. He was born in 1948 at home in a two-room shack in a Puerto Rican sugar field. Growing up, he thought the cane plants outside his door were very beautiful. In the fall, the *guajana*, or cane flower, would blossom, making a field of shimmering fifteen-foot plants. Those sugar stalks ordered everyone's lives with their needs—to be replanted, burned, reaped, and hustled to the mill. Jorge was raised in their thrall.

Families like Jorge's patched together shacks out of scrap wood, old sacks, remnants of boxes, and leaves of the cane plant itself—"whatever you could find," Jorge said. He would wake in the morning with smoke in his eyes from the lamp, a glass bottle filled with burning oil. Outside, over a pit filled with stones, kerosene, and fire, his mother would prepare breakfast—coffee and grilled yams. His father and mother would step out before seven to work, armed with machetes. At the end of the day, Jorge, the oldest, would help cook dinner—usually yams with cornmeal, occasionally with codfish or sardines or the crabs the kids caught after a rain in the sloppy mud of the riverbanks by the cane field. Jorge's family grew food—potatoes, cassava, plantains, avocados, pineapples, bananas—but the only thing they could count on for a meal year-round was yams—always yams—and Jorge came to hate them. After dinner, at sunset, a curtain of blackness swept thickly onto the fields, until there was nothing to do but sleep.

Sugarcane had been planted all over Jorge's island. Cane stalks climbed slopes—even though the plant prefers the flat, coastal land and its rich alluvial soil—edging out the coffee and tobacco that had once grown so well in the hills. Sugarcane grew in narrow river valleys all the way down to the water, among the houses and up to the roadsides, in any of the flatter places among the ranges of the sierras of the eastern highlands. The local planter would give workers an acre of land to build a shack and farm some food, along with barely subsistence wages in the cane field.

Jorge was nine years old when his parents took him out of school to labor in the fields alongside them. "It wasn't about what

I wanted or didn't want—I had to do it," he says. A slight, small child, he joined grown men *bregando con la caña,* or doing battle with the cane, soaked with sweat as they hacked through the hot, reedy jungle that was their backyard. He started as a water boy, scooping river water into a coconut or gourd shell for the workers to drink for eight or nine hours and a salary of a quarter a day. Jorge was the oldest of thirteen, and as each of his brothers aged into cane work—at about seven, eight, maybe nine—each took his place in the fields. For Jorge, the system of farm work on an un-mechanized family plantation in Aguas Buenas seemed to stretch infinitely into the past and the future.

The planter would set fires on the farm, burning the leaves of the cane plants to make it easier to cut through their stalks. The wet, tropical swelter would be compounded by the fire's ripping dry heat. From his family's shack, Jorge could see thick black smoke whirling up over the crops. Later, when the sweet-smelling smoke had cleared, the workers would follow a blackened path into the field. There in the char, Jorge would gather the sugar plants, finding, again, that the thick skins of the stalks had protected the precious juice from the flames.

Work like this leaves its marks on the body. Fine hairs on the cane stalk implant themselves in the skin, causing a desperately itchy kind of pain—like rubbing up against fiberglass in the heat—and sometimes ulcerous sores and infections. Laborers like Jorge endured cuts on the hands and arms, sciatica, leg pain, and, too frequently, serious injury by machete. No one wore gloves. Thick, tall rubber work boots shielded the legs of those who could afford them, but Jorge worked barefoot. When he cut his feet on sharp cane husks, his father would salve the wound with a wad of chewed tobacco. Jorge became a carrier, forever stooping, heaving, bundling, and throwing cane like a javelin into the truck bed, and then a cutter—by his reckoning, a thousand times harder than any other field work.

His cane would be trucked to Central Santa Juana, a mill in Caguas, where it was crushed. The juice would be extracted and cooked into syrup, crystallized, and divided into raw sugar and molasses, ready for export to refineries. People describe the thick smell of the air around the *central* as a sweet burn, like cooking caramel. To Jorge Torres, it smelled like honey. It was the smell of transformation, as the stalks of a familiar plant became heaps of yellowish crystalline export. It was a smell that could mark the raw sugar all the way to places like New York, where that smell, and every indication of a growing plant rooted in a place, would be refined away.

Jorge's family didn't buy much in the way of food from the store, but sugar was one of the items, along with salt, rice, salted cod, and oil. Jorge would scoop up pure white refined sugar from unmarked sacks and carry it home in a folded-up piece of paper. He never knew the brand. In the middle of a sugar field, muscles aching from cutting cane, Jorge ate sugar that could have been from anywhere.

Eighteen years old, exhausted from sugar, Jorge had been working in cane half his life and wanted to retire. The year before Jorge's birth, the Puerto Rican legislature—acknowledging that the island's economy could not support its people—had created the Employment and Migration Bureau to help them to leave. Migration was increasing, and Jorge heard of a Department of Labor program: Sign up, and employers in places like New York and Connecticut and New Jersey will send for you. Your night flight will be paid, and you can double your wages the next day.

The first independent decision Jorge made as an adult was to leave. He packed a heavy, handmade wooden suitcase with work clothes and little else, stepped onto a plane, and soon found himself in rural Pennsylvania, bending to pick asparagus just as he used to double over to collect cane. Soon, though, after a few more short-term contracts in agriculture, he moved to a "broken-down" neighborhood in the Bronx to work in a picture frame factory, in construction, in restaurants, never to return to the fields. There were big meals of *pernil*, chicken, pork chops, sweet flan—no yams if you didn't want them. Jorge met his wife, Margo. Life seemed better than it had ever been.

IN 1799, William Havemeyer, a young sugar boiler from Bücke-burg, near Hanover, was laboring in a hot sugarhouse in London, the world's refining capital, when word of his skill crossed the Atlantic to New York, where the art of boiling sugar was still not very well known. William knew how to clarify the sweet extract of the cane plant with ox blood, clay, and albumen, bake his mixture for hours in a kettle, and pour it into a mold, producing an off-white crystalline sugar loaf to sell as a hard cone. His product was in high demand in New York, where people kept sugar locked in a box, like a collection of tiny gleaming diamonds, a chest of wealth.

The Seaman sugarhouse on Pine Street contracted William to come from London and run the refining, and his brother Frederick soon joined him. Not long for wage labor, the brothers decided to open a business of their own. They found a site on the very edges of the city on what would become Vandam Street, north of Canal and a few blocks from the west side wharves, a place so

isolated that the stagecoach passed by mainly to transport prisoners. They built a two-story sugarhouse, as well as homes for their
own families and two hired hands, and they began to roll barrels
of tan-colored raw Caribbean sugar one by one in from the ships
at the wharves. As was the custom, William and Frederick Havemeyer passed their trade on to their sons, William and Frederick
Havemeyer Jrs., and they passed the trade to *their* sons, so that
cousins and brothers and uncles at various times ran the company
together. The account of which son-in-law came into the partner-
ship when, adding an ampersand to the name of the Havemeyer
firm, can read like a dense biblical list of who begat whom. The
point is that the Havemeyers ran permutations of the sugar company for more than a hundred years, and their business would
reshape the sugar landscape of the Americas.

At midcentury, New York was already entering a new urban
age. "It is really now one of the most rucketing cities in the
world," wrote Washington Irving. Buildings grew taller; more
ships passed through the port. William Havemeyer Jr. retired
from sugar as a leading businessman and in 1845 became mayor
of New York—evidence of the growing reach of the city's sugar
interests. Frederick took a hiatus and traveled to Europe, observing new developments in the great sugarhouses. "I have been here
only 3 days + have seen more of London then I have seen of it in
the nine years I lived in it before," he wrote in an 1839 letter to his
wife.

He was on the hunt for technology to speed and ease the con-
version of cane juice into pure white crystals. The vacuum pan
permitted sugar to crystallize faster, without burning or caramel-
izing. Char, or bone black, derived from animal bones, provided
a filter that left sugar a clean, expensive white. As production

switched from man to machine, the sugarers saw that they could produce a year's worth of goods in a month. Their children would make in a day what they once made in a year.

This mechanization helped make sugar cheap. Working people began to frequent little dry goods stores selling every manner of exotica—coffee, oranges, lemons, cochineal, camphor, hemp, nitrate of soda, and also sugar. The wealthy covered their dinner tables with "confectionary and gew-gaws" so elaborate that they barely looked edible. The poor, meanwhile, bought candy from street peddlers and hucksters. The Erie Canal connected the city directly to the Midwest and opened up new markets hungry for sweets. Per capita consumption of sugar leapt from about four pounds in 1815 to twenty-one pounds in 1860. As more and more people aspired to keep sugar on their tables, the Havemeyers strove to supply them.

In a move to be oft repeated by Manhattanites seeking space, the Havemeyers went to Brooklyn. Williamsburgh had recently been little more than dense thickets of cripplebush on swampy lowlands, but in a generation it had filled with distilleries, rope makers, shipyards, tanneries, a glue factory, and a fire insurance company. The Havemeyers' million-dollar whiz-bang refinery opened on the East River in 1856, with its own docks and warehouses, and instantly made the inland sugarhouses obsolete. Other refiners followed to the Brooklyn waterfront, and soon the Havemeyers and their dozen-odd local competitors were producing half the sugar consumed in the United States. Sugar was the city's most important industry, and Brooklyn was the country's refining capital.

What was seen then as advanced technology looks pretty medieval today. The new refinery dedicated one building to boiling bones for char, which produced a stench like rotting meat, but whose product could be used to filter sugar and make it clean and white. The bones at such establishments came from nearby slaughterhouses, and also from wandering urchins. The children pawed through mounds of fetid garbage on the street, searching out discards from abattoirs, butchers, and the tables of meat-eaters. They might gnaw their findings, or boil them into a soup, and then sort, store, and sell their osseous wares. Big bones, such as the jaw, the shin, and the foreleg, were worth more; small bones from table scraps were worth less; chicken bones were useless—and sorting it all meant careful piles stowed under the bed, on tables, and on chairs in apartments smelling of rancid meat. "Bones is hard business now," declared a thirteen-year-old girl who had stashed her putrid collection under the bed until it could be sold for thirty cents a bushel.

Sugar refineries had always been accident prone, built as they were on an ever-larger scale with the latest, untested machinery in an era without workplace regulations. In the Havemeyer plant in Brooklyn, you could get burned and bruised by an exploding boiler, crushed by a falling elevator, or you could lose a limb to a revolving wheel. You could stab yourself falling on a hook, scald yourself in the overflow from a vat of boiling sugar, drop a box of sugar on your foot, or find yourself pinned under falling sugar bags. You could certainly faint in the intense, 110-degree heat generated by 135 boilers. Amid flammable sugar, the greatest threat was fire, which could burn an unlucky worker "to a crisp," as one newspaper cheerily reported, and blaze through the sugar stores.

The worst flames ripped through the Havemeyer-owned Williamsburg refinery in 1882. Some four thousand barrels of sugar incinerated while walls and floors, brick and iron, collapsed into their own seething furnace. Alarm after alarm rang and dozens of firemen hosed arcs of water into the smoke—but they could not best the fire. As night fell, a mess of flame reflected off the black water of the East River.

Naturally, the family's response was to rebuild. "Colossal," headlined the *Brooklyn Eagle* when the new refinery was finished. "We are here in the midst of the greatest sugar refining centre in the world," the paper breathlessly wrote later, describing a plant that could, in a single day, convert four million pounds of raw material into 12,000 barrels of refined sugar. The refineries were "the most striking objects on the whole of Brooklyn's waterfront," and their "towering outlines on a foggy day, or in the last of the twilight" suggest "the lineaments of a Rhenish castle." Having built a sugar castle, the Havemeyers began to govern like kings.

Henry O. Havemeyer, the younger, dominating son of Frederick Jr., had thick lips, a fat mustache, a growing gut, and pale, slightly bulging eyes. Harry, as he was known, had begun work at the family firm as a child after he was expelled from elementary school for fighting with the principal. He proved just as aggressive in business. The man who named his fine-lined yacht the *Impatience* fostered such an antagonistic relationship with his workers that when small fires broke out at the refinery, he assumed employee arson. When a group earnestly presented a petition for eight-hour workdays, Harry responded, "I cannot grant your request, boys," and then banged his fist on the table. "No, I will not." He accused his brother Theodore of leaking information about prices, and threatened to break up the family firm. "Get it down as a fact that Harry is King of the sugar market," their father presciently wrote to Theodore.

Now Harry managed a new refinery, whose very size made it more efficient, which made it more profitable, which made it better able to withstand dips in the sugar market and the pressures of intensifying competition among the city's sugarhouses. All of this put Henry O. Havemeyer in a position to dictate terms not only to his own family and employees, but to other refiners. In 1887, he convinced seventeen refineries in Brooklyn and beyond to merge and control prices with a Sugar Trust, patterned after the Standard Oil Trust of John D. Rockefeller. Every refiner got a share based on the value of his company, and Harry shut down the least efficient of them. At least one refiner hesitated to join the trust because of Harry: "He considered him a brute," admitted the trust's own lawyer. By the end, Havemeyers & Elder had consolidated with a next-door refinery to form one gargantuan factory extending five waterfront blocks, the largest of its kind in the world. The price of refined sugar immediately went up, and the trust proceeded to crush competitors. Refinery workers who labored long hours, shirtless, wet with sweat, and at risk of fainting in the terrific heat, called their job "hell." A prosecutor called the Sugar Trust "a conscienceless octopus, reaching from coast to coast." Harry saw it differently, saying: "I think it is fair to get out of the consumer all you can."

Annoyingly, rivals persisted. Independent investors opened a refinery in Yonkers, and others followed suit in Long Island City, Queens. The Arbuckle brothers, the coffee magnates, also set up a refinery in the New York area, when Harry incorporated a coffee company.

Harry fought the Arbuckles "with all the enthusiasm of a schoolboy," an observer noted. The Arbuckles, in turn, sold sugar at a loss to drive down prices. Newspapers would publish daily updates on the battle: "So far as the coffee end of the war is concerned, all is quiet to-day," wrote the *Brooklyn Eagle* in 1900.

"Do you see any possible way of coming together and conducting the sugar business in harmony?" a reporter asked Henry O. Havemeyer.

"None whatever," he replied. He thought the sheer size of his operation would allow him to outlast the competition. "We think it is best to lay to, like a ship in a storm," he said.

Finally a truce was announced that seemed to revert to the previous status quo: Havemeyer would be left alone to regulate the price of sugar, while the Arbuckles would fix the price of coffee.

The Sugar King earned his moniker when he consolidated with all three nearby remaining competitors into a near total monopoly that controlled 98 percent of the refined sugar sold in the United States. The ground was laid for the kingdom to extend its reach on the world stage.

BY the close of the nineteenth century, the Sugar Trust was fed up with the vagaries of revolts, revolutions, and European disputes that could close one Caribbean island and open another. Mostly, the trust was fed up with the U.S. government tariff on importing foreign raw sugar. New York sugar men wanted a close and steady source of raw sugar, preferably for free.

In 1898, the United States went to war with Spain, and in July, a fleet of gray armored U.S. Navy gunships quietly floated up to the southern coast of Puerto Rico. Days later, the first Americans arrived to build a sugar company. "Every man, woman, and child in the United States is directly interested and beneficially interested as a consumer," argued a young U.S. congressman from New York named Jacob Ruppert, advocating in the House to remove tariffs on sugar from Puerto Rico.

Soon the American desire for sweetness planted the place full of cane. Havemeyer's corporate giant, the American Sugar Refining Company, was able to raise unprecedented amounts on Wall Street, and Havemeyer and others busied themselves with erecting mills, improving ports, and building railways right into the sugar fields.

Puerto Rico was not new to sugar production—it had opened its first grinding mill in 1523—but operations had languished as Spain, plundering Mexico and Peru, had lost interest. It took three hundred years to develop a real sugar economy, and by that time, the great market was no European power, but the United States. In the mid-1800s, New York shipped Puerto Rican planters- sugar-mill machinery and sugar-hauling locomotives, and even machetes specially made by the nearby gun manufacturer Collins & Co., stamped CALIDAD GARANTIZADA. After slavery was abolished, New York City capital also helped to renovate ox-powered sugar mills into steam-powered *centrales*. In return, in ever-larger quantities, New York bought raw sugar, especially after tariffs were removed in 1901.

Now New York sugar men could make more direct investments, and Puerto Rico's annual production of sugar jumped tenfold from 1899 to 1910. Soon that single crop provided about two-thirds of the island's income, and employed more than a third of its labor force. Other aspirations for agriculture and industry could not compete. After Cuba, little Puerto Rico became the second largest producer of sugar in the Western hemisphere.

Back in Manhattan, on Pearl Street, at the Coffee and Sugar

Exchange, men huddled around a blackboard and monitored tickers, teletypes, and telephones, the air carrying the aroma of coffee roasting nearby. "These traders almost never see, handle, the food commodity they may buy or sell," wrote one observer. "These are like mathematicians, in that they deal only in 'figures.'" Yet their calculus could easily reach all the way to rural Puerto Rico. As one observer noted, any honest, astute man among them, if asked what he was doing, would say: "We're making the price."

Banks such as the National City Bank—later to become Citibank—helped finance the operations. The City Bank of New York had been conceived in 1812 by a group of men including Frederick Havemeyer, and prominent sugar traders and refiners—including Henry O. Havemeyer—served on the board for generations, offering credit for Caribbean sugar. In the 1930s, when sugar prices plummeted, National City almost went bust.

Change came even to isolated Aguas Buenas, where Jorge Torres's great-grandparents' generation watched pasture and underbrush suddenly sprout cane. In neighboring Caguas, Belgian investors built a new sugar mill, Central Santa Juana, where Jorge Torres's sugar would one day be processed. The company lawyer drew up contracts with local farmers to produce cane. Yet the farmers began to realize that even when sugar prices soared on the New York market, the profits did not reach them. They raised funds to build their own, independent *central,* which they called La Defensa, hoping it would fend off foreign imperialism. Instead, La Defensa soon closed, and the Belgian mill eventually came into the possession of National City Bank, the New York–based, marble-colonnaded citadel of sugar power.

The old records of the Coffee and Sugar Exchange were destroyed in the collapse of the World Trade Center, and so now it is difficult to confirm exactly where Jorge Torres's sugar was shipped when it left the port of San Juan—but it's safe to say that some reached the gargantuan refinery on the Brooklyn waterfront.

SUGAR never really generated well-being for Puerto Ricans. From 1910 to 1934, the weight of the sugar produced in Puerto Rico more than tripled, but the number of people employed in the industry remained roughly the same. Sugar harvesting included a dead season each year, when there was no work, and more than 60 percent of the workers of Puerto Rico were unemployed either all or part of the year, said Theodore Roosevelt Jr., the governor of Puerto Rico and the son of the president. Many working people earned little; for decades, cane cutters' wages stayed level, lower than elsewhere in the Caribbean. The average daily per-person food budget for the family of a cane cutter was only twelve cents—"four cents more than the food expense required for feeding a hog in the United States!" noted one reformer. Some 71,000 people left the island between 1909 and 1940, mostly to find work, many in New York.

They came at first by steamship, on vessels such as the *Borinquen*, the *Coamo,* and the *Marine Tiger,* following the route established by the sugar executives and financiers and, of course, the raw sugar itself. The trip began in San Juan—passenger ships docked in the harbor beside cargo terminals, where workers loaded sugar, molasses, and rum. People planned and saved for years to pay the cost of a ticket. Men boarded the ships in their best suits and hats, women in heels with matching handbags, girls in frilly white dresses, and boys in creased short pants, as though already, on the sea, they were living the better life of Nueva York.

Card games and Bible readings and formal dancing and *canciones* with drums and guitars—and seasickness—passed the hours on the choppy trip up the Atlantic.

In a previous era, Spanish Caribbean immigration to New York had two notable strains: sugar attachés and revolutionaries. Merchants sent their sons to study at Fordham University in the Bronx, known as the Colegio de San Juan. Political agitators against Spain established New York newspapers such as *Patria* and *La Revolución*. But that epoch was over—the newest arrivals just wanted work. They settled near cargo jobs at the waterfront and by factories and cigar workshops—the latter of which employed *lectores* to read novels aloud to the workers, just like in the Caribbean. They bought winter coats on credit from Old Man Markofsky and ate *chuletas*, or pork chops, at restaurants such as El Paraíso. They slurped shaved ice bathed in sweet tropical fruit syrups, just like in the town plazas back home. In underheated, tight-packed tenements, musicians composed plena songs of longing for the rural tropics, such as *"Yo me vuelvo a mi bohío"* (I'm Going Back to My Hut). It's not clear whether that idyllic life still existed, even in Puerto Rico. Some of what passed for homesickness in New York was nostalgia for a previous version of the island, before the dollar economy, before sugar.

Newcomers kept coming. Salaries in Puerto Rico stayed roughly level for decades, while the salaries Puerto Ricans could earn on the mainland jumped dramatically, amplifying the rewards of departure. As city factories recruited workers, tens of thousands began arriving each year. Billboards in San Juan and Ponce advertised a "Job and Home in New York," and Puerto Rico's Department of Labor set up an office on East 116th Street in Manhattan to find jobs for the unemployed. By 1960, Puerto Ricans made up 8 percent of New York City residents.

Puerto Rican cane workers helped create migration by air. After World War II, former GI pilots bought battered army surplus planes from the War Assets Administration to fly unscheduled wildcat trips from San Juan to New York. Bare-headed laborers wearing short-sleeved work shirts sat on beach chairs on the windowless planes chartered by particular firms as though ready to leap straight to work in the field, which essentially is what they did. The trips could cost as little as thirty-five dollars a ticket, but they were subsidized by "employment agents" proffering sometimes nonexistent New York jobs and charging fees that could consume a cane worker's life savings. The dubious charters were soon replaced by frequent, cheap airline flights on DC-4 planes collectively known as *"la guagua aérea,"* or the flying bus. Tens of thousands of Puerto Rican workers flew the 1,600 miles from San Juan to Idlewild Airport in Queens to harvest northeastern crops during sugarcane's springtime dead season, then back to the island for the cane harvest. A night on the hot, slow, bumpy, unpressurized Thrift Flight from San Juan to Idlewild cost only $52.50, though English-speaking tourists who inquired were advised to spend the extra $11.50 and travel in comfort on a pressurized plane. Whereas in the 1930s, the annual rate of migration had been 1,800, by the 1950s, 43,000 people were leaving Puerto Rico for the United States mainland each year.

Sugar production on the island peaked in 1952 and then slowly dwindled. As the harvest became more mechanized, the sugar industry laid off 42,000 Puerto Rican workers during the 1950s. Another surge of Puerto Ricans flooded New York, and the city's mayor, Robert Wagner, visited San Juan to discuss migration. Labor costs had increased, the mills had been poorly managed, and a new program sought to industrialize the island rather than promote agriculture. The local mill where Jorge Torres's sugar had been processed closed in 1967, and other big *centrales* followed.

BY the time Jorge Torres came to New York in the late sixties, the old Havemeyer sugar plant, now known by the brand name Domino Sugar, was still chugging away on the Williamsburg waterfront. The Havemeyer family no longer had any connection to the refinery. Sugar had become ubiquitous, not only sweetening soda and ice cream, candy and cake, but also enhancing flavor in processed and fast foods like TV dinners and McDonald's burgers and buns. As a new sweetener, high-fructose corn syrup, gained market shares, Domino's parent company changed its name from the American Sugar Corporation to Amstar Corporation so as not to be limited, specifically, to sugar.

Joe Crimi worked for twenty-five years in the Domino plant, starting in 1976, when he was twenty-two. He was a machine operator and a forklift driver; he worked the packet line, where he loaded paper packets into a spinning machine that filled them with sugar, and the five-pound line, where sacks of this size were filled and sealed. For a while, he hung powder, as they called it, pressing a button so hot confectioner's sugar flowed in waves into hundred-pound bags. Sugar for him, too, was a family business. His mother-in-law worked as a telephone operator at Domino for three decades, and his father-in-law was a blacksmith in the Domino repair shop. Four of Joe's wife's cousins were truck drivers who delivered sugar. Union members all, they enjoyed working conditions that had improved far beyond anything Henry O. Havemeyer would have allowed. "I loved the place. It was phenomenal," says Joe, who recalls good vacations and other benefits and fair treatment from the owners. The company hired college kids to work summers when employees went on vacation—and some stayed. People kept right on working into their eighties. "It was like you don't want to go," says Joe.

The factory's doors were open to the East River, where ships packed full of raw sugar came in from all over the world. Most of the factory workers didn't talk much about the sugar's origins— they just knew it kept coming. Scrolls, or pipes with spiral stainless-steel turning blades, circulated the product through the buildings. The heart of the beast pumped sugar through steel and brass arteries to every limb of the eleven-acre plant.

Workers in the factory used to eat the raw sugar by the handful. "There's everything in it," says Joe. "It tastes earthier." They used refining techniques the Havemeyers would have recognized, pouring brownish sugar syrup into bone black filters two stories high and watching it come out clear. Aged machines had been refitted with stainless-steel parts and painted hospital green. Many of the machines, imported long ago from France, Germany, and Switzerland, were so outdated that there were no spare parts, and workers in the maintenance shop had to build them. "They may not have had the high school, they may not have had the college, but they can work with their hands," says Dennis Richards, another Domino employee. Every night, they would shoot hot water through every machine to leave them clean.

The warehouses could hold millions of pounds of raw sugar— plant managers were careful never to halt production by allowing supply to run out. Containers moving sugar from one place to another closed like jaws, with a clank, and made a *psssss* sound when they opened, and workers could tell by the rhythm if something malfunctioned. Sugar slammed down from a height into the bin below with a hollow bang, like a drum. Powder mills hammering away to make a fine dust of confectioner's sugar produced a jet engine roar. So much sugar dissolved in the air like a candy fog that a special circulation system was designed to suck it out. A film of sugar settled on the workers' skin, so that the sweat dripping down their faces in the heat tasted sweet on their tongues.

Much of the labor was still manual, but the machines continued to advance, and every decade or two, the number of workers seemed to halve.

Sugar waned as sweeteners such as high-fructose corn syrup, saccharin, and aspartame waxed. The British company Tate & Lyle bought Amstar in 1988. The company, whose founders had contributed to London's Tate Gallery, had become the largest sugar and sweetener company in the world. In the 1980s, Joe, a union leader, watched as new managers slashed benefits, fired employees, and expanded workloads of the holdouts.

After more strikes and layoffs at Domino, the plant was operating at only a fraction of its capacity, with whole rooms shut down. During the last twenty-month strike, what the guys called "rigor mortis" set in on the old machines—with no one to grease and wash them, they cracked and refused to move at all. No more workers were left in the maintenance shop to make repairs. "It was just a matter of timing," said Joe. "We knew it was going to close."

In 2001, Tate & Lyle sold Domino to the Fanjul brothers, exiled Cuban sugar planters managing their own sugarcane kingdom out of Florida. When the Fanjuls announced three years later that they would shutter the plant in Williamsburg, some neighbors thought—despite the smoke whirling from the chimneys—the plant was *already* closed. Much of Brooklyn's industry had long since left. Still the largest manufacturer in Williamsburg, Domino had gone from 4,500 to 300 workers, whom a newspaper called "relics from a bygone era." The last age of sugar in New York, that of good union jobs for Joe Crimi and his friends, had passed.

JORGE Torres is an expert in how to eat cane. First, it has to be cut—he gets out a machete stashed in the casita, poises his right hand, slashes—into a length you can hold. Then its thick bark has to be removed, so he uses the machete as a vertical peeler, hacking all around the stalk, revealing a wet, white center that looks something like the flesh of an apple. You have to bite that fibrous middle to release a bit of juice, and suck and chew and knead out more. It's not as intense as a spoonful of white table sugar, but has a light, fresh, lingering sweetness.

For hundreds of years while sugar refining was big business in New York City, you might have been hard-pressed to find a piece of cane to suck outside of the odd import in Chinatown. But when people from the Caribbean came, they wanted their *caña*. "Out of huge barrels loom red sugar cane, six or eight feet high, which later, cut in short lengths, is eaten as stick candy by children," wrote a visitor to Harlem in 1928. As generations of Puerto Ricans continued to settle in the city, Jewish merchants at East Harlem's markets began to stock tropical produce.

When his children were young, Jorge Torres would go to the bodegas near his Bronx apartment, with their bins and boxes of fading sugarcane, prehistoric yucas, blackening mangoes and plantains and papayas—enough mottled imports for every household between the Cross Bronx Expressway and the Bronx Zoo to produce some pale version of a tropical diet. He brought the cane home to his children, but it had aged in its travels from Puerto Rico. "Old sugarcane smells bad and tastes bitter," Jorge said, and its pure white flesh becomes reddish. The stuff available at the bodegas was, in his assessment, "worthless."

Why the impulse to grow cane struck when it struck is hard to explain. "I like the taste, I like the way it looks," Jorge says. "I like to give it away." Sugarcane juice is good for the kidneys and for blood pressure, he says. "Sugarcane is healthy and it makes you grow," he insists, ignoring all evidence of tooth decay, obesity, type 2 diabetes. People are still shocked when he takes out a machete and slices through the stalks on his windowsill nursery to retrieve some cane for the kids to chew. One day, his brother came over with a camera phone to make a video of the cane to put online.

Back in Puerto Rico, the area where Jorge cut sugarcane is now filled with sidewalks and highways and houses. Yet some people on the island, and Puerto Ricans like Jorge in New York, still remember how a man might say a girl is *like sugarcane in February*—the time of year when the cane is barely mature and the sweetest for plucking. *You're sweeter than molasses,* a man might say to a woman. *You wiggle more than sugarcane in the wind,* a parent might tell to a restless child. *His machete is sharp,* a person could say of a man known for his way with women. *His machete is blunt,* one might say of someone dull. *That's worth less than the*

*chaff. He's stingier than the knot of the cane. It stings more than cane
fluff. May your cane juice always be sweet.*

All over New York City, sugar has left its mark. The sugar
exploiters, men like Peter Stuyvesant and Henry O. Havemeyer,
and the sugar laborers, people like Jorge Torres and Joe Crimi,
have shaped the city. Our whole mercantile, freewheeling, im-
provisational town descends in part from the Dutch West India
Company's sugar-rich investments. Sites where sugar clerks ad-
ministered their sugar kingdom still exist, including the Havemeyers' offices at 117 Wall Street, now renumbered, rebuilt, and
occupied by Citibank. Plans have stalled to gut the sugarhouse of
the Domino plant in Williamsburg to build high-priced condos,
and the smokestacks and the company's iconic yellow sign still
telegraph the industrial past.

Assorted Havemeyers live in the city with Harry's objets d'art,
though the bulk of his collection of Spanish and Impressionist
art, including works by El Greco, Velázquez, and Goya, is in
the collection of the Metropolitan Museum of Art. Citibank has
branches all over the city. On weekends in Central Park, on the
beach at Coney Island, in small community gardens like Jorge
Torres's, bomba y plena musicians sing plaintive songs of another
time and place: "I can see from here/the cane fields . . . where I
was born."

And in Jorge Torres's garden in the South Bronx: a red stalk
of sugarcane with a thick white pith. "My kids don't even know
what it is," says Jorge, before biting into the flesh of his cane plant.
What it is: the early withdrawal from school, the grueling labor,
the hot sun, the blazing fires in the fields, the twenty-five-cents-
a-day wages, the recurring meals of yams, the stunted growth, the
adolescent exhaustion, the decision to leave everything and flee to

a faraway place. His kids don't know anything about those things. "But they eat it," says Jorge, smiling. His gift to them is the cane without its cost. He has found a way to pass on his history without its damage. He offers the privilege that so many others take as a given—that here in New York, his children should never know the debilitating side of the cane, only its sweetness.

BEER

THERE ARE JOSH FIELDS and Jon Conner, standing inside the cinderblock-walled freight elevator off the kitchen in Jon's loft space. They carried kegs into the elevator from their temperature-controlled storage space in the garage, brought the lift to the second-floor kitchen, stalled it, and opened the door. They hung a sign saying: SAVE A DINOSAUR—REUSE YOUR CUP! They pulled over a table and piled it with plastic cups so they could offer beer service from within the elevator shaft.

Now men in plaid shirts and women in tight jeans—sculptors, photographers, painters, cabinetmakers, glassblowers, jewelry workers, graphic designers—fill the bright, cavernous kitchen. A blackboard highlights the beer specials, which Josh and Jon brewed: Land Lover, a dark brown ale with an earthy feel; Frank Lloyd Rye, an India Pale Ale with a floral hint and a spicy note of rye; Robot Small, a rice ale, similar to Sapporo. There's After Glow, a pale ale with an orangey haze, and Shark Attack!!, a bitingly high-alcohol IPA made with hops with a tropical mango flavor. There's Eric, a mild smoked porter, named after Jon's friend Eric Porter, who extracted a promise of eponymous tribute for all porter beers. It's months of effort they're offering, many mornings of huddling over the brew kettle. Now as Black Mountain and Lil Wayne provide a soundtrack, Jon and Josh remain in the elevator shaft, pouring.

When the lights dim naturally as the sun fades from the kitchen skylights, Jon turns on two neon lights he made himself— one a yellow ear of corn with a green husk, and one a red and orange spiral. A red-light-district-red bulb hangs over the bar in the elevator shaft. In the dim light, people laugh more, drink more. Someone breaks something; the volume rises. A black-eyed woman in a denim skirt comes back to the elevator, beer in hand, saying, "I love this." A crowd gathers around Josh and Jon.

The party lasts until the early hours of the morning, until the beer runs out.

Josh and Jon began brewing in 2002, when they were roommates in this 4,500-square-foot loft, drinking enough beer that they decided to save money by making five gallons at a time on the kitchen stove with a kit—a can of syrupy malt extract, pre-mashed grain, and hops: just add water. "Beer in a bag," says Josh, "like buying a cake mix instead of baking from scratch."

Soon they switched to grinding their own grain so they could have more control over the flavor. Over the years, they graduated to a larger pot for heating water, balanced over two burners on the stove, and a plastic Igloo cooler, which kept the grain and water at a constant temperature during mashing. Then they built their own more advanced system that allows them to be more precise in their control and more prolific in their output.

At the very first beer party, to celebrate Jon's birthday, friends had swigged fifteen gallons of blond ale and asked, "When's the next party?" A couple months later, they held another, and then another, and each time the volume of beer and the number of people increased, until about a hundred and fifty people were showing up in the loft to consume eighty gallons of beer. "We were busy," Jon said. Once, some Swedish guys stole from the bathroom wall a framed replica of the Constitution that came from Colonial Williamsburg. But mostly it was friends and friends of friends, who kept coming back, contributing their own small gifts of homemade pickled eggs or soft, baked pretzels. "It ended up being a fun way to share the beer and be able to brew more of it," said Josh. They could nail down recipes, try new things—and get instant feedback. When Josh moved out of Jon's loft to live with his girlfriend, he and Jon continued to brew.

Josh has the kind of warm, easy smile you like right away, a soft, blunt-featured face, a ponytail, strawberry-blond stubble, and a faint brush of brows. He's a conceptual artist who has worked with sculpture, paint, and drawing. As the economy fell apart, he realized that most of his work made him dependent—on art markets, which plummeted; on gallery owners, who became conservative; on other artists, who could no longer hire his help. Beer, on the other hand, was a constant. When times are good, people drink it to celebrate. When times are bad, it promises consolation.

Jon's schlubby, paint-splattered aspect—brown plastic glasses, loose, graying curls, a mask of a beard, layers of T-shirts—belies his precision work as a sculptor and fabricator. He has shown his art in prestigious galleries and taught at Yale, but as commissions slowed, he found himself cutting and building three-dimensional objects to other people's specifications, "like a short-order cook." His grandmother's grandfather had been a brewer in Dayton, Ohio, and legend says the family drank beers on the roof of the brewery during the city's Great Flood. Jon's grandma also told stories of sipping tea during Prohibition with the ladies when a series of booms rattled their teacups—exploding bottles from a homebrew setup in the basement. "Embarrassing!" she said.

Drinking beers at the kitchen table after long days of brewing, Jon and Josh would assess the situation: Not enough work in art. Not enough faith in the art world. But they had plenty of small-business skills and enthusiasm for beer. Why not be independent, they thought, and make art of something their friends can drink? Why not start a commercial brewery?

Over the course of a year, to the crooning of Sunday-morning Sinatra on NPR, Jon and Josh hammered, welded, drilled, insulated, encased, wired, coiled, computerized, and reformed a thousand dollars' worth of odd parts into a functioning brewery, adding new components all the time.

At one point, they talked about lawyering up in order to legally sell growlers—half-gallon glass jugs of draft beer—out of the ground-floor garage. But they were put off by arcane regulations and overlapping bureaucracies. Then Jon's landlord announced that she wanted to sell. Spaces like the loft had become rare and valuable, even with its open elevator shaft in the kitchen, its rattling windows and skylights and its cracks in the walls. Jon thought about trying to raise money to buy the place himself, but then he heard the asking price: three million dollars. "No way," he said. So while Jon's landlord looked for a buyer, Josh and Jon started looking for a new place to brew.

ONCE, in the late 1800s, New York was the brewing capital of America. Beer-loving Germans made up a third of the city's

population in 1875, and they poured lager in saloons and grocery
stores, beer gardens and beer halls, at picnics and parties and parades, helping to support as many as 125 breweries in Manhattan
and Brooklyn.

But across the country, a new breed of Prohibitionist cam-
paigned not only against whiskey and rum—but also, specifically,
against beer, and the urban immigrants who brewed and drank
it. During Prohibition, many small and midsize city breweries closed for good, hastening waves of consolidation that made
beer the province of giant corporations. When Prohibition was
repealed, the Midwestern brewers, who had developed national
distribution systems, took over. In the following decades, the last
neighborhood breweries in New York City went out of business,
including that of Jacob Ruppert, who had owned the New York
Yankees and built Yankee Stadium, and Rheingold, which spon-
sored a Miss Rheingold beauty contest that in the mid-twentieth
century had garnered a third as many votes as the recent U.S.
presidential election. Beer ceased to be a neighborhood commodity.

The last of the old New York City breweries closed in 1976, at
a kind of low point in American beer, when Miller Lite had just
emerged, low-calorie light lager beers were driving the market,
and brewers were on their way to consolidating into only forty-
four companies. But in 1978, President Jimmy Carter signed a
law legalizing home brewing for the first time since Prohibition.
Experimental new breweries began to produce small batches of
distinctive beers. The craft brewing movement had launched.

Now light lager still dominates nationally, but its sales are
declining, as craft beer sales grow. There were more than 1,927

breweries across the country at the end of 2011, 1,877 of them craft breweries, with 855 more in the process of getting licensed—which is almost 50 percent growth.

But in New York, real estate is expensive, and brewing takes up space. Delivery trucks crossing in and out of the city have to pay costly tolls (as much as forty-two dollars for an eight-wheeler to cross the Verrazano Bridge), and factor in traffic jams and parking tickets. Taxes are higher and so are wages. New York has become a hard city for breweries.

Still, hundreds of hobbyists now brew their own beer in closets, by their bedside tables, in their kitchens and bathrooms, and in airshafts between buildings. Unlike when Josh and Jon first began brewing, specialized homebrew supply shops, along with plenty of other outlets, even Whole Foods, sell ingredients and equipment. Homebrewers organize competitions, tastings, and boozed-up twenty-five-dollar house tours. The New York City Homebrewers' Guild convenes at Burp Castle in the East Village, in a room decorated with murals of orgiastic beer feasts, where homebrewer presses against homebrewer, pouring new beers. In Park Slope, Brooklyn, a partner in the beer bar Bierkraft grows his own hops in his backyard, tending plants that look like sweetpeas, climbing and curling around themselves—but instead of pods, they have pretty little pale green cones.

The city seems primed for Josh and Jon's beer. As of 2011, there are still only six professional breweries in New York City, depending on how you count them. Little Portland, Oregon, less than a tenth of New York's size, has almost ten times the breweries. Josh and Jon are situated smack in the middle of what could be the country's densest agglomeration of the craft-beer curious. It's easy to imagine a little brewery with a tasting room filling with a rush of people at four p.m. on a Friday, the brewers finishing up their work to drink alongside their customers cum friends. "It would really be awesome," Jon says.

"This is the best beer I've ever tasted," friends would tell Josh and Jon when sampling their boozy experiments. Some would donate money toward ingredients and tell them they should start a neighborhood brewery where everyone could hang out. The enthusiasm bolstered Josh and Jon's dream of making a viable working brewery.

Josh realized that with beer, unlike with art, he could "be creative and share the product with a large group of people who could afford it and who really enjoyed it." Beer, unlike art, was gratifying.

IN 1626, the year the Dutch purchased the island of Manhattan, a visitor from Holland wrote that they "brew as good beer here as in our Fatherland, for good hops grow in the woods." In those days, impure drinking water made people sick, while fermented beer was safe. Yet even in a tippling time, the Dutch stood out. The settlers of New Amsterdam brewed so much beer, the story went, that there was no grain left for bread. Leading citizens— magistrates, merchants, aldermen—ran breweries on Brouwers Straet (now Stone Street, in the Financial District), and one report noted that a quarter of all the settlement's buildings sold alcohol. Women and men met in taverns and bars to play games like backgammon, handball, and bowling. Yet all this was not to last. The British took New York, and switched to English-style ales and stouts and porters, and over time, rum and whiskey became the drinks of choice. Beer declined—until the Germans came to Manhattan in the 1840s with their love for lager.

Bavarian brewing techniques date back to 1487, when the ingredients of beer were limited to barley hops and water, in a ruling that was soon codified as the Reinheitsgebot, or purity regulations. Later laws also limited times for brewing to winter and spring, necessitating storage, or *lager*, in German. The result was a fresher, lighter-tasting beer, with more carbonation and lower alcohol, made from a different yeast that thrived in the cold. It's not clear exactly when lager came to America, but various brewers likely boarded boats on the Rhine carrying their own packets of *Saccharomyces pastorianus,* or bottom-fermenting lager yeast, to found separate breweries across the country in the 1840s. Those who came to New York arrived in a city just outgrowing its small-town past and setting up conditions to brew massive quantities of beer. Kleindeutschland, where many Germans settled, was becoming the first immigrant neighborhood in an American city—later to be known as the Lower East Side. The city had just built a system for piping in pure water (the purer the water, the more control the brewer has over the beer), from the Croton Aqueduct. As the first of the new breweries opened, a recent immigrant named Franz Ruppert became the city's first maltster, the person who wets the barley, allows it to germinate, and roasts it to preserve its sugars—making malt, a crucial ingredient for beer.

Franz was too ambitious to stick to manufacturing a single ingredient. With New Yorkers mad for lager, in 1851 he bought the Aktien Brauerei, on Forty-Fifth Street near the East River, then a small German settlement where people lived in log cabins and old railroad cars. As dozens of other lager brewers launched elsewhere in Manhattan and in Williamsburgh, Bushwick, and the Bronx, Franz Ruppert installed a backyard beer garden and reopened his own Turtle Bay Brewery.

Brewing was an incestuous world, as marriages bonded families of brewers, maltsters, and upstate hops growers. Franz Ruppert's son Jacob worked in the brewing industry from age ten, and when he was old enough, he married the dark-haired, large-eyed Anna Gillig, the daughter of a brewer. Jacob's sister Carolina married a hops grower in upstate New York, who became the country's chief hops trader. His other sister Eliza married the brother-in-law of the brewer George Ehret.

And when Jacob wanted to strike out on his own, he followed the path that George Ehret had blazed. The handsome, audacious newcomer from Baden had ventured to the north of Manhattan Island, where he could drill seven hundred feet through solid schist for water pure enough to produce a convincing Munich lager. Jacob Ruppert bought an adjacent plot of land and became his neighbor. What is now the far Upper East Side was then a forest where officials had planted marble markers and iron rods amid the pine, tulip, and hickory trees to denote a grid that would someday be built into streets. Jacob chopped down trees with an ax, and in 1867, with his own hands, built a fifty-foot-square brewery, for a time the only permanent structure on that particular block other than a few scattered squatters' shanties. That August, Jacob's wife, Anna, gave birth to a son, also named Jacob, starting a dynastic line of brewers who would craft beer on that spot in upper Manhattan for the next eight decades.

Success was a question of timing. Jacob Ruppert and George Ehret were positioned at the right moment to slake the thirst of the arriving waves of German immigrants. The newcomers spoke

Swabian and Upper-Rhenish, Berliner, Saxon and Westphalian, but all swilled down a stein of cool lager beer. The United States Brewers' Association, which conducted all its meetings in German, had just been founded to lobby for the industry. As national beer consumption grew from about 36 million gallons in 1850 to about 855 million gallons in 1890, George Ehret became the top producer in the country, with Jacob Ruppert not far behind. Milwaukee and St. Louis combined produced a mere drop in the buckets of beer flowing in New York. In a sense, beer marked the city's shift from an English place, with English-style ale, to a city of immigrants.

Yet lager had trouble winning its due esteem. Shady establishments sold women to their male customers along with the beer, and even respectable *Lokals,* German-style saloons, shocked outsiders by serving whole families. "The little boy, who is just tall enough to reach the table edge, has a mighty tankard of 'lager,'" wrote a non-German, adding, "The Herr Papa views his youngest with satisfaction while the Frau Mama stuffs his mouth with pretzels and refreshes herself with a cool drink." Lager sellers would advertise with signs depicting King Gambrinus, the patron saint of beer. "Sometimes he is presented life size, bearded and crowned, and holding in one hand a stupendous beaker of the national beverage, the froth of which bulges from the rim like a prize cauliflower," wrote one observer. In a city with 7,071 establishments legally licensed to sell alcohol in 1870, the elite saw beer as nothing more than another way for the rabble to get drunk.

The Germans, however, thought it tasted like home. On hot summer nights, tens of thousands attended lantern-lit festivals fueled by beer, Schumann, and Schubert. Sunday evenings were spent at the great German American institution of the era, the beer hall. Fifteen hundred waltzers and schottischers filled gilded rooms decorated with gaudy frescoes depicting mythical Germanic scenes of "naked goddesses, grim knights, terrific monsters." Some halls, such as the Concordia and Germania, such as, included bowling alleys, slot machines, and rifle ranges. Far from their homeland, Germans thrived on *Gemütlichkeit*, a sense of hominess and cheer—the enveloping camaraderie of beer.

So the Ehrets and the Rupperts prospered. They hobnobbed with congressmen over dinners of pigeons and steaks. They took off midweek for upstate fishing trips. They spent thousands of dollars on wild-eyed, fast-trotting stallions, which they harnessed to liveried carriages to commute a few blocks to work. They did not live among the city's old-money elites. ("We Germans do not mingle with Americans in public," some said.) Instead, they moved uptown near their breweries. George Ehret built himself a florid home on Ninety-Third Street and Park Avenue. Jacob Ruppert erected a turreted, gabled, mansard-roofed four-story mansion at the corner of Fifth Avenue and Ninety-Third—"coarse and ignorant," said *Real Estate Record and Builders Guide*, but also nostalgic for old Germany. A dining room mural portrayed a procession of Rhineland children among sprays of vine and barley stalks, dancing, singing, and trundling a barrel of beer. In the basement was a *Kneipstube*, or drinking room, in German tavern–style, and over the Fifth Avenue window was a German inscription: MALZ UND HOPFEN/GIBT GUTE TROPFEN, or "Malt and hops/ Make good drops." Mounted on the wall was a spigot that had released some of the Jacob Ruppert Brewery's very first beer.

At the beginning, the Ruppert mansion was surrounded by newly engineered streets slicing through flattened, empty fields. But throughout his childhood, Jacob Jr. watched the brewers' fiefdom grow to fill the Yorkville section of the Upper East Side. Brewery managers and accountants bought genteel row houses and brownstones. Ruppert-owned tenements filled with coopers and maltsters, barrel washers and rackers, and droopy-mustachioed apprentices showing up with Old Country references. Soon came German meat markets, saloons, apothecaries, and music halls. When the winds were right, the smell of fresh beer drifted many blocks away toward the brewers' grand houses of Fifth Avenue like a thick, low fog coming in from the east.

IN the Williamsburg loft, Josh Fields stirs a tub of heating water with a giant paddle. "It's a cream ale," he tells me. "It's called Cream Master." It turns out the beer's appellation is an art world reference, named for Matthew Barney's cycle of films, *Cremaster,* whose conceptual departure point, Josh explains, is the male cremaster muscle, which raises and lowers the testes in response to temperature. "Ours is poking fun at him," says Josh, a bit sheepishly. He and Jon Conner also make Bankrupt State, a California common, or steam beer. They free-associate beer names while they're brewing, and came up with Frank Lloyd Rye for an IPA made in part from rye when Jon was working on a sculpture related to Frank Lloyd Wright's Fallingwater house. "We were cracking up," says Jon.

Every brewer follows similar steps to make beer: Take malt— barley that has been wetted so it germinates, and then kilned in an oven so that germination stops. Add water and steep it to extract as much sugar and flavor as possible, creating the mash. Add the flower of the hop plant, which provides flavor and bitterness, and also acts as a preservative. Cool the mixture, and drop in yeast, which converts sugar to alcohol. But exactly how to accomplish each step is a matter of centuries of contention.

There are dozens of varieties of barley malt and hops, and brewers can also malt other grains or skip hops altogether. Yeast is a living microorganism that must be tended, and specific varieties are used for different beers. Even water can be challenging: How soft is it? What else is in it? The choice of mashing temperature affects how the ingredients combine into flavors. For a drink synonymous with laid-back enjoyment, beer's manufacture is a precision chemistry experiment in which every element is critical.

The founder of the groundbreaking New Albion Brewery in Sonoma, California, famously drove all over California, Oregon, and Washington in the 1970s, stopping at scrap yards, dairies, and farms to pick up discarded pumps, pipes, and tanks. Decades later, on the other side of the country, Josh and Jon had eBay, Craigslist, and the junk piles of Brooklyn. One tank came from all the way up near the Manischewitz wine production plant at Canandaigua, and they collected tidbits from the inventories of old soda distributors and ice cream makers. They picked up two 535-gallon tanks from a maple syrup producer in the Berkshires, also a home brewer, who poured them a couple pints and assured them that the tanks were safe for food. "There's a little bit of brotherhood," said Jon.

Josh found a ten-gallon, dried-out oak barrel on the street in the Sunset Park section of Brooklyn. "It's a little risky," Jon said, but they figured it had likely been used for wine and ended up cleaning and sanitizing it and soaking it in water, so the wood expanded to fill gaps between staves. Then they barrel-aged a few beers—a Belgian dark strong ale, and a Belgian witbier that they said was delicious.

For today's cream ale, Josh pulls a vacuum-packed bag from the freezer full of hops pellets, ground and molded from the bitter flowers of the vinelike plant. He selects Northern Brewer hops, which smell green, and Saaz hops, which smell deep. Just off the kitchen, a small storage room is crowded with tubes and kegs and empty fermentation vessels, like a modern-day apothecary. The actual brewing takes place in the center of the loft's main room, which also houses a welding station, an art studio, fabrication equipment, and a wood shop. Josh sets the hops on the table and heads down to the garage, past a tiny, insulated fermentation room under the stairs, outfitted with a computer-controlled heater and air conditioner that keeps the temperature within a degree of the target.

In the garage, below a poster of a Colt 45 girlie looking coy in her underwear, Josh throws his whole body into milling grains, hand-cranking a clay slab roller left over from an art project of Jon's. The rollers crush the grains, cracking their kernels and exposing their contents. Each grain alters the chemistry of the brew slightly, allowing Jon and Josh to fine-tune flavors. "Flaked corn adds sugar," Josh says, measuring out two pounds, "and the more sugar, the more alcohol." He adds flaked rice, for the same effect. Two Row base malt, nutty and light, provides a kind of canvas for flavor. A brandname malt called Carapils, Josh says, untying a giant vinyl bag and measuring out two pounds to dump into the machine, provides body and head retention. "That's nice," Josh says, sweating, when suddenly the wheel turns freely—he's done.

Josh and Jon recently worked out a new brewing system, and this is their first time brewing on it. They're in mechanic mode, ready to fix what might go wrong. They mix the milled malt barley and rice with water—now it's called the mash—in a stainless steel keg they call the mash tun. Mashing is a slow heating process that allows enzymes to turn starch in the grain into sugars; it is punctuated by occasional pauses, or mash rests, when the temperature hits certain levels. This new system provides a different way to control temperature—not in a cooler, but by pumping the mash through a fifty-foot stainless steel coil that runs through a hot water tank (called, confusingly, a hot liquor tank), in a principle similar to that of a double boiler. At the end of the process, Josh and Jon will pump cold water through a similar copper coil they place in the boil kettle, to chill the wort, or unfermented beer, to a temperature optimal for yeast.

The workshop, with its high ceilings, skylights, and many windows, has the glassy feel of a greenhouse. It's cold outside, and the thermometer on the wall of the unheated loft reads 40 degrees. The only heat comes from the liquid barley, bubbling up toward 140 degrees in the mash tun in the center of the room, and we gather around the brewing beer as if it is a hearth.

Josh uses a giant piece of cherrywood as a paddle to mix the mash—another leftover from some art project. "Kind of amazing it becomes beer," he says, gazing into what looks and smells like a giant vat of breakfast porridge. He picks up the thermometer—144 degrees. They're approaching the critical target temperature of 150, which they want to hold for ninety minutes.

"We gotta get all smart," says Jon. "This is the moment."

You have to hold the temperature as close to the target as possible, Josh tells me, to allow the enzymes to do their work. Temperature at this stage affects the body, flavor, and dryness of the later beer. A couple degrees Fahrenheit translates to a world of difference in taste. The thermometer edges to 147, 149. Jon and Josh move around their equipment, checking and rechecking it.

They had wired up a computer-controlled temperature monitor to turn the burner on or off as the mash temperature drops below or above their target. Now Jon cuts the fire on the burner under the vat. "We might want to put on some insulation," suggests Josh, and so Jon fashions a beer cozy, tying old moving blankets around the mash tun with bungee cords, leaving just the temperature dial sticking out. Jon turns on the new pump.

This new system keeps the temperature steady, and after the specified time, they pump the mash into the boil kettle. Josh gazes into the steaming twenty-gallon pot, where the foam of bubbling wort has made landmasses that crack and separate and recombine, like tectonic plates at high speed. "It's ready," Josh says. Jon drops in the hops pellets one by one. "The hops will help it to coagulate," he explains, "so it looks like egg drop soup." Great yellow bubbles turn over in the brew, and visible bits of protein twist and turn and attach to each other, forming something like floating congealed snowflakes. Josh adds the Irish moss, a plant-based gelatin that helps the proteins attach to each other and leaves the beer clear—an update on the isinglass, made from fish bladders, used in the past. The surface of the wort becomes foamy, with deep wrinkles, like the skin of a shar-pei dog, but greenish, like pond scum. And the characteristic aroma rises: fresh, green, bitter.

As the brewing finishes, the system is dismantled into its component parts. Hoses are detached from the vessels they had filled and they drip out their liquids, limply draped over the brew tank. Lids creep off pots and clatter to the floor. Vessels, pipes, pots, and burners return to closets and shelves, receding to join the rest of the tools on the periphery of the loft. It's as though these dissociated pieces of equipment had not, for a few hours, formed a brewery.

And when it's all done, Jon dumps the water that had been used to cool the wort into the washing machine, and fetches a basket of dirty laundry. No sense wasting hot water.

THE lager breweries in New York started as small operations, with a brewmaster and five to ten German *Landsleute*, or countrymen, sweating over a kettle on an open fire. But the new technology of the Industrial Revolution transformed their careers. Mechanization was polarizing, as the early adopters expanded and became rich, while brewers who could not afford the costly machines shut down.

Early on, Jacob Ruppert's business included new malt house machines to clean the barley with forced air and mix it with other grains. Pumps moved the wort into giant brew kettles heated with coal or steam. More beer, less labor. Soon the operation became so large that Jacob Ruppert no longer worked as the brewmaster. Instead, he managed money, external relations, labor, technology, affiliated companies, and a growing portfolio of real estate acquisitions: instead, he became a capitalist. It wasn't just brewers—in the middle 1800s, bankers, brokers, exporters, importers, manufacturers, and real estate and publishing men all amassed fortunes. "Wealth," wrote New York lawyer George Templeton Strong, "is rushing in upon us like a freshet."

The story of the Industrial Revolution is a story of the fall of the individual and the rise of the machine. "We brewery workers have already reached the lowest level of social existence," read one letter to a German-language newspaper in New York. "We are told that work ennobles, but in the breweries it debases him and makes him dumb." Unlike in Europe, where laws forbade summer brewing, American brewers worked year-round, from before dawn to as late as nine at night. Everyone was usually drunk, and often the brewmasters beat the workers. When finally the workers tried to form unions, Jacob Sr. and other New York brewers locked them out. Men who had thought of themselves as craftsmen in an ancient fraternity learned that to their bosses—the new beer barons—they were nothing more than replaceable factory workers.

Meanwhile, the well-groomed, modern Jacob Jr., with his hair slicked back in geometric layers, had joined his father's brewery in the lowest position of bottle-washer. "Show this apprentice no favors," his father reportedly told the brewmaster. "If he does good work, promote him. If he won't go along and do the work we require, dismiss him." Jacob Jr. soon advanced to carrying hundred-pound sacks of barley in from the delivery wagons, and a few moves later, he was manager. The system was changing: No bottle-washer could save up enough to buy the massive equipment and tracts of real estate necessary to operate a modern brewery; the owners just promoted their sons.

The saloon at the time was the smallest local political district, and the bartender was not only confessor and raconteur—but also a kind of community mayor for those who drank his beer. Surely Jacob Jr. knew that Tammany Hall, the Democratic machine, was fleecing the public—one 1892 denouncement had termed its leaders "polluted harpies that, under the pretense of governing this city, are feeding day and night on its quivering vitals." Yet he threw his lot in with the Democratic powerbrokers, hosting glamorous dinner parties at the brewery's Tap Room for Tammany district men. He knew that his father kept the brewery lawyer Congressman Ashbel Fitch happy with such gifts as a five-hundred-dollar watch charm with a cat's-eye gem. In the "silk stocking" brigade of the National Guard, Jacob Jr. served New York's governor as an aide with the rank of colonel—a title he insisted others address him as for the rest of his life. He ran for U.S. Congress on the Tammany ticket, and he represented Yorkville for four terms.

And he continued to sell beer. Like other brewers, the Rupperts would purchase corner storefronts, install mahogany booths and brass railings, paint murals on the plaster walls, hang mirrors and nudes, and mortgage the places to the barkeeps, bringing them into their debt. Beer came with a free lunch—Bismarck herring with onions, vinegar, and Tabasco, sandwiches of fresh-cut bologna full of garlic and cloves, highly seasoned wursts, and limburger, mustard, and horseradish. Of course, Ruppert-owned saloons sold, exclusively, Ruppert-made beer.

Something had happened to lager beer in America. Bavarians had relied on their heavy, nourishing beer as food—they called it liquid bread—but New Yorkers disliked the dense flavor and found the heavy hoppiness sour and bitter. They wanted something lighter and less filling. The brewers answered with light-bodied, low-alcohol, translucent, foamy Bohemian lager. In underregulated America, the Rupperts, like other brewers, broke with European tradition, stretching the mash with corn to create a cheaper, lighter brew. The Rupperts named their beer Knickerbocker, after the mythical Dutch New Yorker. No doubt about it, theirs was a New World beer.

With his political connections in place and a growing customer base, Jacob Jr. helped organize the Rupperts into efficient vertical production, investing in an ice factory (for cooling), horse stables (for transportation), forestry concerns (for making wooden barrels), real estate (for saloons), banks (for credit), and the German-language paper the *New Yorker Staats-Zeitung* (for favorable press). The Rupperts' double-team horses clip-clopped up and down the cobblestone streets of the city, and sales soared for Knickerbocker, Ruppert's Extra Pale, and Ruppiner.

The Industrial Revolution had helped create a city of extremes. Tenement blocks for the new class of workers sprouted up the whole East Side and through the middle of the West Side, each tall, narrow, slapped-together building packing people so densely that strangers shared their secrets, their odors, their heat, and their illnesses. Meanwhile, among the new tycoons, lavish parties included "black pearls in oysters, cigars rolled in hundred-dollar bills, lackeys in knee breeches and powdered wigs," as publishing houses churned out etiquette books to guide social climbers. The city's high society was opening to people like Jacob Ruppert Jr., a nouveau-riche industrialist who had led such an insular life in America that he had a German accent.

Slumming was in vogue, and men in evening dress would wander the impoverished East Side late at night with police escorts. You could stop at chop suey houses or hole-in-the-wall saloons such as Chick Tricker's Flea Bag, the Billy Goat, and the Cripples' Home. Opium, morphine, and cocaine were available in drugstores. Jacob Jr. was a member of the prestigious Larchmont Yacht Club at a time when fellow members held a stag dinner at Sherry's restaurant in Manhattan, where guests chased a young stripper called Little Egypt and party favors took the form of drug-ready syringes.

Jacob Jr.'s sisters received lavish weddings under canopies of lilies of the valley and roses, consolidating the family's status and promising brewery heirs. Anna wore a diamond-studded veil and received her father's gift of a fully furnished house. Amanda wore orange blossoms woven into her dress and her hair. But Cornelia, a beauty with dark, soft eyes and pale skin, had been expected to marry George Ehret's son Frank, finally merging the next-door brewing dynasties. Instead, she eloped with Nahan Franko, the renowned Metropolitan Opera concertmaster. As well as failing to be a brewer, he was divorced, Jewish, a musician—entirely inappropriate for a Ruppert heiress—and the newlyweds were barred from the Ruppert home thereafter. When Cornelia died suddenly less than two years after her marriage, the sensationalist Hearst-owned *New York Journal* had a field day. "True Romance of Cornelia Franko," the newspaper headlined. Her father had removed her body to a private mausoleum without her husband's consent, and Hearst filled in all the salacious details: *"Chap I.*—How the Lover Robbed the Brewer of His Daughter. *Chap. II.*—How the Brewer Tried to Rob the Violinist of His Wife. *Chap. III.*—How Death Robbed Them Both. *Chap. IV.*—How the Brewer Robbed the Bridegroom of His Dead Bride." None of this had been part of the business plan, but in an era like today's when scandal meant publicity, the Ruppert enterprise soldiered on.

The ascendant Jacob Jr. cultivated the aristocratic habits of his class. He paid thousands of dollars for blooded Saint Bernards—Marvel, Remnant, and Lady Bountiful III, broad of chest and rough of coat—and the dogs' births and deaths and matings made the sports pages. In 1902, when the term "automobile" had only recently been coined and laws were just being enacted to regulate their use, Jacob Jr. was arrested for "running an automobile beyond the lawful speed limit." He sipped glutinous turtle soup with the men who moved New York and he danced with society women in brilliant gowns of grenadine and brocade silk. Finally, after two generations, Ruppert beer wealth had bought acceptance into the highest reaches of New York society. A former mayor jokingly gave the up-and-coming Jacob Jr. a pet ocelot called Tammany—Tammany Hall had been caricatured as a corpulent tiger devouring the body of the republic. Jacob Jr. was an insider.

But a new period was just around the corner. The big German brewers of the Midwest, who lacked the luxury of a giant local market, were already seeking to expand their distribution to New York taprooms. Pabst, Miller, and Schlitz in Milwaukee and Anheuser-Busch in St. Louis reached out nationally as soon as technology allowed them to bottle their beer and send it in refrigerated railroad cars. They created networks of depots and warehouses, salesmen and agents; the portion of all U.S. beer brewed in New York City decreased from 22 percent in 1880 to 16 percent in 1900. Local brewers like Jacob Sr. tried to stop rivals from offering rebates and loans to their saloonkeepers, but their grip was loosening. Wrote the *American Mercury:* "Adolphus Busch would drop into town, take over a floor at the Holland House, and make the local brewers look drab before departing with his pockets crammed with orders for Budweiser."

IN a studio space for artists on a strip of old brick warehouses in the Gowanus section of Brooklyn, judges for the Brooklyn Wort home brewing competition are preparing to taste thirty beers. Their table is graced with yellow and white roses, a pitcher of pens, scorecards, and palate-cleansing Poland Spring mini waters. Local amateur brewers have entered the biannual homebrew competition by paying fifteen dollars and submitting five gallons of beer for the chance to win one thousand dollars in prizes.

The judges—all brewers—sit in faded jeans and T-shirts and

plaid flannel work shirts, sequestered in a hallway. They hold up the first round of glasses to the light to see the clarity and color of the brew. Peer. Sniff. Sip. Swallow. The sense of bitterness, a defining aspect of beer, is at the back of the tongue, so unlike with wine, you have to actually drink in order to taste.

"The first beer's always the hardest to judge," says Kelly Taylor, brewmaster of the Heartland Brewery and his own Kelso. "It's got some birch, like a root beer spice."

"It's playing funny with the hops, smelling one way—playing another," says Ben Granger, a partner in Bierkraft, the Park Slope emporium. He sniffs and gazes into his glass at the same time.

As well as the panel of judges, members of the public can taste and judge the beers for a thirty-dollar ticket. Clatter and chatter travel in from the crowds in the next room, where people are packed so tightly that they can barely move from table to table and beer to beer.

Beer one is cleared and beer two arrives before the judges: darker, foamier, stickier.

"It really lingers on the tongue," says Danielle Cefaro of Brooklyn Homebrew, who is judging along with her husband and business partner, Benjamin Stutz. "Yeah, it hangs out," agrees Ben Granger.

Danielle, who has russet hair and an armful of tats (including a pig marked with a butcher's diagram missing one leg and leaning on a crutch), positions her nose over the glass and keeps it there. Mostly the judges sip and write in silence, but sometimes they go back and forth to suss out the essence of a beer. "You get that tinny, metallicky—" begins Kelly. "Green apple," suggests Ben. "Yeah, green apple, right at the beginning," says Kelly. "It's a candy apple." "Yeah, candy caramelly apple," says Ben. "In a can," says Kelly. "Yeah in a can," says Ben. Finishes Kelly: "It's not bad—it's just interesting."

"Number four," says the bearded server, setting down the next round.

A woozy smell begins to fill the room, the aromas of many kinds of beer rising and mingling. The judges sip through a quick succession of beers and issue their assessments. It smells like a Band-Aid, it tastes slick, it has "an earthiness, almost like dirt." "I like that soapy dryness," "that aspirin/Tylenol bitterness," "like some gourmet store on the Lower East Side . . . a bit of dust on it." It's like chocolate, like nail polish remover, like the plasticky smell of bubbles you had when you were a kid. "Smells a little oxidized or papery or something," someone says. "Smells like they burned the bottle," someone responds.

Danielle is tapping her pen on her iPhone in time to a Fela Kuti song. Benjamin picks up the same rhythm and taps his end of the table. Ben, sitting across from him, begins to tap his fingers too.

Beer twenty-one smells like peanut brittle. Beer twenty-two is reddish, very sweet, unfinished. "I hit a wall," says Danielle. "I'm getting there," says Ben. Beer twenty-three is the same light, golden, hoppy beer again. "Smells a little vegetal," says Ben. Beer twenty-four tastes like "Worcestershire, definitely Worcestershire," says Ben. "Sam Adams Triple Bock with soy sauce." By beer twenty-eight, the judges are complaining of cottony tongues. "It smells like spent fireworks," says Ben. Everything smells like spent fireworks. Beer twenty-nine arrives with more fanfare than flavor: Someone reaches for a glass, someone else knocks it over, and the whole thing spills onto Ben, seeping foam into his pants.

Finally, beer thirty. "Interesting amber aroma," says Kelly. The others, glassy-eyed, tapping the table in rhythm, have little to add.

FEW people were better prepared to fight the temperance movement against alcohol than Jacob Ruppert Jr. The Colonel was short—five foot four inches—but charming, and tough. He remembered everything, spoke quickly, and even walked with an "aggressive step." He was endlessly rich and could call upon his onetime colleagues in Congress. He often displayed a twinkling, distant smile, exuding the cultivated privacy of a man who grew up in the public eye, protected by his social stature, and knew how to reveal nothing. He was bold and confident. And he was accustomed to winning.

The temperance movement had been organizing since long before he was born in 1867. His father happened to have purchased the land to build the Ruppert brewery from the widow of Bible printer Daniel Fanshaw, a sober man who opposed tobacco and alcohol. In Fanshaw's time, the mid-nineteenth century, there had been uncertainty about where precisely lager stood on the ladder of alcoholic evil. In 1858, when a Brooklyn brewer and beer garden owner were brought to trial for violating the city's Sunday drinking law, his lawyer argued that lager was not intoxicating. Witness after witness testified to drinking stupefying quantities of beer—fifteen glasses before breakfast! a hundred and sixty quarts in a day!—with no ill effects. A reporter from the *New York Times* reasoned, "If it takes a pail-full of bier to make a person drunk, and the same person could get drunk on an eighth of the quantity of rum, then lager is not an intoxicating drink, but may be a wholesome beverage." The judge agreed, and the brewer was acquitted—but the legal battles continued.

To temperance advocates, beer was code for immigrant filth and sloth, unemployed men who abandon their women for the saloon. The brewers were foreign interlopers who came to America to fatten themselves on sales of their vile lager, leaving a trail of drunk and debauched citizens in their wake. In the 1880s, an evangelist from the Women's Christian Temperance Union greeted immigrants as they disembarked in New York City, distributing temperance literature in sixteen languages. In the 1890s, the temperance organization advocated restricting immigration to stop the influx of "the scum of the Old World."

Jacob Jr. moved into the new century with a clear two-pronged strategy for his brewery: expand and defend. The Rupperts and the Ehrets were still at the helm of New York brewing, but the Doelgers, Hupfels, Clausens, Trommers, Piels, and Liebmanns were at their heels. So when he took control of the Ruppert brewing empire from his father, who died in 1915, Jacob Jr. developed the capacity to produce two million barrels a year and lead the pack, working closely with his younger brother George. He promoted the idea that beer was harmless and wholesome. "You may walk the streets of New York City for hours and not meet with a drunken man or woman," he assured his critics. "Legitimate and orderly saloons do not encourage or create intemperance." He enlisted medical testimony that beer was safer than milk, and as nutritious as food.

He described his craft as drawn from an ancient and noble tradition, yet also explained to journalists that his beer was brewed with the most sanitary and modern techniques: "aged in glass enameled tanks to ensure perfect cleanliness," "drawn through sterilized copper pipes, never exposing it to outer air," "put through a pasteurizing process," and finally, "carefully examined under electric light."

He lived in a neighborhood where beer was beloved. "I drank beer from little up," said one woman in Yorkville, where a child's household duties included "rushing the growler," or filling tin pails with beer at the saloon to take home for parents to drink. Sometimes the elderly would attach the pail to a rope to lower out the window to the street and call for a child to ferry it to the bar. A part of family life, beer was also often the quickest way to dull the pain and indignities of assimilation.

Yet at some point, Jacob Jr. realized that it was not beer, but the entire German community that was under attack. Across the country during World War I, mobs attacked Germans, and one Lutheran minister was publicly whipped. About 10 percent of New York City was of German descent. Yet in Yorkville, anti-German hysteria led the names of the German Savings Bank and the German Hospital to be changed to the Central Savings Bank and Lenox Hill Hospital. "You couldn't walk the street with a German paper under your arm," said one Yorkville woman. "You'd be abused from one end of the block to the other."

By late 1917, symphony orchestras were refusing to play the music of Beethoven and Brahms, people were calling saukerkraut "liberty cabbage," and the government investigated Jacob Jr.'s closest relatives for "disloyalty." The State Department was concerned that Anna Ruppert, his mother, might be related to the Hohenzollern family of the German kaiser. Agents of the Bureau of Investigation made inquiries, only to conclude that while Anna Ruppert was not a threat, her son George and his wife,

Emma, might be suspicious. "George Ruppert's wife met Count Von Bernsdorff at a dinner party at the Astor Hotel in the Fall of 1915," noted a government document, which went on to state that she "gave vent to some expressions favorable to Germany and the cause of Germany." The officials promised to investigate further as necessary.

The fate of brewer George Ehret showed how much was at stake. His daughter had married a German baron, and he was visiting her in Germany when the United States entered the war in 1917. The eighty-three-year-old planned to leave for New York with the U.S. ambassador, but doctors advised him against the long journey, so he stayed put. Soon the Custodian of Alien Property, mandated to seize and administer U.S. properties owned by enemy nationals, took over George Ehret's $40 million estate (worth nearly $700 million in today's dollars), including his home, his art, his properties, and, of course, his brewery.

German Americans had been strong and vocal opponents of Prohibition, but with a rising anti-German sentiment, their influence was lost and their protests ignored. Government officials found records showing that German brewers including Jacob Jr. had together lent hundreds of thousands of dollars to the editor Arthur Brisbane to buy the *Washington Times*. The brewers said they were just trying to promote articles supporting beer and opposing temperance. But their representatives were hauled in to testify at a Senate hearing in late 1918 against charges that they were propaganda agents of Germany. The *New York Times* headlined, "Enemy Propaganda Backed by Brewers." That very day, the president signed the popular Wartime Prohibition Act, which cited the need to preserve grain for food and banned the sale of alcohol, easing the country into the full-blown Prohibition soon to come.

JACOB Ruppert Jr. sued the federal government to exclude beer from the new Prohibition law. His lawyer was his friend Elihu Root, who had represented the Sugar Trust before serving as secretary of war and secretary of state and winning the Nobel Peace Prize. In *Jacob Ruppert vs. Caffey*, Jacob Jr. claimed that beer with an alcohol content of less than 2.75 percent was not intoxicating, and in any case, the new law overreached Congress's authority. As before, men of science showed up to testify that one could drink more than a dozen beers without inebriation. But this time it didn't work. The Supreme Court dismissed Jacob Jr.'s injunction restraining the government in 1920. Near beer would be allowed, at 0.5 percent alcohol, but anything more would be verboten. Most beer at the time was about 7 percent alcohol, and Jacob Jr. and other brewers found themselves in limbo—their product was illegal, but they were allowed to exist.

Where can you buy alcohol in Manhattan? asked the *New York Telegram* in 1929, far into Prohibition. The answer was extensive: "In open saloons, restaurants, nightclubs, bars behind a peephole, dancing academies, drugstores, delicatessens, cigar stores, confectionaries, soda fountains, behind partitions of shoeshine parlors, back rooms of barber shops, from hotel bellhops, from hotel headwaiters, from hotel day clerks, night clerks, in express offices, motorcycle delivery agencies, paint stores, malt shops, cider stubes, fruit stands, vegetable markets, taxi drivers, groceries, smoke shops, athletic clubs, grillrooms, taverns, chophouses, importing firms, tearooms, moving-van companies, spaghetti houses, boarding houses, Republican clubs, Democratic clubs, laundries, social clubs, newspapermen's associations." Beer and wine, whiskey and gin, were clearly still around. But something did vanish: the corner saloons, the beer halls where people lingered all evening among friends—the casual working-class culture of beer.

Instead, mobsters organized to produce hard liquor, which brought in many times more money. Cocktails came into vogue as bartenders and experimenters grew expert at using fruit juice, syrups, and sugar to mask the taste of bad booze. A whole generation came of age swilling down a Manhattan after a Sidecar after an Old-fashioned.

Still, some mobsters became bootleg beer specialists. The blue-eyed, beak-nosed Owney Madden ran the Phoenix Brewery on Tenth Avenue and Twenty-Fifth Street in Manhattan, where he kept more than forty fermenting and storage vats with 25,000-gallon capacities, some connected to the sewers for easy draining in case of a raid. As an outlet for his "Madden's No. 1" beer, Owney also bought the Cotton Club in Harlem—where black dancers entertained white customers amid antebellum décor including bales of cotton and a plantation shack. Meanwhile, the sloppy, brutal Dutch Schultz, in his cheap, baggy suits, sent beer delivery caravans "thundering up the cobbled pavement on the West Side free from interference," to make predawn deliveries to beer drops like "The Tins," rows of metal garages near Mott Haven in the Bronx. One brewery on Pulaski Street in Brooklyn developed an elaborate system to pipe its beer underground to the garage of a moving company a full block away.

Gangsters waged beer wars with spectacular violence. Men

would force their rivals to take sledgehammers and axes to destroy their own fleets of delivery trucks. They would stalk drivers and payroll men at night and kill them at home in their bedrooms. Mobster brewers built offices behind double sets of doors: a regular-looking door to the street, and another, internal steel-armored door, with a peephole covered in bulletproof glass.

Upstate, near Cooperstown, New York, in an area that had produced 90 percent of the country's hops, farmers pulled up their plants to make room for new crops. Like many of the longtime German brewers in the city, Jacob Jr. soon diversified into non-intoxicating products such as ice, a kind of fermented milk, and classic malt syrup. The syrup was used to make ice cream and candy—and home brew, or *heimgemacht,* the most popular beverage in Yorkville. Grandmothers made it, children sipped it, and speakeasies trafficked it.

Jacob Jr.'s chief chemist dutifully bought beer de-alcoholizers and struggled to find the most efficient technologies to strip alcohol to create near beer, a virgin barley drink that no one ever really liked. It is not entirely clear whether the Rupperts, like other brewers, also quietly bottled and sold full-alcohol brew. The Colonel kept all his workers on the payroll—Out of charity? To keep them quiet? To keep them up late at night when no one would notice them brewing full-alcohol beer?

Jacob Jr. had also expanded into another, more popular industry. Just after the war began, the Colonel had been solicited to purchase the scrappy, losing New York Yankees. He went into the 1915 purchase "in a sporting spirit," he later wrote, "like buying a lake, or a shooting preserve." By the early 1900s, baseball had become a national institution that was supposed to represent the best of American values—country born, class neutral, good, clean fun. The game was thought to have the power to make immigrant children American. In a sense, that's what it did for Jacob Jr. as an adult.

After buying the team with a partner, he briskly acquired new management and purchased Babe Ruth from the Boston Red Sox. In 1917, days after Congress authorized American entry into World War I, the Yankees had their opening game of the season. The Colonel had his team members pass for review before Army men, shouldering their bats like guns. When the Yankees were evicted from a shared, rented ballpark, Jacob Jr. purchased ten acres of brush-filled land across the Harlem River and built his own $2.5 million Yankee Stadium with 67,000 seats. It was the largest ballpark in the country, the first enclosed structure called a stadium in U.S. sports—and the first place where the owners could control sales of hot dogs, peanuts, and, yes, eventually, beer. The Colonel showed up at games with glamorous guests like Amelia Earhart and the king and queen of Siam. Unless the Yankees piled up at least a ten-run lead, one journalist wrote sympathetically, "He shivers, turns up the collar of his coat, and leaves the park with an, 'Ach, I can't stand it.'"

So the imperious, Teutonic-accented Colonel became the back-slapping Jake. Despite his beer and his German roots, the Colonel emerged during wartime as the popular patron of America's favorite pastime.

MARCO Boggio Sella, an artist friend, was sitting in Jon Conner's kitchen drinking a beer. He had just purchased a decrepit industrial building in the Bushwick neighborhood of Brooklyn and was about to launch into renovations, intending to develop artist studio spaces. As he was telling Jon about the project, he had a thought: Could his space be made into a brewery? "Hey, this could be an option," he told Jon. "It's an awesome offer," Jon said.

With Brooklyn luck, it turned out that Marco's building had originally been constructed as a brewery. Marco didn't know much about the history, but he thought it would be a poetic reversal to return the building to its former function. A couple weeks later, he showed Jon and Josh around. It was a cavernous space, with fourteen-foot vaulted ceilings, walls of naked brick, a cast-iron spiral staircase, and light flooding the place from long windows. Someone had scattered glitter across the floor, adding to a strange bright sense of enchantment in ruin. "This is amazing," Jon said. "It's nuts."

This floor will be artists' studios, Marco said. Then he led them upstairs. There were no lights in the stairwell, and a shock of wires burst from the wall. On the second floor, where more studios would be built, the ceilings were almost as tall. Even the attic had beautiful light, and the slanted wood rafters would make a charmed alcove where Marco would build an apartment for himself.

Finally Marco took them to the basement. Half of it, he said, could be theirs for brewing. The other half would be pub space. The whole floor was a fraction of the size of Jon's 4,500-square-foot loft; half of it could work to start off—but they hoped to expand.

Jon got out a tape measure and pressed it against entryways, walls, elevator doors, and stairwells, noting the dimensions on a pad of paper. Where would a forklift deliver pallets of bottles? How would they move the kegs up the stairs? There wasn't any clear way for the loading dock upstairs to access the cellar. If we wanted to do this, we'd need the whole floor, Jon thought. The old brewery used to take up the whole *building,* he thought. "You really need space, that's part of the deal," he said.

Later that week, at a beer pairing at a restaurant in Tribeca, Josh mentioned the possibility of moving into Marco's old brewery. "No way!" said his friend Matt Levy, excited. Matt, an exuberant, mustachioed tour guide, had lived in Bushwick and become fascinated with the big, old, elegant brick industrial buildings that looked Photoshopped onto the aluminum-siding landscape he passed on his bike.

He had discovered his neighborhood had once been riddled with German-built breweries, along with the odd turreted brewer's mansion. He happened upon Will Anderson's out-of-print book *The Breweries of Brooklyn* and learned that at one point, brewers had filled Williamsburg—which had been two-thirds German—and Bushwick—then known as Dutchtown, from "Deutsch." Meserole Street had been known as Brewers' Row in the nineteenth century, when eleven German brewers operated corbelled breweries at once. They were former revolutionaries and innkeepers, brewers and farmers, who had washed up on Brooklyn's shores looking to start businesses. In a city of short, often wood buildings, theirs stood out as grand institutions of heavy industry, with their tall chimneys and enormous icehouses and large properties for beer gardens. In his enthusiasm, Matt had created the Bike Brooklyn Beer Blitz, a six-mile bike tour of defunct breweries.

So when Josh mentioned the address of the place, Matt whipped out his iPad. He came up with a historical picture of the old Diogenes Brewing Company, built in 1898 in a last burst of German enthusiasm for lager, and closed after Prohibition. From the outside, it hadn't changed that much: four stories tall, pretty brick arches over the windows, brick blocks on the sides. "Is this the building?" he asked. No doubt about it, that was Marco's place.

Jon went back for another visit. ERECTED 1898, he noticed it said on the side of the building, and then he saw the interlocking monogram DBC, Diogenes Brewing Company. He had read enough about beer to know something about the structure of early breweries. The Diogenes Brewing Company would have used a gravity-fed system, milling the grain on the top floor and allowing it to pour down into the mash tun on the floor below, then to flow as a liquid down to the boil kettle below that. "I'm sure it was made that way—that's why most of those buildings were tall and had multiple floors," Jon said: architecture in service of a recipe. He and Marco wandered around looking for places where holes and chutes might have opened between floors. Jon discovered an old tunnel that once led from the basement to the end of the lot through a wall that had been cinderblocked over. Was it a Prohibition tunnel for secret deliveries? Had he uncovered an archaeology of vice? Or was it simply a way out to a loading dock?

Josh and Jon called the State Department of Health, the State Liquor Authority, and a small business startup help line run by the city to learn more about codes and regulations. Did their equipment need to be certified safe for food, as with restaurants? In the meantime, could they actually sell beer out of the garage in the current loft, since the place was zoned industrial? No one seemed to have clear answers.

At thirty-one and thirty-nine years old, respectively, Josh and Jon had been in New York for most of their adult lives, and had networks of friends and associates. They knew that Marco's space could help them to make a brewery work in the city.

But Jon began imagining driving a truck through Brooklyn and Manhattan to drop off beer at bars and restaurants. He envisioned getting stuck in traffic, searching for parking, paying off massive tickets. "I would say I don't want to get into a truck and do that," he said.

They imagined struggling to move the mash tun and the boil kettle down the narrow steps into Marco's basement, never mind the weekly deliveries of grain, and, eventually, carrying out the beer itself.

They worried about the neighborhood around Marco's building. Parts of Bushwick may be filling with bars and restaurants, but this block struck Josh as industrial and pretty drab, kind of worn out, not a place where lots of people would frequent a pub anytime soon.

In late-night conversations over beer, Josh and Jon forged and canceled business plans and clarified their own ambitions. They wanted to start their brewery on a low budget, all by themselves, without investors, and build up from there. They might open as a brewpub, and then distribute more widely, but their eventual goal was to be a local or regional brewery—not to ship beer all over the country. "A lot of breweries make this massive initial investment and owe a lot of money so constantly need to crank out more product to start making money," said Josh. "You get trapped in a cycle of growth where once you get all that initial equipment paid off, you're expanding, and getting rid of the equipment, and buying all new equipment, and it seems like a never-ending expansion process." They wanted somehow to avoid the endless expansion that has determined much of brewing since Jacob Ruppert's time. "We're putting our lives and souls into this," said Jon, "and if there's any success or rewards for this labor, we'd like to do it our way and get that back."

Meanwhile, another option was on the table. Jon's father offered them space on his large rural vineyard in Oregon to start their brewery—for free. They would be able to brew off a gravel road in view of grape vines and the distant smoky blue of the Cascadian mountain range—the antithesis of the high-density hassles of Brooklyn. It was something to think about. It meant they didn't need to jump on the first opportunity.

They wanted to start a brewery, but it wasn't clear that it should be Marco's old brewery in Bushwick. "All those old breweries closed for a reason," said Jon.

PROHIBITION proved hugely unpopular, especially in big cities like New York, and after more than a decade, the beer world was banking on repeal. Aged horses were readied for wagon deliveries; big copper vats were cleaned and polished; and the United States Brewers' Academy in Midtown reopened to teach trainees the chemistry and technology they would need to become master brewers. But the landscape had changed. Gangsters ran some breweries. Others had closed. "They are not sure their salesmen can meet the competition of gangsters' machine guns, sawed-off shot guns and bombs," the *Times* reported when the brewers sent lobbyists to Washington to discuss combating organized crime.

When beer finally came back, the triumph was incremental. A beer bill allowed states to decide individually to legalize a low-alcohol 3.2 percent brew, which was suddenly classified as "nonintoxicating," giving it a status similar to soft drinks and allowing it to be sold to minors in grocery stores and drugstores, as well as in restaurants and clubs. And so at 12:01 a.m. on April 7, 1933, after thirteen years of proscription, 3.2 percent beer, at least, returned to New York.

Anxious that "there be no carnival or untoward celebration," Jacob Jr., the head of the United States Brewers Association, ordered members across the country not to deliver beer right at midnight, but to wait until six the next morning. "Beer may not be intoxicating, but its promoters do not intend to take responsibility for any orgies that may accompany its return," noted the *Washington Post*.

Just after the ban lifted at midnight, some speakeasies in Manhattan managed to provide sips of beer reputed to have come by taxicab from "an uptown brewery," but there was little open revelry. Instead, six grave, hatless men dressed in tuxedoes staged a Midtown funeral for near beer, carrying a keg of the de-alcoholized brew out of a restaurant and into a waiting hearse. A six-piece Bavarian band struck up a dirge as the car cruised slowly through the streets, attracting a cortege of more than two thousand impromptu "mourners." The real show was at the breweries, where quiet crowds assembled to watch trucks load up cases and kegs for distribution at dawn.

Later that very day, the Colonel's new threat took shape in the form of six Clydesdales, their manes decorated with red and white roses, pulling a shiny red Anheuser-Busch wagon carrying three hundred wooden cases stamped **BUDWEISER** across Thirty-Fourth Street. Out-of-town brewers were staking a New York claim. Beer needed massive reinvestment, and the Midwesterners, with their national networks of equipment, salesmen and advertising, were positioned to dominate.

The Rupperts' beer thrived for a while. In the days after the ban was lifted, restaurants and cafés offering free beer with meals had to post STANDING ROOM ONLY signs. Thousands of New Yorkers took the elevated train to Coney Island to sip a beer by the beach, though it was freezing outside. Local brewers hired two thousand new workers to pour beer all night and still failed to keep up with orders. They quickly ran out of bottles and barrels and resorted to buying them used from speakeasies. Veteran beer drinkers showed up to rush the growler, like the elderly man with a handlebar mustache who was cheered when he emerged from the Ruppert brewery with a brimming tin pail in each hand. In days, beer taxes from New York City alone added a million dollars to federal, state, and local government coffers.

At first it looked as though the Colonel had come out on the winning side of consolidation. The Rupperts' old friend and rival George Ehret had never recovered from the seizure of his plant during the war, and when he died in 1927, his children closed his factory. The Ruppert brewery bought it, more than doubling its size to thirty-five fortresslike redbrick buildings, occupying most of four blocks from Ninetieth to Ninety-Fourth streets between Second and Third avenues.

But soon the eaters get eaten.

A generation had skipped beer and grown up with sweet, fizzy soda pop and hard liquor. Saloons, the lifeblood of the local brewer, were gone, and the Midwestern brewers, far more experienced with marketing, came up with slick new campaigns. An uneasy Jacob Jr. ran his own educational advertising to tell people how to drink beer. One ad showed a formally attired, debonair, white-mustachioed elderly man with a handsome young couple. "Take it from an old-timer—this is the *real* Ruppert's Beer!"

Another showed a woman setting a table and suggested including beer in fine dining: "The dainty glass bottle of Ruppert's harmonizes with fine linen, delicate china and sparkling glass." In the fall, Jacob Jr., aware of the power of a grand public gesture for a popular cause, donated $250,000 to support Admiral Byrd's expedition to the South Pole. The freighter for the voyage—the *Jacob Ruppert*—left port loaded with 180 husky dogs to pull the explorers' sleds, as well as 20,000 cases of Knickerbocker lager.

In December 1933, when Prohibition was finally fully repealed, there were only twenty-three breweries left in the city, down from seventy before the ban on alcohol. Across the country, the great brewing families were getting out of the business: Hensler and Krueger's and Ballantine's in Newark; Fort Pitt, Duke, Silver Top, Old Shea, Dutch Club, and Tube City in Pittsburgh; Jax Beer in New Orleans and San Antonio; and hundreds of others. Old-fashioned, city-based brewing companies with high land and labor costs were set up to market their beer in corner saloons, not to capture national markets.

Prohibition had created an army of liquor-and-beer specialized thugs. Seeking to go legit, some took out licenses to open breweries, only to use the same old tactics. Hijackers kidnapped a Ruppert driver and stole the beer. A Ruppert employee exchanged shots with four men carrying army revolvers and sawed-off shotguns.

A Brooklyn barkeep was terrorized by thugs demanding he stock their brand of beer, in a conversation the *Times* relayed in classic gangster style:

"What's wrong?" asks the barkeep upon encountering a gangster in his establishment.

"Nothing," says the gangster, "or, not just yet anyway. What sort of beer are you handling?"

The barkeep names a brand. The gangster chuckles.

"You mean you was," says the gangster. "From now on you're selling ours, get me?" he declares, naming his own brand.

When the barkeep demurs, the gangster threatens: "Oh, that's the way it is, eh? Wanna be persuaded, do you?" Then he turns to his companion and says: "Give him the works!"

"The works," unfortunately, include a ruptured scalp for the barkeep's wife, who intervenes.

Meanwhile, the era of consolidation was just beginning.

GET New York City brewers together to talk about beer today and you hear a strange mix of pessimism and fervor. At the Craft Beer Jam in the performance space of a local NPR station, representatives of four local breweries sit under studio lights talking about the explosion of home brewers and craft beer connoisseurs, and how somehow, the enthusiasm just hasn't bubbled up into many city breweries.

Homebrewers have long formed the ranks from which craft brewers emerge. Some of the professionals at New York City breweries today started as Bud Lite fans in college who wanted to guarantee their own cheap supply of booze while still underage, or produce quantity for sale by the plastic cup, or add a hint of West Coast hip or European sophistication to their rote weekend beer consumption.

Steve Hindy, a cofounder of the Brooklyn Brewery, first got the idea for homebrewing while working as a journalist in Saudi

Arabia, where alcohol is banned. The Brooklyn Brewery has become a kind of model for small business development in New York City, complete with its own manual, *Beer School*, a case study in entrepreneurialism written by the founders. But the brewery, opened in 1988, initially made all its beer upstate and only began brewing within city limits eight years later. Land was cheaper then, and about a dozen breweries operated in the city around that time, a recent peak. In the early 2000s, the Brooklyn Brewery tried for years to expand its Williamsburg plant, succeeding only when the economy tanked, rents went down, and the state contributed an incentive grant. The owners want to expand further, so the current plan is to build a bigger brewery—upstate.

Sixpoint started brewing in 2005, in the Red Hook section of Brooklyn on the site of a former brewery, pressing its enormous old stainless steel fermenting tanks into service until the brewers could afford replacements. Putting his brewery to double duty, Kelly Taylor operates both the Heartland Brewery and Kelso, the brand he runs with his wife, at one site near downtown Brooklyn.

In a kind of local shoutout, Kelso puts out a Putrid line of beers named after putrescent city waters—the Newtown Kriek, a lambic; the East River porter; the Fresh Kills brown ale; the Saint Gowanus Belgian pale ale. Distribution has expanded and now some Duane Reade drugstores sell Kelso growlers. Recently Kelly did a beer tasting at the Duane Reade in Williamsburg. "One guy had two packs of condoms and three growlers," Kelly said, grinning. "Saturday night, man!"

THROUGHOUT his life, the Colonel drank little, worked hard, and remained vain enough to avoid being photographed wearing glasses. In his middle age, *Bachelor* magazine considered him glamorous enough for a jubilant if slightly misogynistic feature. "Colonel Jacob Ruppert says men marry only when they are lonely or in need of a housekeeper—He is neither!" said the headline. "He likes the ladies. He's glad when they are married to someone else," the magazine wrote. A photograph shows him taking his breakfast from a silver tray, alone at a long table.

But at seventy-one, he fell ill with phlebitis. In 1938, while his brother George ran the brewery, he followed the Yankees on the radio from his sickbed and was so captivated that he ordered all home games thereafter to be broadcast, in what sportswriters would later note was his last official act. In early 1939, Babe Ruth was among the last to see him alive. The beer baron had always called the baseball player "Ruth"—which sounded, with his slight German accent, more like "Root"—never using the famous nickname. Now the older man held out his hand to clasp his protégé's. The Colonel said one word: "Babe." The next day he died.

He left behind the Yorkville neighborhood his family helped create, where German butcher shops sold wiener schnitzel, German newsstands sold the *New Yorker Staats-Zeitung*—and, of course, German-style taverns served frothy lager in pewter-lidded beer steins. Up in the Bronx, Yankee Stadium was known as the house that Ruth built—but more accurately, it was the house that beer built.

The German neighborhood faded away as its children assimilated and moved on, and the old Yankee Stadium has been destroyed. But the Colonel also left behind a cultural shift, an idea so natural that it now feels inevitable: it can be argued that it was Jacob Ruppert who married beer and baseball as the most American of pastimes. He certainly tried.

. . .

JUST past nine a.m. on a Friday in June finds Josh Fields and Jon Conner and two friends pushing stainless steel containers up a ramp into a twenty-six-foot yellow Penske truck. They move the boil kettle, and then comes the biggest 535-gallon mash tun. The task is to lower each beer vessel into the next largest, the 108-gallon hot liquor tank inside the 360-gallon boil kettle inside the 535-gallon mash tun, protecting each layer with moving blankets and custom-made foam—and to do it all by hand. "We're gonna make a Russian doll of beer," says Jon. Every time they nudge it, the largest vessel emits a deep clang like a steel drum, or some hulking, metal-voiced beast. "Geronimo!" Jon calls as the men slide the two inside the third with a hiss. The next question is whether the ramp to the truck can support the weight of all the vessels at once. Three men push and one pulls. "This is so dangerous, and they're so fearless," says Gilda, Josh's soft-eyed girlfriend, a graphic designer. When the vessel-encrusted vessel is safely stowed in the truck, the rest follows: a capper machine to lid beer bottles, big plastic tubs of grain, boxes of empty bottles, a vacuum pack machine for preserving hops, a handful of kegs. I help load in mini kegs—dozens of them, still smelling of beer. Some of the kegs are positioned a bit precariously, but Jon shrugs it off. "If it breaks, we can fix it," he says—he's packing the welding equipment. Passing cars slow down so the drivers can stare at the unusual contents of the moving truck. "You guys starting a fucking brewery or something?" someone calls out.

In fact, they're moving one, to Oregon, that promised land of brewers. Of course, they're not the first to give up on New York City. In 1966, the Jacob Ruppert Brewery shut down. In the next decade, all the other local brewers closed too; it had become too expensive to produce beer in New York City.

In Portland, Josh and Jon will find cheap space, that most important and difficult commodity for a person interested in brewing beer. They've taken up the offer from Jon's dad to use his big rural property, where they can live in a trailer in a field and incubate their brewery in the barn until they can rent a permanent space in Portland. Equipment is cheaper. Things are easier to transport. There's parking.

As they pause to gulp water, a man asks Josh to move the truck so he can get his car out of his garage, but as soon as there's room, the UPS guy slips into the open spot. "It's so aggro here," says Jon. "Everything's a think."

Jon and Josh, sweating through their T-shirts, hug good-bye. Josh will go first with Gilda in this truck, and Jon will follow in a few weeks with his brother in a convoy of two more twenty-six-footers full of brewery equipment. Jon slaps Josh's back: "I'll see you on the other side." Gilda's waiting in the cab of the truck. Josh scrambles up into the high seat and starts the engine, and the yellow Penske pulls out of the parking space into traffic.

FISH

THERE'S MAR GONZALEZ, throwing a spider crab through the air so that it arcs against the blue sky, its eight black, silty legs kicking all the way until it lands from whence it came, in the salt surf off Coney Island. "Wow," says a woman nearby, watching the soaring crab. "I play football, that's why," Mar says, shrugging off the compliment. You've got to return the rejects.

Back at her bucket, she pokes through her cache. A half dozen blue crabs, pincering each other, and two meaty-looking fish, all of them floating in seawater. "What she's got here is rare," says a shirtless man with a concave belly and slicked-back hair, peering into the pail. In fact, what she's got here is her standard take, good when boiled with a little salt and some Old Bay seasoning, and enough to last until the next Saturday finds her back on the pier.

"How old are you?" another kid asks. "Twelve," says Mar. "No way!" says the kid. She looks bigger and older, and it's just not that common to see a twelve-year-old city girl, hair braided off her face, skin the color of sand, wearing a white T-shirt, orange shorts, and soaked red socks, sinking raw-chicken-baited crab traps thirty feet off a pier.

"I've been fishing since I was one month old," she says. "My dad had me in one hand and the fishing rod in the other." Like centuries of fishers in New York City, she knows how to read the water and anticipate her prey. To her right is a sign that says, PREGNANT WOMEN, WOMEN OF CHILDBEARING AGE, AND CHILDREN UNDER 15 YEARS OLD SHOULD NOT EAT FISH OR EELS CAUGHT IN THESE WATERS. Mar pays no attention.

"Fishing is free," she says. "It's the only thing in the city you can eat for free."

New York is full of people like Mar, fishing because they like to and they need to, because fish are free and gear is cheap and every day you have to eat. In the far East Village, a couple of boys sit in a bus shelter on Avenue D, holding heavy, wet plastic bags shifting with pincers, waiting for the bus to take them to Chinatown markets to sell crabs they just raised up from the East River. Along the banks of the Harlem River, homeless guys have set up tarp tents as shelter for their fishing. "I don't have time to fool around," says Philip Frabosilo, a taxi driver who keeps three rods "pre-rigged" in his trunk—loaded with pale, stinking bunker fish—so that when a fare takes him toward the waterfront, he can set up in less than two minutes, fish for half an hour, and get back in his cab.

All around the city's edges, Indians, Jamaicans, and Italians eat the smaller fish, the little shiners. Puerto Ricans and Bosnians and Poles go for the bluefish and striped bass, the bigger the better. People will bring a black trash bag to the docks and toss in everything they catch. They will hitch a Styrofoam cooler to a luggage cart to pack with seafood. They will cozy their fish against an ice pack for a long subway ride through the boroughs.

Most are not destitute, but they look to the waters to help them in their struggle to get by. A hundred years ago, a small-time pushcart peddler on the Lower East Side was called a *luft-mensch*, a Yiddish word meaning literally a person who lives off air. The word could be used today, but it would be more apt to say people live off water.

The problem is that these fish, and these waters, contain toxic chemicals. The state Department of Environmental Conservation recommends that most women and children not eat *any* fish or shellfish from most New York City waters. The guidelines permit men to eat various fish in limited quantities, according to the species—once a week, once a month, or in some cases, never. A study of Hudson River fishers found elevated levels of PCBs and other toxins in their blood. Sustaining oneself by the last wild meat in New York City is no longer advisable.

No one has surveyed precisely how many people subsist on local fish in the city. In Manhattan's East Harlem, a poll of two hundred women enrolled in the federal Women, Infant and Child program, an assistance program for low-income mothers, found that 10 percent of them eat fish caught in city waters. When the Environmental Protection Agency investigated cumulative exposure to toxins in Brooklyn, officials were shocked to learn that many people in Greenpoint and Williamsburg depended on a diet of East River fish. "This was the first time the U.S. EPA had heard of this potential health hazard," wrote an academic who studied the project. A community group spent several months one summer polling two hundred Greenpoint and Williamsburg anglers and found that they caught an average of fifty-seven fish a week each: blue crabs, eels, bluefish, and striped bass. The fishers' family members each ate an average of 9.5 fish per week.

New York is a city on water. Once, seventy miles of streams veined the island of Manhattan and twenty-one ponds pooled in it. A freshwater creek flowed from a marshland under the current offices of the *New York Post* and met another creek beneath what is now the Marriott Marquis. Another channel flowed from Times Square to the Hudson, near the entrance to the Lincoln Tunnel. The present-day Maiden Lane was a pebbled brook where Dutch girls washed clothes. The marshy Lispenard's Meadow left soft ground in Soho and northern Tribeca, which for many years made it impossible to construct tall buildings.

Now the old Minetta Brook, which still runs underground north of Washington Square to near Union Square, burbles up into the lobby of an apartment building on Fifth Avenue, which reportedly displays it in clear plastic tubing that looks something like a bong. Other West Village cellars, built on wetlands, flood. Willow trees flourish on the high watertable of the Lower East Side, which was built on landfill. In Flushing, Queens, the planners of the 1939 World's Fair filled a tidal marsh to make ball fields, which often flooded—and which became, again, wetlands: Around the barbecue area, marshy plants such as spikerushes and water purslane grow in soft, depressed, eternal puddles, and bullfrogs croak.

Manhattan, Brooklyn, Queens, and Staten Island are all islands or parts of islands, and the Bronx is surrounded on three sides by water. New York for hundreds of years was more famous for its oysters than for its tall buildings. The distinctive odor of the Fulton Fish Market at the southern tip of Manhattan—long among the world's biggest—was often immigrants' first impression of the city upon disembarking from the ferry from Ellis Island. "When my sister picked me up, I asked her if all of New York smelled like rotten fish," said one newcomer.

When it comes to fish, the city has a dual history of consumption and destruction. For centuries, the growing and industrializing city suffocated the fish with its wastes even as it continued to eat them. "The bulk of the water in New York Harbor is oily, dirty, and germy," Joseph Mitchell wrote in 1951. "Men on the mud suckers, the big harbor dredges, like to say that you could bottle it and sell it for poison."

Since then, the waters have improved. Follow the city's perimeter, 578 miles of it alongside water. No one keeps official count, but tens of thousands of people likely fish each year. On the right day, if you circle the islands, you will find fishing rods and crab traps dipping off the edge of the city all the way along, seeking out wriggling life from the other side.

ON the edge of Queens facing Manhattan, Canada geese fly up over the East River straight into the sun in a V. From the Gantry Pier in Long Island City, a row of rods and lines of fishing wire block the postcard view of Midtown across the water. John Ruffino unpacks his preferred bait—bunker, otherwise known as menhaden, a bony, oily fish he cuts into pieces large enough to whet the appetite of a good-size striped bass. "You buy as many bunker as you could, you *bunk out!*" John says, noting the shortage of baitfish. Leaving the table sparkling, covered in sharp, iridescent fish scales, he hooks into the bait. In a single motion, he casts out gracefully and effortlessly far into the water toward Manhattan, as he explains his technique.

"I don't *never* fight hard—I let him do the fighting," John says. "I don't horse, I don't pump the fish, I just keep the tip in the air and let him pull, I tighten it, and let him pull," John says, as though summoning a fish with this talk. "And it feels so good, it really does, 'cause he's still fresh, he's got a lot of *tempo* left, you know what I mean?"

John is in the small-time business of peddling East River fish, with a cell phone call to people who've wandered by the pier and expressed interest in his salty, oily wares. "A lot of time they walk down and they witness me fighting the fish," John says. "I always blurt out, soon as I see it, I give it an amount number: twenty dollars, thirty dollars, fifty dollars, you know? And the guy says, 'Oh, you sell them?' I go, 'Yes, sir!'"

John won the 2009 Brooklyn Fishing Derby, a monthlong, borough-wide competition to capture the largest fish, with a 40-inch striped bass. Sometimes he gets up at six in the morning to come to the pier and doesn't leave until eleven p.m. One night he fished till three a.m. in a rainstorm, while his friend crawled under the fish-cleaning table.

He caught a bird once and had to unbraid the line out of its wing; he has caught a log, a boot, a shoe, various pieces of tire, a rusted can, a pair of old-fashioned bloomers, a sunken board, a shirt, half a fender. He caught a hacklehead, a fish that looks like a toad. He often catches plastic bags and used condoms—"Coney Island whitefish," the anglers call them. He looks up at one of the few places in the city where you can see an expanse of sky, as big as a Wyoming or Montana sky, sweeping above the East River. Then he looks down. "This whole river is *covered* in a carpet that looks like the most dirtiest cotton," he says, gazing out at the fuzzy white surface of the water, from whose depths he extracts food. For the first time, he goes quiet.

.　.　.

HE doesn't talk about Newtown Creek, a partial border between Brooklyn and Queens, whose waters empty into the East River just around the corner from John's fishing spot. But the history of this creek, as well as its fetid, chemical water, embodies all the reasons not to eat the fish he catches. The creek is a four-mile Superfund site, one of the most contaminated bodies of water in the country. It contains raw sewage from twenty direct sewage portals and oil and toxic chemicals from a century of industrial waste.

On one of his regular patrols, John Lipscomb, a boat captain for the Riverkeeper environmental organization, takes me upcreek on his Chesapeake Bay deadrise workboat. We enter a netherzone of floating pieces of cars, collapsing bulkheads, and rusting pipes that can emit sewage from the city sewers during a rainstorm. Along the creek banks are crumbling redbrick, smokestacked buildings, like a watery museum of nineteenth-century industry, alongside hulking twentieth-century plants. About a mile in, I see viscous black oil pooling onto the Queens side of the creek and spilling out of the booms, floating plastic barriers designed to contain it. The beast from below is burbling up.

It's the site of the Pratt oil refinery, one of the oldest on the creek, which once took up eighteen acres making kerosene for lamps. Later, on the phone, a Riverkeeper investigator conjectures that the recent installation of metal bulkheads could have punctured the soil, creating a path for oil to seep from the groundwater to the surface water—perhaps a very large plume.

A vast underground lake of contamination more than fifty-five acres wide has already been identified alongside the creek, containing spills, leaks, and waste oil companies dumped long ago. "Like the Blob," wrote Daphne Eviatar in *New York Magazine*, "it keeps changing shape and moving—bulging south beyond the Brooklyn-Queens Expressway, slithering north toward Greenpoint Avenue, ballooning west to at least Monitor Street." The oil in the groundwater along the creek banks adds up to the largest urban oil spill in North American history—estimates range from seventeen million to thirty million gallons, or three times the size of the *Exxon Valdez* spill.

It wasn't always so contaminated. "Exceedingly refreshing," wrote Edward Neufville Tailer of a quick swim in its waters, where he also caught weakfish, in 1848. But in following decades, the Industrial Revolution exploded on its banks, and the water served as a transitway and waste disposal. The American oil industry invented itself on this little waterway, where kerosene was first produced, and where John D. Rockefeller's Standard Oil eventually consolidated control over more than a hundred creekside stills. By the early twentieth century, the creek carried more freight than the thousand-mile Mississippi River. Storage tanks leaked, solvents spilled, and the waste products of distilling oil to produce paraffin wax, kerosene, naphtha, gasoline, and fuel oil seeped into the ground and water. It was a slow-motion spill of disastrous proportions.

More recently, a survey of industry along the creek noted cement factories, food and waste processors, gasoline storage centers, thirty facilities for storing extremely hazardous wastes and one more for storing radioactive waste; seventeen petroleum and natural gas storage facilities; and ninety-six aboveground oil storage tanks. The city's sewer overflows still dump millions of gallons a year of raw, untreated sewage directly into the creek.

Of course, the thing is that water moves. You can go out on Newtown Creek one day and see oil slicks and gassy swirls colored violet and blue and brown, like an iridescent bruise, while you sniff out uriney ammonia, the stink of feces, and the chemical smells of asphalt and petroleum and rubber cement thinner. The next day the tide will come in and a certain wind will blow through and the creek suddenly looks just like any natural passage, flowing clean and supple as water.

Obviously, then, Newtown Creek also flows freely into the East River. Its myriad toxins and carcinogens carry through the water to Gantry Pier. Its fish swim out to John Ruffino's line.

"IT is not possible to describe how this bay swarms with fish, both large and small, whales, tunnies and porpoises, whole schools of innumerable other fish, which the eagles and other birds of prey swiftly seize in their talons when the fish come up to the surface," marveled Jaspar Danckaerts in 1679. He described tasting foot-long oysters, harvested from Brooklyn's Gowanus, as good as those in Europe. "I had to try some of them raw," he said. In his day, tuna, perch, sturgeon, striped bass, herring, mackerel, halibut, weakfish, blackfish, stone bream, eel, sheepshead, oysters, and sole, as well as whales, porpoises, otters, and seals all filled the waters of New York Harbor.

The city was a nexus of fish routes, as some fish moved up from ocean to river to spawn, and others swam down from river to ocean. The tidal straits, creeks, kills, narrows, bays, inlets, marshes, reefs, streams, basins, coves, and wide-open ocean of New York City form one of the most intricate and ecologically complex estuaries in the world. "With all the interlacing of waterways hereabouts, we could have had a wonderful national park," mused one nature lover in 1980, considering the extraordinary

confluence of waterways that contributed to more than fifty ecologically distinct areas, including pitch-pine barrens, peatlands,
and eelgrass meadows. "Think of the fishing, the boating, the
wildlife marshes, the oyster beds, the shad runs, the scallop beds.
All that room for marinas. The cool ocean breezes. Those mag-
nificent and smogless sunsets, which sustained an entire Hudson
River school of painters."

Instead, when the Dutch moored their ships in the East River
shallows and trudged to shore in their leather boots, they saw in
the waterways the ideal infrastructure for commerce. They built
homes facing the water, and from the start, they ate of it.

When Europeans arrived, the Lenape people native to New
York sold them fish. The Lenape had long fished with spears and
milkweed nets and launched tulip-tree canoes off the west side of
Manhattan to drop lines with bone or stone hooks into the water.
They sun-dried shad and striped bass on tree bark to preserve for
the winter, gathered oysters from the shallow waters and dug with
the balls of their feet for clams in the soft mud. One of the very
earliest ways to make a living in Manhattan was as a fisher and
fishmonger.

Within a century, regular fishing fleets were setting out to
catch cod, mackerel, and sturgeon—more than a thousand fish
at a time. Manhattan farmers sought prime waterfront land so
they could fish and trap off their own shores. They cooked shad
(whose Latin name, *Alosa sapidissima*, means "most delicious of
herrings") nailed over an open fire. They called soft-shell clams
"pissers" because they squirted water like a boy peeing. The original charter for the Trinity Church in Lower Manhattan includes
rights to whales that stranded themselves on the nearby beaches
of the Hudson.

By the 1700s, the city huddled by the water was growing north, yet lower Manhattan still had the feel of a waterfront town. African American street vendors trawled the narrow, newly cobblestone streets, calling out, "He-e-e-e-e-e-ere's your fine Rocka-a-way clams." The youngest known fisher in town was the son of Mr. and Mrs. Moles Lynn, tavern-keepers: at two and a half years old, he fished from Moor's Dock with a tiny rod—until September 1773, when he fell into the water and drowned.

For hundreds of years, visitors arriving in the city would be advised to "enjoy the oysters." In 1800, oyster houses advertised Jamaicas, Rockaways, and Amboys, named for the places they were harvested. Saloons offered all the oysters you could eat for six cents on the "Canal Street Plan," and there was an oyster and clam stall on nearly every block. In one contest held in Grand Central Station in 1885, the winning shucker opened 2,500 oysters in two hours, twenty-three minutes, and thirty-nine and three-fourths seconds. "All along the East River are places, rude huts, paralytic shanties, where oysters are sold at a penny apiece," wrote one chronicler. Then as now, everyone had free access to the fruits of the local waters. For the poor, these wild meats were a staple protein. As hungry immigrants began to pour into the city, all around Manhattan, "anyone with a length of string, a hook, a railroad nut for a sinker, and a bit of clam purchased at a fish market could expect to catch a fine dinner," wrote one fisheries historian. Oysters were a rare instance of rich and poor eating the same food at the same time prepared the same way.

Fishing was a growing industry with ever more efficient technology. Commercial fishers dropped purse seines, circling around a school of fish and pulling the tops of the net together, like a ladies' purse. They used gill nets, with holes large enough for fish heads but not fish bodies, so they would get stuck and the net could be pulled up full. Like sensible predators, fishermen moved in and out of New York Harbor following their migrating prey. In March, the fleet of southern mackerel seiners set out from New England ports for the waters off North Carolina, to meet and trap the first schools of fish swimming north and deliver them to the marble display counters of the Fulton Fish Market. The first catch would get the highest price of the season. The boats brought the living fish to the city in a wet well, a large wooden fish tank built into the hold. By late April, the schooners would be off of New Jersey, making two or three trips a week to the Manhattan market. When the mackerel were farther north in the summer, the schooners would deliver them to the markets of New England. Overfishing was nothing new; shell records show that even the native people, the Lenape, had used up the largest oysters. What was new was the scale.

Demand for fish was rising. Just past the turn of the century, newcomers dined on the fish of their homelands as though trying to preserve here on the East River the cultures of the Caspian, the Aegean, the Tyrrhenian, the Adriatic, and the Black Seas. Herring peddlers carried wooden buckets of fish through the streets, yelling, "Hey, best here! Best here! Best here in de verld!" People from far-off places would dig deep into the wagons of the open-air fish markets for the clearest-eyed specimens—perhaps unaware that despite the bounty, by this time, only about 10 percent of these fish came from nearby waters.

"EHH, plenty of time you lose the fish, because every day is fishing day, every day is not catching day," says Milton Serrattan, a construction worker from Trinidad who is fishing on a strip of grass between the water and the road out in the Rockaways, in Queens, hoping to make his daughter a dinner of kingfish cooked in curry powder and oil. All over the city, immigrants like him are fishing for their suppers.

They stand on Coney Island piers, listening to tinny merengue songs from speaker phones holstered to their belts, watching for the fat crabs they used to catch in the Dominican Republic. They venture out onto rocky ripraps in Queens that remind them of island fishing villages they left off the Korean coast. They gaze into the degraded East River and see not the bits of Styrofoam and sheeny plastic bags, but the idealized South China Sea of their memories, where you could reach in and grab fish with your hands.

Along the East River in Manhattan's Chinatown, elderly ladies with jade bracelets and umbrellas-cum-parasols patrol the waterfront in their flip-flops. Families peel lychees together, littering the ground with rosy, reptilian skins. A few girls lie on their backs on the benches, looking up into the eyes of their boys. And old men impale fat, grubby pink shrimps on their hooks and cast out toward Brooklyn.

They are from the fishing towns along the coast of Fujian province, where boys would fish most every day with homemade rods and all the village lived off the water. Fung Xiu is six feet, four-inches tall, with white-streaked hair slicked back into a pouf, sad, distant eyes, and a handsome, chiseled face that lights up when he talks, through a translator, of the water.

Xiu has kitted out his bike with a crate to hold fishing supplies: the raw chicken bait, rusted scissors and shears for adjusting the fishing line, a towel for cleaning the fish, and several pairs of pliers for freeing the crabs from the twine. He and a few other Fujian men are filling bait cages with chicken skins and casting their snare traps out with a fishing rod. As soon as the hungry crab extends one of its claws to the bait, it becomes ensnared in loops of fishing line and they pull it in. One man in a cap that reads FISHERS HAVE LONGER RODS speaks no English but holds the line up so the blue claw crab hangs aloft, dancing for passersby with its eight-legged shadow. People wordlessly crowd in, taking pictures with their cell phones as though a sea monster has just come up from the lagoon, until the fisher places the crab on the ground, firmly presses a flip-flop-clad foot onto its back to limit its pincer motion, and carefully removes the wire from its claws. He points to a bandage on his big toe where another crab's pincers did their work: a mere distraction en route to steamed crabs with sesame oil, soy sauce, scallions, and rice.

Up in the eastern Bronx, by the bridge to City Island, in a weedy, swampy lowland, a man comes out of the bulrushes onto a small beach, three friends emerging one by one after him. He moves with sleek, amphibian fitness into the muddy-bottomed water, dives down with a net, and rises up, spilling silver fish. He shakes the water out of his hair, his smooth brown arms streaked with seaweed. One friend, in a black wifebeater, black nylon pants, and black running shoes, walks waist-high into the water beside him, smoking a cigarette.

Their net is twenty feet long, with poles at either end stretching the five-foot width. The first man holds one end, his friend the other, and they wade in deeper, chest-high, then turn around and walk back, slowly pulling the resistant net with them, gathering in their fish. They step back to the beach and come together as if they were folding a long sheet, bringing the ends of the net close.

Trapped in the middle with clumps of seaweed are many dozens of tiny, black-eyed fish. Flopping and leaping, they reflect sun off their silvered scales like so many netted lightning bolts.

On the pebbly dirt beach, all of them—the men and the fish—glisten wet in the light. Steve Sankhi lets the fish flop from the net into a white plastic bucket filled with water from the sea and hundreds more Atlantic silversides. He covers the bucket with a handful of leafy plants so they don't scorch in the sun. He tells me that this is how they all once fished as kids in Guyana. There, you throw out a piece of bait on a string with something heavy—a huge washer of molded lead—and bring back fish, every time. You dip a net in anywhere you want and come up full.

"I've been coming here since I was thirteen years old," says Steve, now in his forties, and working as a custodian in Long Island City. In the 1980s, he says, the waters suffered from hypoxia, when dissolved oxygen rates dropped so low the little, sensitive silversides they like to catch could not survive. These men became ichthyic experts, following the ebb and flow of various fish over dozens of years—snappers, baby bluefish, full-grown blues, which you can fry with butter or use to make fish soup. Perhaps they were the first to note the return of their favorite sardine-like silversides. "You got to fry them, and they're real crispy, cause there's a lot of bones."

They fish March to October, and after cleaning all the fish, they freeze some of them to fry in the winter during football games. Fishing here is relaxing, they say. "You can see an eagle come down and catch a fish," says Michael Lockram. They stay all night sometimes, bringing sheets to lay out on the sand and blankets to cover themselves. They build a fire and sit around it, the bright moon and the streetlights reflecting off the water.

"We have friends who were born here—they don't like to leave the block," says Michael. It's something they never understood about New York: how its people could be so uninterested in the nature creeping in from all the edges of the city. "We're not like that. We like to go outdoors," Michael says. "We came from a country where everybody spends time outside. We love the openness." He says he dreams of finding a girl to marry and buying a house someplace with wide-open vistas and good fishing.

And then he dives into the water, his running shoes thrashing at the surface as he does an awkward front crawl away from his net.

EARLY on, New York turned its back on its waters. Alongside the story of the city sustaining itself by the water is a story of the city trashing it. The Dutch built deep canals to connect the middle of Manhattan to the rivers, then dumped their garbage in them. Europeans girdled the island with bulkheads and studded it with piers, destroying wetland fish habitats and natural sandy beaches. Over time, the streams and ponds were covered and filled. Bridges were built up and tunnels dynamited. The waters were fished so intensively that they contained fewer and fewer fish.

Human waste filled the waterways as the population jumped from a little over 33,000 people in 1790 to over 1.4 million in 1890. Garbage scows trucked out into the harbor to open their mouths and drop out refuse, much of which would only drift back to shore. Dead horses and cows were also thrown into the rivers, where their bloated and stinking bodies floated in and out with the tides.

As industry and commerce took over, all the city didn't

want was shunted to the waterfront: breweries, brothels, bars, slaughterhouses, shantytowns. The people who came in from the water—rough and rowdy fishermen, clam men, boat men, and oyster men—were the most disreputable elements in any crowd, as though the water itself could taint a reputation.

Waterfront districts earned names like "Poverty Lane" and "Misery Row." Vagrant children called "dock rats" bedded down under the East River piers "amidst the stench of the oozing tides and sewage," wrote *Harper's New Monthly Magazine.* They sometimes survived by pilfering from the cargoes of anchored ships, using rowboats as their getaway vehicles, and vanishing into the open pilings, too narrow for the larger ships pursuing them to follow. Meanwhile, Fifth Avenue in the dead center of the island, at greatest distance from the water, lined itself with mansions.

The industrial age had to have an outlet, and in New York City, the country's manufacturing center, it was the waterways. Manhattan Island by the mid-nineteenth century was rimmed with meatpackers, coal yards, gasworks, ink factories, ribbon makers, iron works, breweries, bottling plants, bone boilers, dairies, slaughterhouses, glue factories, stockyards, tar dumps, garbage transfer stations, rubber factories, masonry yards, flour mills, icehouses, lumberyards, sugarhouses, distilleries, oil refineries, plumbing supply houses, and elevator and dumbwaiter manufacturers. They located on the water so they could ship in supplies and raw materials and move out their finished products. Yet the water was also their dump.

The Gowanus Creek, a mile-and-a-half-long finger jutting into western Brooklyn from New York Harbor, had once produced Brooklyn's first notable export to Europe, oysters the size of dinner plates. In 1869 it was dredged to serve as an industrial canal, and by 1880, residents a mile away called it "a repulsive repository of rank odors," suffering from the same abuse as New-town Creek. Along with the canal's tanneries, machine shops, sulfur producers, and one of the first chemical fertilizer facto-ries was a dye works that colored the water the hue used that day in production, giving the canal the nickname "Lavender Lake." Joseph Mitchell later wrote that sightseers would come to coal and lumber quays along the Gowanus to watch the black, bubbly water where the "rising and breaking of sludge bubbles makes the water seethe and spit."

At the same time, the odor on Newtown Creek was becom-ing unbearable, even to people passing by on commuter trains with the windows closed. In the summer of 1881, *Harper's Weekly* ran a three-week series of exposés describing people choking in their sleep from the stench. "Children grow pale and languish; the mother sees her babe sicken and die in her arms, and feels that it is the foul air that has stifled it." Finally, the Fifteenth Ward Smelling Committee traveled up the creek to sniff out the source of the foul odors. Passing cargo ships, manure scows, a dog pound, and sausage factories where heaps of flesh rotted in open doorways, members of the committee judged the odors to be unremarkable. At last they reached a point near the oil refineries where "the stenches began asserting themselves with all the vigor of fully developed stenches." What they had discovered was that the area had become an ecological wasteland.

Fires started easily at waterfront refineries off of Brooklyn, Queens, Staten Island, and New Jersey. As a standard precau-tionary measure when a fire approached, workers would open the spigots for thousands of gallons of oil to flow out into the sea or just jettison barrels of petroleum and kerosene wholesale. One time, flames a hundred feet tall leapt from a gasoline barge on the Hudson near Midtown. Another time, a boiler on a Standard Oil tank steamer exploded off the coast of New Jersey and the vessel drifted out into the Upper Bay of New York Harbor, a blazing shell trailing in its wake burning naphtha—the chemical from which napalm takes its name—the water "lighted by some strange grotesque sun."

But such environmental calamities were possibly secondary to the impact of human sewage. By 1910, the number of people living in New York City had increased to more than 4,700,000. In the past, some of the city's sewage had partially decomposed in streams and cesspools, so that whatever was eventually dumped in the harbor was less potent. Now new indoor plumbing efficiently piped raw waste directly to the rivers with no treatment at all.

Chemicals and sewage made for a toxic brew for the city's famed oysters. Specific beds off Staten Island became known for the oysters' petroleum taste. Cholera outbreaks could often be traced to a particular oyster bed, which would be shut down. People caught typhoid fever, a disease transmitted through exposure to feces, merely from oyster handling.

FISHERMEN were among the first to organize against water pollution. They "have been grumbling considerably recently about the pollution of New York Bay," wrote the *Times* in 1899, conceding that fish became scarcer every year. The fishermen decided to propose bills to the legislature and organize people in every assembly district to lobby their representatives to protect fish from chemical pollution and to prevent commercial menhaden fishers from casting nets that indiscriminately captured all kinds of fish for fertilizer. By the next year, the Protective League of Salt Water Fishermen was a lobbying force claiming to represent 100,000 city fishers.

There was so little idea of environmental preservation at the time that eradicating habitats for fish was seen as a sign of progress, a legitimate trade of nature for industry. When a canal was built to provide passage for big ships from the Harlem River to the Hudson, the *New York Herald* cavalierly wrote, "The life of the bobtail clam, which has had its haunts in the marshy meadows of the Harlem River, is fast drawing to a close," as its habitat would be destroyed. "No more will the blithesome clam digger, clad in long rubber boots, a short fustian coat, and a red necktie, hie himself to the flats when the tide is out and dig himself a bucketful of this fruit for breakfast." At the opening of the canal, Mayor William Strong said: "This canal has spoiled my fishing ground, but still, I am willing to do away with another fishing ground upon account of the city of New York."

By the turn of the century, families swimming on the beaches of Staten Island found themselves covered with "a smelly black substance" that lingered in the water for weeks at a time—the dregs of crude oil. Garbage and waste filled public swimming pools floating in the East and Hudson rivers. Kids would dive off a sewage pipe into the East River and swim a kind of locally practiced breaststroke to swipe away the excrement.

There's an old maxim: Don't shit where you eat. Eventually, that wisdom became apparent to New Yorkers. In 1910, the Metropolitan Sewerage Commission set out to assess the impact of dumping six hundred million gallons of untreated human waste into the city's waters every day. In a well-stocked floating laboratory, with shelves full of beakers and bottles and books, the commission's scientists took samplings of grease and fecal matter from the water. They analyzed velocities of sewage traveling on tidal currents, "in which V is the velocity of the ascending sewage . . ." They mapped the locations of hospitals in relation to sewage outlets (unhealthily close by), and charted the incidence of diseases such as typhoid in New York compared to other cities (disturbingly high). They even sent portly, mustachioed men down into the sewers to examine white stalactites of mold.

They found that the bottom of the harbor was deeply harmed, wrote John Waldman, a professor of biology at Queens College who focuses on the ecology of the city's waters. It was coated with a layer of man-made muck "black in color from sulfide of iron; oxygenless; its fermentation generating carbonic acid and ammonia waste; and putrefying continuously, giving off bubbles of methane gas, so actively in some places 'that the water takes on the appearance of effervescence accompanied by a sound like rain falling upon the water.'" In some places this black substance was an impenetrable ten feet deep. Fields of sewage surrounded Manhattan as far as fifteen miles from shore.

It took a while for assumptions about the superiority of fresh fish to catch up with the realities of pollution. Kids would catch bergalls by the George Washington Bridge, and their grandmothers would make cold sweet-and-sour fish with raisins. People gathered to dig fat, soft clams at low tide at 110th Street. At night near 130th Street, the boats set out to catch the beautiful silver shad with the line of shrinking black circles down its sides that looked like phases of the moon. But the shad catch from the Hudson was about a tenth of the size of a few decades prior—and no one could say exactly why. Men began to notice that they could no longer find the fish they had reeled in as boys.

Mr. Charles H. Townsend, director of the New York City Aquarium, offered the commission his expert testimony: When he kept fish in tanks filled with water pumped in from the harbor, they died. When he kept them in imported ocean water, they lived long lives.

MANY people fishing in the city today don't eat what they catch. The prospect of contaminated fish usually stops Jane Borock, who casts all up and down western and southern Brooklyn, often near the sewage overflows that attract striped bass. She has seen the brochures warning that a mother's consumption of local fish can harm a developing fetus. "I want to have kids someday," she says.

Wearing red, round oversize sunglasses and a white helmet, she wheels down the India Street pier in Brooklyn on her 1969 red Solex motorbike. At the end of the pier, she hops off and reaches for her sturdy fake crocodile purse, overflowing with fishing rods and tangles of line.

"You got bunker?" she says, walking down the pier to another fisher already setting up his gear. There's a shortage of baitfish, and she wants to cut a deal. "I'll give you double market rate."

Jane tries to think like a striped bass. She works in advertising, so she knows how to imagine herself in the position of a creature she wants to lure.

"Like, if you want a three-year-old to run over to you, you're gonna offer a cookie. And if you wanted to lure in a thirty-year-old, you would offer really fine whiskey," says Jane. "You just know how to go after your demographic."

Her demographic, in this case, is the mature striper, the ocean fish that can grow to sixty pounds or more and come to the Hudson to spawn: the trophy of New York Harbor. A lot of people use artificial lures, says Jane, as if it's nobler somehow, as though catching a big fish with a little fish requires less human skill. But the big fish of the season have all been caught with bunker, says Jane. "Scientifically, *that's* how you catch them."

Jane is not driven by hunger, but is by the thrill of the hunt, yet she also likes fish, and hates waste, enough to overcome her misgivings about consuming the fruits of local waters. She might smoke her catch or fry it or curry it—she used to do that a lot when she went out on fishing boats. She might put her FRESH FISH sign on her bike and ride it around town. She might give it away to some hungry person fishing near her on the pier. She once gave a big fish to a friend, with a warning about where she caught it, but he cooked up a fish stock for his wife who was eight months pregnant. She notes that a lot of people can't afford to buy protein, and she imagines that eating fish from the East River is a good option.

"I'm an addict," Jane says of fishing. Sometimes she stays out till morning and watches the sun come up. Other times she binge fishes for as long as thirty-six hours at a time, updating her Facebook page with pleas to her friends to bring warm clothes, and then turning off her phone to preserve the battery. Her favorite piers are littered with Tyskie and Żywiec beer bottles, which the Polish guys leave behind like a trail of bread crumbs denoting the best fishing spots this side of Brooklyn.

Her hands chafe from the cold and are punctured, repeatedly, by hooks. One of her fishing crew, it turns out, had been a doctor back in Poland, and he said he would take a look. When Jane held out her raw, scabbed, cut-up paws, he stepped back and said, "You're not a woman!" Jane promised herself a manicure at the end of the month.

One day, Jane cast really, really far—into a pickup truck, and when she reeled back her hook and sinker, they came flying with boomerang force into her face, bludgeoning and piercing her nose—which she accepted with good cheer as nothing more than a slowdown. "Holler when you want to hit the pier," she texted her friends on her way out of the hospital.

When two cops gave her a summons for fishing alone one night past closing at the Valentino Pier in Red Hook, she wrote on her Facebook page: "Today: The Fisherwoman VS. The City of New York. Wish me luck." Later she updated: "The judge let me off the HOOK." A friend commented, "Sounds like you fed him a LINE."

Late at night, she sometimes goes to the Secret Place, a private property in Brooklyn with a long dock deep into the East River, whose warning signs are not visible in the dark—DANGER KEEP OFF PIER, DANGER NO TRESPASSING. Someone holds up a cyclone fence and she slims her body underneath it to reach shifting slabs of concrete, the cracked remnants of a crumpled Williamsburg pier. Jane walks gingerly from slab to slab while each piece rocks underfoot. When the slab seems to slide toward the blackness of the water, she shifts her weight. She doesn't speak, in order to avoid the attention of the property's night watchman.

Carrying fishing rods like rifles in some kind of commando operation, she and the other fishers run down the next section of the pier, which is nothing but narrow I-beams extending like balance beams over a hole of black water. At the end, Jane finds herself on solid cement at the farthest extremity of this part of Brooklyn, with the deepest water and, she hopes, the biggest fish. The shapes of the guys she is with disperse around the edges of the dock to set up fishing rigs. She hears the pale jangling of the bells on the ends of fishing rods, the wind, the whooshing noise of the cars across the river in Manhattan on FDR Drive—like the noise inside a seashell. And she stands, facing Manhattan amid seagull shit and bones, and she waits to catch a fish.

Baiting with bunker one day on a pier off North Fifth Street in Williamsburg, she finally reels in a legendary striper, with the characteristic smooth lines of dark and silver scales. "Yeah!" she yells as the fish flops onto the wooden deck. Measured tail to fishy lip, it is 28.5 inches. Barely legal. Soon she catches another, and another. "Just caught a nice striped bass," she writes on Facebook. "Will deliver to your home or office. Let the bidding begin."

MANHATTAN'S legendary Fulton Fish Market was dedicated to fish only in 1822, when local fish were already becoming noticeably scarcer. In 1826, a New York newspaper announced the novelty of a shipment of fresh salmon from Lake Ontario coming up the Erie Canal, to be exhibited for sale in the Fulton market. Soon, steamships and railroads routinely carried fish cargoes, so that New Yorkers ate salmon from Maine and Scotland, prawns from the Carolinas, and black bass from the western rivers and lakes. By the 1830s, Peter Cortelyou, the head of a Long Island fishery, lamented, "All the fisheries in New York harbor are nearly destroyed, and the fish which now supply the markets of that city are brought from the distance of 60, 80, and even 100 miles." The wild meats of the lands had long since disappeared; now those of the waters were receding from reach.

A century later, in the 1930s, much of the fish coming into the Fulton Fish Market arrived by truck "rattling and jolting along the cobblestoned streets," and some were flown in by airplane. People wanted less fish as beef and pork arriving from the West in refrigerated railcars became cheap and readily available. Giant slatted pine boxes still bobbed afloat in the East River behind the market as holding cells for live fish. But increasingly, even the boats, sloops, schooners, and smacks brought fish dead, filleted, and even frozen, to be sorted in an icehouse off Pier 17.

Three clangs of a gong announced the start of fish sales at six a.m. "Whale and five chickens," a rubber-booted salesman would shout in the argot of the market, meaning a large halibut and five small ones. "Pin blues" were small bluefish, and "scrod cod" were small codfish. Buyers practiced the centuries-old ritual of look-ing into a fish's eyes for clarity, checking the color of its scales, rubbing a piece of its flesh between their fingers to determine its oiliness, tasting it. They wanted fresh.

The clam and crab men would arrive early at the market, be-fore dawn, and then trawl the streets of the city, calling, "Ho! Clahmmmmmmmmmms! Ho! Clahmmmmmmmmms!" One African American fish seller explained his technique for reeling in customers. He would invent fish-related lyrics and sing songs like "Yo, ho ho, fish man!/Bring down your dishpan!/Fish ain't but five cent a pound./So come on down." He tried to game his audience: In Jewish neighborhoods, he would sing to the tunes of songs like *"Bay Mir Bistu Sheyn,"* the popular number from a Yiddish musical. In Puerto Rican neighborhoods, he sang in Spanish. Among black people, he used a swing tune, and sometimes, when he sang, he said, "the kids be dancing the Lindy Hop and Trucking." Fish sales were strong, and he credited his music. "To be any success at all, you had to have an original cry," he said. "You got to put yourself in it. You've got to feel it."

Meanwhile, the local commercial fishers practiced a certain New York-style fishing. Lobstermen had to check their pots very early in the morning, every day of the week, so that no one would steal the lobsters. Crabmen dredged for blue crabs by the Statue of Liberty, and navigated their haul into the Fulton market, where they would tie their boats together in a bobbing waterborne queue and sleep in them overnight to await the market's opening. Legend says that a scallop boat once docked in a storm at Pier 17, bringing in thousands of pounds of scallops and a mutinying crew that refused to go back out on a rough and forbidding sea. The story says that the captain, waving a gun, rounded up his men by chasing them through the fish market.

The last large-scale commercial fishing ended in the decades after World War II. During the war, the government had shrouded the harbor in nets to keep out enemy submarines—incidentally entrapping schools of fish. An enthusiastic fisherman with a military deferment to catch shad could drop down a simple pound net and lift in a bonanza. After the war, Eastern Europe's enormous factory ships came to the edge of the continental shelf and sucked up fish. In the 1940s, the *Times* ran recipes for shad caught in view of Midtown Manhattan (baked and stuffed with bread crumbs, celery, and sage), but the shad population soon plummeted. A clam, crab, and lobster industry thrived in Staten Island

and Brooklyn, but by the 1950s, local fishing was winding down. "Scarcely anything but weak-fish" sold at the Fulton Fish Market had lived any of its days in the waters of New York City. The last ship to call regularly with fish was the *Felicia*, a Brooklyn-built wooden dragger, which quit deliveries in the 1980s.

Philip Frabosilo's father and maternal grandfather were fishers and fishmongers into the 1960s, and later worked in a smokehouse, where they smoked sturgeon and herrings and whiting. They would also take out a small rowboat and circle with a giant net near the Rockaways. Once, as his son watched, Philip's father put the net in his mouth and swam with it, pulling a wake of fish with his teeth through the edge of the salty Atlantic. He would collect hundreds of fish in a day, fill a cart, and roll it around Manhattan, calling out "Porgies!" and "Bluefish!" and "Striped bass!" He was the last of a kind.

WITH no hope of receiving boats coming in from the waters, the Fulton Fish Market moved in 2005 to the Hunts Point Market in the Bronx, where there was better highway access for trucks and a new, modern indoor market building, with loading docks, temperature controls, and level floors for Hi-Lo forklifts. Just past three a.m., I came in from a black, cold winter night to find the market at its height, flooded with white lights under 40-foot ceilings as Hi-Los speed down the central corridor.

The sellers wear their J-shaped fish hooks over their shoulders. The long wooden handles burned with their names—DAVE, ANTHONY—hang down front over their collarbones, and the sharp, short hook ends tear holes in their shirtbacks and wound the raw skin of their shoulderblades. They hook into the slippery fish to throw them from box to box, or present an especially fine one to a potential buyer for inspection. If a big fish sells, the vendor might wrap it up in a 50-pound unused dog food bag (they're cheap), or in a waxed box, which he will carve out to make a hole for the fish tail. The soft smell of fresh, cold fish mingles with the sweet smell of cigars the sellers smoke at their stands.

The fish and shellfish come in from all over the world. Perfect ridged oyster shells are transported on a black tangle of seaweed from Harpswell, Maine. Black-eyed lobsters, their armored weaponry disabled with a few rubber bands on the claws, come from eastern Canada. The gray scales of a single 200-pound, $1,400 swordfish from Australia stretch across a whole table. Scarlet stripes of tuna from Thailand fill a row of plastic bags; Chilean sea bass from the deep ocean waters off Peru fill an icy four-foot box. The foreign fish enter the country on ice packs on planes with monitors that record their temperature throughout the flight; if the temperature rises above a certain level, the fish are condemned on arrival. "Price on skate!" a man walks into a stall and announces, gazing down on fleshy, freckled, grayish-red wings of skate on ice. "A dollar twenty-five, my friend," comes the offer.

Of course none of the fish here are from local waters, and as fewer fish are available at all, prices continue to rise. Americans eat less seafood, restaurants and grocery stores set up their own direct supply lines, and fish companies at Hunts Point go under. "No one seems to want to be in the fish business anymore," says Joseph Scibbara from a glass-walled, heated "office" on the fish floor. "When our forefathers came here, all they had to eat was fish. It's not part of the American dream anymore."

. . .

WITH salty air and docked boats, and fish for sale when the boats come in, Sheepshead Bay in Brooklyn still feels something like a fishing port, though the eponymous sheepshead fish no longer fill these waters—nor do the commercial fishing boats that once trawled them. Instead, "party boats" go out—the *Marilyn Jean*, the *Sea Queen VII*, the *Ocean Eagle V*, the *Capt Dave*—to take groups of people fishing out on international waters for fifty or sixty dollars a day, as they have as far back as the 1940s. The *Brooklyn VI* is a white boat with blue trim, a 110-foot supercruiser, powered by three turbo Detroit diesel engines. The ghosts of fish of yore are tangible in the stink from the moment you step on deck.

Wearing rubber overall slickers they call skins, these thirty-odd men—and they are *all* men—are hunting bluefish, a darker, oilier fish, something like a massive sardine. Not so delicious, unless you know how to deal with the oil by smoking or broiling or barbecuing.

The boat sets off leaving the dim line of the Rockaways behind us. The *Brooklyn VI* dips and then soars, breaks through each wave taking on the rhythm of the sea, sending spray and foam to the sides. When the horn sounds, two dozen lines are in the water within seconds.

You get out into the deep, and you're surrounded by gray. You feel the salt on your skin, which becomes a film over all your body until you too are of the sea.

Every boat has its core guys. They are cops, firefighters, real estate guys. Glen Evans goes out as much as possible—Friday, Saturday, Sunday. He used to have a girlfriend, he says, but he didn't want her to join him fishing. The punch line comes as expected: The relationship didn't last. The fishing did.

The boat has Furuno fish-seeking radar, so the captain moves when the fish do. Three other boats hover around the same spots. This way, everyone gets his money's worth in fish.

We're ducking and soaring. Throwing bunker into the blue sky so it lands in the gray sea. A whirring and then a plop.

One man doesn't bother closing the door to the tiny bathroom and stands there pissing, the metal door flapping in the wind, the saltiness blowing in, and then turns to walk out, still zipping up his fly.

Sometimes the conversation turns serious: "Do you consider yourself an alcoholic?" "I'm one hundred percent alcoholic—I admit that." One man says, "My wife died eight years ago, of cancer. I became addicted to fishing, like any other drug." But most talk is of trivial things: "The only thing worse than cherry Pepsi is Dr. Pepper." "I kind of like Dr. Pepper." Days could pass in this kind of talk—and they do.

You cross into another medium, the wet, the dark, the sliminess of it, and you extract life. Back at the dock, you walk off the boat carrying a plastic bag bulging with fish.

"HIS face was dead gray, East River gray," Saul Bellow wrote in the 1970s, and in fact, by this time the city's waters had lost life. Summer after summer passed when bluefish failed to move north into New York Harbor. Almost no porgies or sea bass swam in, and only a few summer fluke hovered near Sandy Hook Bay just south of the city. "Inshore, it's dead," said one Long Island fisherman. "You have to go out 68 to 72 miles to find the ocean alive." Many of the fish that could be found could not be safely eaten. In the 1970s, the State Department of Environmental Conservation banned most commercial fishing in the Hudson River and advised children and women of childbearing age against eating any Hudson River fish because of unsafe levels of cancer-causing PCBs.

Yet here are three Bronx men lying on the silken green grass in a park by the water on City Island with their rods against the fence and their lines in the water, talking about fishing the dank, mucoid waters of the half-abandoned city where they grew up.

They remember in the 1970s kitting out a Blue Ribbon or Schaefer or Rheingold beer can with some twine weighted down with rocks or spark plugs they found on the street, for a makeshift fishing rig. They would turn the can like a reel. They would bait with raw dough from the bodega.

They remember tying rope to the window frames of a sunken car and heaving it up out of the Bronx River—just the metal frame, no tires, no motor, no dashboard, no seats—to find it full of fish, clams, and crayfish, so that became the fishing technique, dragging stripped cars from the water, an automobile-caught seafood stew.

They remember catching big perch, crayfish, shrimp, green frogs, and, once, a snapping turtle in the Bronx River where it runs through the botanical garden and the zoo. "The frogs usually come out when it rains hard," says Emmanuel Nwogu, "the kind of frogs they sometimes sell at delicatessens—not a bullfrog."

"My mom used to say, 'Papi, where you get this from?' I say, 'I get this from the Bronx Zoo,'" says John Rivera, who's wearing a whistle and a wooden cross around his neck.

They remember using clams, bunker blood, and sand worms as bait—"The fish will strike," says Emmanuel.

Miguel Miles remembers going pro very young, catching crayfish in a bucket from the pond in Central Park for a man who offered him a dime for every dozen. "The other kids would come see what I caught, and they would say, 'Can I get that, can I get that?'" says Miguel, a window installer, wearing a wifebeater, shorts, athletic socks, and no shoes. Soon he would toss into the water whatever container he could find—a crate or an empty garbage can—and pull out crayfish to bring to his mother to make a cream crayfish stew, says Miguel. "Turns out just like lobster."

By the mid-1970s, when Miguel and his friends were fishing, levels of PCBs, mercury, dioxin, and pesticides in New York Harbor were often hundreds of percent higher than the benchmark that would harm fish. People avoided the waters. There's a kind of cycle of decline, in which people stop fishing because the waters are dirty, and then, with fewer people monitoring the waters, they get dirtier.

By the 1980s, there was a kind of backlash against fishing altogether. Fish markets hung posters to reassure customers that their catch was not from local waters but from distant, cleaner places. Meanwhile, people complained that fishers on bridges lassoed boaters, hooked joggers, and even in one instance took out a woman's eye. A fishing line wrapped around the neck of a woman passing under the bridge to City Island in a small boat. "I was nearly hanged," she said. "We want to end the chaos on the city's bridges," said a politician. Yet whenever the city tried to stop fishing—building impenetrable rails on the bridges, fencing off waterfront areas—people kept figuring out ways to access water.

MOST of the city's waters are olive-colored and turbid. You can't see fish. Maybe that's why it can be difficult to fathom exactly what is wrong with them—or to understand why eating them can hurt us.

The Clean Water Act of 1972 slowed the dumping of pollutants, but the existing pollution hasn't disappeared—instead, it entered the food chain. Plankton—microscopic plants and animals—absorb chemicals from the water through their cell membranes. An Atlantic silverside eats plankton that contain tiny amounts of mercury and PCBs. A striped bass eats many of these silversides over its lifetime, accumulating the mercury of each one in its body. The toxins tend to remain in body tissue, meaning that the more plankton a small fish eats, the more small fish a big fish eats, and the more mercury and PCBs the big fish contains. Fish can be contaminated at levels hundreds of times higher than what is found in the surrounding water. When people cast out and catch a fish in New York City waters, take it home, fry it up, and eat it, they absorb most of the contaminants the fish contained.

It's an issue of choice, officials say. Government advises; people choose. The problem is that study after study has shown that many subsistence fishers are not aware of the risks. "I think if we do not reach out in every way possible," a citizen representative told a city council hearing in 2002, "we are in serious danger." Since then, with budget cutbacks, educational campaigns have been scaled back.

"I've been eating East River fish all my life, and I never get sick," fishers will say, not realizing that the danger of PCBs and mercury is a long-term accumulation that can lead to serious illness, not a short-term stomachache. "I clean the fish really well," they assure, failing to address the chemicals bound up in the fish's very flesh. Some people say the regulations are so complicated—

they change from year to year for specific fish, and differ for adjacent bodies of water, or sometimes even in one body of water that straddles state lines—that it's hard to believe they mean anything.

A pilot study by the Mount Sinai School of Medicine in Manhattan found that blood and hair samples from local fishermen in a fishing club who eat their fish show elevated levels of PCBs, dioxins, chlordane, DDT, and mercury. Those who ate more fish had higher levels of toxins. But no local study has closely examined the physical impact on those most vulnerable: poor people, many of them immigrants, who eat dinner after dinner of fried fish, fish stew, crab curry, all summer long.

The pollutants are stored in the fish's fatty tissue and in its filter organs, such as the liver and pancreas. To avoid toxins, you want to get rid of fat. Skin the fish, because fat clings to skin's underside. Remove any lingering clumps and globs. Don't fry a local fish or throw chunks of it into soup or stew, where the fat cooks with the meat. Instead, grill or broil the fish so the fat drips away. In many cuisines, the yellowish substance in a cooked crab, often called the mustard, is considered a delicacy—but it's the crab's hepatopancreas, the organ that filters impurities from the crab's blood. Its flavor may be distinct and delicious, but it is a concentrate of chemical contaminants. Don't eat it. Pull it out before you cook it, and after you boil the crab, dump out the liquid.

Yet every sunny summer day, unaware of these risks, people travel to the edges of the city to fish. A New York City subway car full of people on their way to the beach on the weekend has a light, happy sound: children's voices, laughter, a cell phone playing music—it's like the beach has come to the train. You know it's the beach stop because of who stands up to get out: little girls wearing bathing suits with running shoes and carrying neon pails stuffed with plastic octopuses and sea horses, teenage tough boys with gold teeth and knuckle rings spelling BRONX, carrying pink inner tubes. If you look closely, you will almost always see old men with a handful of rods and a pail of bait and a cooler now full of cold drinks but later to transport the catch of the day.

ONE fat, sun-dazed baby on her lap, another growing in her belly, Yolene Joseph raises the crab trap out of the water off the Coney Island pier. Her year-old nephew watches on her knee in fascination as the pincers reach out of the metal cage, followed by the rest of the spiderlike body.

Yolene and her twin sister, Yoland Thomas, have brought a whole watermelon and some drinks to the pier. They've spread out a yellow pad on the boardwalk where the baby can crawl. Yolene has three daughters to Yoland's three sons, and the older kids are wading in the sea. Their mothers are up on deck, lowering empty crab traps and raising full ones.

They're from Trinidad, where they used to live right by the beach. The crabs were always fresh—sometimes you could buy them right out of the nets off the boat. They would eat callaloo, a coconut stew made with crab meat, pumpkin, okra, coconut milk, and the leaf of the callaloo plant that gives the dish its name. Their mother, Darner Joseph, remembers shimmying up to the top of the coconut tree in a yard to grab fresh fruit and picking dried coconuts off the ground to cook into curry crab.

Yolene baits the trap with fresh chicken in a flexible wire basket whose hoop net will collapse and flatten on the bottom of the seabed. The water is clear enough that you can hang out over the railing and watch the crab walk right into the trap. Yolene manages two traps, so as soon as she frees a crab from one trap for deposit in the bucket, she walks over to raise up the second. There's a rhythm to this. Sit, talk for a while, pull up one trap, pull up the second trap. Sit, talk, trap. It makes for stilted conversation but an impressive haul.

Though she has already netted several dozen crabs, Yolene says it's not impressive enough. "I've been here where every time you pull up your basket, you have five or six crabs," she says. Today the sisters will go home salty and hot and tired from the beach, and stuff the crabs in the freezer. They will have to make several cross-Brooklyn trips from their home in Crown Heights to catch themselves enough meat for curry crab, cooked with curry powder, coconut milk, onion, garlic, thyme, scallions. When they don't trap crabs themselves, they buy them in Chinatown: enough for a big meal for the extended family could easily cost seventy dollars. Maintaining Caribbean traditions in New York City can be expensive.

Sometimes the sisters take their children to catch crabs at Sheepshead Bay at night. They shine a flashlight onto the water so the crabs freeze; then they scoop them up. "They're kind of creepy-looking," says Yolene. "It's fun." Sometimes they come here to Coney Island and stay till late at night. They bring a tent for the kids and put them to bed on the pier, letting them whisper and giggle until they finally sleep, beside the steady plop of the trap going into the water and the dripping crab coming up, claws thrashing silently in protest. They work hard during the week, all of them—Yolene, a caregiver in a group home for adults with disabilities, Yoland, who does data entry for a health care company, and Darner, their mother, who also works as a counselor in a group home. They've heard the advisories, but even eight months pregnant, Yolene pays no mind. "A lot of people cook them just how you see them there, but we actually break off the back and we use like a scrubbing brush, and we scrub out all the stuff from inside."

Yolene herself seems to glow in the sun in her red and pink sundress, her belly swollen with her fourth child, her hair braided back off her face in rows, and her relaxed smile. She holds no stock in PCBs. Is she worried at all about consuming bottom-feeding scavengers that ingest the accumulated problems of the waters of New York City? "Not me—I've been eating it for years!" she says. The water flows in and out, it's not sitting still, she reasons, so contaminants must simply drift out with the tides. "I'm still alive, and I've got a lot of meat," she says, patting her thighs. "So!" she finishes, as though her own flesh is proof.

WINE

THE REDBRICK HOUSE on Ninety-Second Street on the Upper East Side of Manhattan looks unremarkable. Narrow, four stories tall, with iron railings on the stairs, and a wood-paneled front door. You could walk by it every day and never know that in the back-yard, there is a vine. The vine bears grapes, which climb all the way up the back side of the house and onto the roof. The family harvests the grapes on the rooftop and by reaching out the windows. The fruit makes wine.

The winemaking began decades ago. Latif Jiji, a mechanical engineering professor at City College, had ceded the narrow backyard of his family's townhouse to his wife, Vera, for gardening. But one day in 1977, on an impulse, Latif brought home a cutting from a grapevine—just a bare branch, really—and stuck it into the soil. Soon, he said, "it took over." Vera, a retired English professor, likes to point out the Freudian symbolism of a man with a stick who dominates. In any case, the scraggly vine gradually leaned forward, attached itself to the redbrick house, and grew tall, slithering upward like some kind of magic beanstalk. In time, it yielded fat bunches of green Niagara grapes—commonly found in northeastern backyards and supermarkets, not so frequently in wineries. Latif and Vera's four children didn't like them because they had seeds, and Latif found himself with a grape surplus. At some point around 1984, the thought occurred to him: "Why don't we make wine?"

His father had made wine when Latif was a boy growing up in the small Jewish community in Basra in southern Iraq. His childhood vine was also tall—two stories high—and rooted in the central courtyard of the family home. The winemaking technique was "primitive," Latif says now, and his father "violated all the rules" that Latif later learned from books. He didn't take care to seal the wine barrel—Latif used to lift the cover and inhale the pungent fumes of fermentation. He didn't siphon the wine to leave behind the sediment, but scooped it straight from the barrel into bottles. You would have to drink around the sediment in the bottom of your glass.

During Latif's own first attempt at winemaking, he and his daughter Lissa pummeled grapes with their hands and produced sixteen half bottles of a drinkable wine. Later the family used a tool Latif devised, something like a potato masher. Eventually, as Latif grew more serious about the process, he got a mechanical crusher and presser. "It was never virgins dancing barefoot on the grapes," says Vera.

As the vine meandered its way to the top of the fifty-foot-tall townhouse, Latif built an arbor on the roof so it could continue to grow horizontally, spilling its grapes in a shady overhead canopy. In the spring, bundles of hard, bright green orbs begin to dangle, like someone's plastic centerpiece, or the idealized Form of the grape, too perfect to be the real thing. By early August, the grapes are pale green and thin-skinned, with a translucent, fatty quality, already giving off the scent of ferment and wine.

Timing is critical. Latif used to decide the fruit was ready only when the starlings began to nibble at it and a heavy winey smell wafted down to the upper floors of the townhouse. Now he works more scientifically, rubbing a sample grape against a refractometer. White hair flying all mad professor, eyes narrow against the light, he reads the displayed sugar content. He looks toward me, and pauses. "The sugar levels are high," he says. It's time to set a harvest date.

"Wine making alert," says the subject line of the email he sends to notify his crew.

On harvest day, the workers—Latif's children, friends, children's friends, children's children, and friends of friends—are organized into teams, each with a dedicated task. On the roof, the pickers stand on crates, reach overhead, and snip and shear and pull. The grapevine makes a curtain so thick that it shuts out the high-rises of Midtown from view and creates a cool, green-tinted haven.

"Smells like the Muscat grape–flavored gummy candy," says a twenty-one-year-old neophyte, frowning at the vine.

Hurrying up to the roof, Latif contrasts his achievement with those of the great winemaking civilizations. "The Greeks, the Romans, the Arabs, they had short vines—my vine is tall," he says, out of breath from the stairs. "Do you have scissors?" he asks me. "Here," he says, grabbing a rusty black-handled pair someone had discarded.

It's hard to pick grapes overhead. The vine weaves around itself, braiding in its fruit, so no one bunch is entirely free. You have to drag fat, delicate grapes through narrow openings in their own wood—you are fighting the vine itself. Your eyes fill with dripping grape juice. Your hands get sticky and black from wet bits of wood. Your arms tire. Your crate slips underfoot on the grape-slickened tar.

Latif fusses over tactics and execution, interrupting himself to greet friends of friends with kisses. He directs his longest-limbed child, Brian, an arts consultant, to grab particular hard-to-reach bunches and shun others: "Don't reach too far!" As his capable daughters, now in their forties, sort out a rope pulley system to lower a basket of grapes from the roof, he cautions them: "Don't lean out!"

Kids on the roof scream, "Coming down!" as they lower the first basket of grapes into the backyard. "Ready?" they call, after it lands.

"No!" the men on the ground answer, too late.

Down in the yard, the crew chief, Genio Rodriguez, a cook, weighs incoming loads of grapes by standing on a scale with the plastic bags in his hands and subtracting his own weight.

Fresh water fills a laundry tub from a garden hose, and Latif's ten-year-old grandson, Jake, swishes his hand around, making currents, washing fruit that becomes slick, pale, and glassy. "It's raining grapes," he complains, as people picking bunches on the roof spill a shower of large green drops with the impact of ball bearings.

Another grandson pours the clean grapes into the hopper of the Italian-made crusher and de-stemmer while Jake turns the crank. Two rollers smash the grape clusters, and the whole mess falls into a trough where propellers separate out the stems from the pulp. The pulp goes into the presser, where thin juice streams out, clean and sweet, to be sent over to the chemistry lab deeper in the yard.

Latif himself hovers over the lab, a rickety patio table set up in the back, where a few of his most trusted aides work a hydrometer, a calculator, a bag of supermarket sugar, and an agent to kill yeast.

After juice, sugar, tannins, pectic enzyme, and the yeast-killing agent have been combined in precise proportions, the mixture will be sealed into five-gallon glass demijohns to ferment and seethe for a month, then it will be bottled and aged for about a year. A good harvest makes as much as a hundred and fifty bottles of wine.

By the end of the day, the vine has been plucked clean, as though plundered by a flock of starving birds. Down in the dining room, the kids drink sweet, fresh grape juice. A few of the workers spike theirs with grappa a friend made from the seeds and stems left over from last year's winemaking. Latif retrieves a bottle of last year's wine from the basement, Vera raises her glass, and he pours.

LATIF left Iraq in 1947 to attend college in Michigan. Just days before, the United Nations had voted to partition Palestine, and the streets of Baghdad had been full of crowds yelling, "Down with the Jews! Down with the Zionists!" As the propeller airplane took off into the hazy air, Latif watched the runway of the Baghdad airport recede into a gray stripe in the brown desert. "I said to myself, 'I will not see this again—I'm not going back.'"

Years later, his parents and four siblings came out of Iraq, a few at a time, hiding their gold jewelry and carrying heavy, rolled-up Keshan carpets. His father died while visiting Latif in Ann Arbor. Latif is not a religious man, but he said kaddish, the Jewish prayer for the dead, every day for a year, mostly in the campus Hillel center, though sometimes, when traveling to a new town, he would open the phone book to look up some Cohen or Levy who could refer him to a Jewish congregation. When he moved to New York City, his mother bought an apartment nearby. His brothers ended up on Long Island and in New Jersey, his sisters in Los Angeles and Israel.

In 1964, Latif married Vera, a young, widowed English-literature grad student with two children. In time, they found the long, narrow brick townhouse on the Upper East Side, a place with many bedrooms, stained glass above the entryway, and above all, a yard where Vera could garden and their four children could play. Only the year before they moved in, the nearby Jacob Ruppert Brewery had shut down, ceasing to cast the smell of beer and hops across the neighborhood. Now the brewery stood empty, like a hulking brick reminder of lost industrial prospects. East Ninety-Second Street in the late 1960s was a place where a couple of City University professors could pay $69,000, take out a mortgage, and just about afford a roomy house to make a home.

For thousands of years, people had been drinking wine in the homeland Latif had fled in southern Iraq. The eighth-century Arab poet Abu Nawas, like Latif, was from Basra, and much of his oeuvre praises the joys of wine, "shining in its glass like a sun." In fact, Arab writers created a whole genre called *khamri-yyat*, or wine poems. But by the time Latif was growing up, few Muslims would publicly associate themselves with wine, as Islam forbids alcohol, and Christians owned most wine stores. The Jews of Basra were known not for wine but for aromatic *araq*, an anise liquor they distilled at home from the sweet, soft dates for which their city was renowned. Latif's family didn't drink much, but at meals his father would pour everybody a glass of the wine made from the family vine.

When Latif left Iraq behind, much of his past was lost, but in New York, he could share with Vera and their kids his family tradition of winemaking. It didn't take long after his first experiments for Latif to begin the slow transformation of house into vertical winery. In the basement, he dismantled a ninety-nine-dollar mini-fridge and used its parts to cool a large wooden cupboard he insulated with fiberglass to refrigerate the fermenting grape juice. He installed a deep sink so he could wash old green bottles for reuse. He turned the brick-arched coal room into an air-conditioned wine cellar: "Wine cellars are supposed to have arched doors," he notes. The vine yields roughly six hundred pounds a year, enough for Latif to produce more than a hundred bottles of white wine. He calls his label Château Latif—a play on the Rothschild Château Lafite.

Latif has a little mustache, white wavy hair that brushes his neck, and kind blue-gray eyes. He has only a trace of an accent in English, and it's hard to imagine that he grew up speaking Arabic. He appeared recently on Al Arabiya television talking hesitantly in a stilted, formal Arabic about the fantastical Iraq he remembers, where Jews, Christians, and Muslims lived together carelessly as neighbors. He has imprinted his nostalgia for that lost world on his daughter, Jessica, a United Nations speechwriter who wrote a novel loosely based on Latif's childhood in 1940s Basra. The first time Latif meets you he will pour you a glass of wine. He will call you family.

More recent immigrants to New York City would make other

kinds of wine. The Fujianese from China would make a red rice wine, which they would serve in restaurants from unmarked plastic jugs. Ethiopians would purchase gallons of honey to make honey wine in glass beakers at home. Hondurans would ferment pan-fried, fibrous chunks of cassava mixed with sweet potato to be served in plastic cups at special occasions. People would make wine out of linden flowers and mulberries and lilacs and knotweed and amelanchier they picked from city parks. Latif could have been Albanian or German, Nigerian or Ecuadorian—the heart of his story would be the same, because the value of homemade wine for him lies in its way of connecting people, and of reaching back into the past for tradition.

"ALTHOUGH they were sweet in the mouth at first, they made it disagreeable and stinking," wrote Jasper Danckaerts, a Dutch traveler, of the wild grapes he found in 1679 by the shores of Brooklyn's Coney Island. In fact, he had his eye on a bit of property not far from Latif Jiji's current house to cultivate European grapes, and wrote that the soil on the rocky hills east of Harlem "would be very suitable in my opinion for planting vineyards." Yet elsewhere in Manhattan, European vines withered, every season they were planted, for decades. No one yet knew they were vulnerable to the grape louse phylloxera, but they knew that they were useless for wine. While visiting the homes of the people of New Amsterdam, Jasper Danckaerts drank wine imported from Madeira.

Local winemakers eventually came around to raising native American *Vitis labrusca* grapes and their hybrids, though they were sometimes derided, in comparison to Europe's *Vitis vinifera,* as "foxy"—an oenologist's term referring to an unpleasant muski-ness, a sharp, extreme-grapey flavor, like essence of Welch's. Around 1816, a woman named Isabella Gibbs from the Carolinas arrived with a cutting of a juicy purple grape, which she planted in her backyard in Brooklyn. The vine thrived, and its grapes came to be known as Isabellas. In Brooklyn in 1827, the horticulturalist Alden Spooner experimented with planting them. "They were much injured," he complained, when his tenants planted potatoes in the same garden bed, but eventually the grapevines prevailed, fruited, and produced fifty gallons of juice, some of which aged into wine that was "pronounced very excellent," he wrote. Another Brooklyn experimenter managed to eke a basic kind of wine out of immature Isabellas, some of them "white and not half grown," adding extra sugar at the end to mask the bitterness and also a bit of brandy to raise the alcohol level. "The flavor I think fine," he finally assessed. It was the ragged beginnings of a New York State wine industry.

Vineyards flourished for a while in parts of Brooklyn and Queens. In the Bronx, people made blackberry wine from berries growing in the wild, and in other parts of the turn-of-the-century city, people fermented dandelions, elderberries, and rhubarb harvested near their homes. At least one vineyard survived until 1901, on several acres in the Queens neighborhood of Long Island City. Presenting a misty, romantic image of Queens rarely seen since, the *New York Times* noted that the vintner, an elderly Frenchman named Monsieur Thiry, who made claret, red wines, and a bubbly akin to champagne, loved to walk "with a basket on his arm and half a dozen children at his heels, clipping here and there a precocious bunch for the table, and handing out every second one to a small boy or girl." But Monsieur Thiry quit when he realized it cost him more to make wine than buy it. As the last large tracts of open space in the city filled with buildings, the era of the vineyard was over, but the age of winemaking was just taking off.

New York is a wine city with two dominant roots: kosher Jewish and Italian. Of course, at one time, many of the city's European immigrants made homemade wine, and some non-kosher commercial wineries thrived. But eventually Jews and Italians were distinguished by the sheer size of their populations—by the turn of the century, 290,000 Jews and 250,000 Italians lived in New York, a city of only about three and a half million people— and their distinct enthusiasms for fermenting the fruit of the vine. A handful of the Jewish wineries persisted for half a century or more, and Italian wine grape sellers and tiny local vintners became community institutions.

In an Italian house, homemade wine was as vital to a good meal as a plate of pasta, and you were more likely to find a glass of *vino* by your plate than a glass of water. The Jewish laws of kashrut, from the Bible and later the Talmud, required that wine used in religious sacrament be produced by observant Jews, leading to a cottage industry of kosher city wineries. For most wineries, it made sense to set up where the grapes were. For kosher wineries, it made sense to operate where the Jews were.

"There really isn't much to say about wine made in New York City," said one expert in the wines of the Eastern United States. "It's not good wine." For the most part, New York City winemaking has not been about quality wine, but about expressing tradition.

. . .

NO rule of Jewish law says that kosher wine shall be sickly, stickily sweet and taste of children's Robitussin and grape Kool-Aid. But the story of kosher wine in America is unfortunately and inextricably tied to that of the peculiar Concord grape, whose juice has a foxy flavor that requires vintners to add copious amounts of sugar to make palatable wine. The Concord was cultivated in the 1850s, just before the great Jewish migration from Europe, by Ephraim Wales Bull, of Concord, Massachussetts, neighbor to Emerson, Hawthorne, and Louisa May Alcott (who jumped his fences and helped herself to his fruit). "I looked about to see what I could find among our wildlings," he wrote. Noting that the birds preferred to eat from a particular grapevine, he propagated select cuttings, in a move that was to sweeten the Passover seder for generations of American Jews. A few decades later, as Concord grape production doubled from one season to the next, its wine was praised as the best in the country.

In the kitchens and basements of the narrow, dark, airless tenements going up all over the Lower East Side, Jews flooding in from the shtetls of eastern Europe crushed these purple grapes and fermented their juice to use for kiddush, the prayer over wine. Upstate New York growers experienced a bit of a grape rush to supply them. "Scores of speculators" and "agents of wine-making houses" bought hundreds of tons of Concords, which they sent to the city in uncovered whiskey barrels. The sturdy, reliable Concord fruited early and never failed, and yielded as much as three and a half tons per acre, the newspapers boasted, a favorable record against the Catawba, the Delaware, the Worden, the Brighton, Moore's Early, and the Hartford Prolific.

Never mind their foxy flavor—Concords were cheap and abundant. The *bubbis,* or Yiddishe grandmothers, brewing up wine in their kitchens didn't know from grapes—they just added more sugar. The wineries followed suit. Sam Schapiro's wine business launched informally out of his basement in 1899, and later developed the slogan "Wine you can almost cut with a knife."

And drink with a prayer: "Blessed are you, the Lord our God, King of the Universe, Creator of the fruit of the vine," goes the blessing recited over the wine in Jewish homes each Friday night, when everyone at the table takes a sip as they enter the holy Sabbath. A full four cups of wine must be blessed, and drunk, at the Passover dinner during the ritual telling of the story of Exodus. Sips of wine punctuate a tale of slavery, gruesome plagues, flight in the night, and freedom—and by the end of the long dinner, the uncles are red-faced, the aunts are giggling, and the cousins are playing footsie under the table. On some holidays in the Lower East Side, when wine was brought into the synagogue, "pious old graybeards leap and dance and drink much of it, to show their joy in God," wrote the novelist Michael Gold.

By the turn of the twentieth century, Manhattan was full of home winemakers, the *Times* noted. "The Hebrews do not seem to be so particular as to the method of making their wine"—pressing grapes between fingers, twisting them in a bag, squeezing them in a clothes wringer, or stomping them with bare feet—"as they are regarding the condition of the utensils which the grapes and the juice are likely to come in contact with." Then, as later, American kosher wine was more concerned with ritual contamination than with bouquet or mouthfeel.

In parts of Europe, kosher winemakers had over centuries developed subtle, dry reds and whites in distinct regional styles. Often Jewish vintners would simply borrow a non-kosher facility, ritually cleanse its equipment, and staff it with yeshiva boys. Yet the Jews who came in a rush to America did not land in a region with highly developed winemaking traditions—they landed in the Lower East Side. And there they worked the grapes they had.

Then came Prohibition. Some argued that Jews should be made to bless grape juice instead of alcoholic wine, but tradition prevailed. Kosher wineries, as well as wineries that produced sacramental wine for Christian churches, were given special dispensation by the federal government to remain open, and rabbis were allowed to order limited amounts of wine for their congregants.

This inevitably led crooked and fake rabbis to go into business selling wine to fake Jews. Vintners would pay a rabbi a couple hundred dollars for the use of his certificate to hang on the door to the wine cellar, suggesting the wine belonged to him. Government agents descended on a licensed kosher winery on Third Street in a sting operation in 1921 and seized an outgoing barrel of wine, as a worker confessed that the winery did its principal "sacramental wine business among the Gentiles." A few years into Prohibition, hundreds of shady wineries and wine stores dotted the Lower East Side, purporting to serve the religious community that had suddenly grown in size and enthusiasm. "Dry Agents Plan War upon Illicit Rabbis," ran a newspaper headline. Even the long-standing kosher wineries dabbled in the black market; Sam Schapiro, whose winery would survive until the 1990s, sold sacramental wine legally to rabbis in the front of his shop on Rivington Street, and hard liquor illegally out the back door. "He was a bootlegger," his grandson said years later.

Into this ferment, so to speak, came a new Jewish winery. Around 1927, Leo Star, the son of a Russian cantor who also sold kosher wine door-to-door to rabbis, rented a double cellar on Wooster Street to bottle kosher port and sherry. His friend George Robinson joined him, and George's brother Meyer became their lawyer. Leo met his wife, Augusta, through her work as a secretary for the legendary Yiddish-speaking Prohibition agents Izzy Enstein and Moe Smith, according to their daughter years later. It is not now clear whether most—or any—of Leo and George's early customers were in fact Jews. But the end of Prohibition left the partners with the Monarch Wine Company, which manufactured a kosher product suddenly not in demand. Leo and George decided to hitch their fortunes to selling a Passover wine they called Mount Zebo. That first year, storeowners sent back what they hadn't sold after Passover. The second year, Leo and George refused returns, and their wine sat on the shelves, until surprisingly, months later, they began to get reorders. They could only conclude that non-Jews had developed a taste for their over-sweet, rabbinically supervised holiday wine. So the kosher wine industry was born.

LIKE Jews, Italians took advantage of a Prohibition loophole. The law did not in fact prohibit all alcohol consumption—but allowed people to make limited amounts of wine to drink at home. Accustomed to a glass of wine with dinner, New York City Italians set about winemaking during *la Proibizione,* observes Michael A. Lerner, author of *Dry Manhattan,* "as they would make bread if the bread shops were suddenly closed." Social workers in Italian neighborhoods estimated that Italian households spent as much as three hundred dollars a year for winemaking supplies, and court records show hundreds of gallons of wine were frequently produced in a single basement to be drunk and sold to neighbors for three to five dollars a gallon. In the fall, the gutters in front of tenements would be stained red by the dregs from winemaking, and shopkeepers would apologize for their grape-colored hands.

As people adapted to Prohibition, shipments of California wine grapes to Manhattan's docks increased more than fortyfold from 300 carloads in 1917 to 14,000 in 1923. So many grapes clogged dock traffic that eventually, all wine grape deliveries had to be banished to New Jersey. There, on the piers just after dawn, hoarse-voiced auctioneers offered up grapes by the thousands of tons to be transferred to the Italian markets on West Street in Manhattan. As carts were loaded and ferryboats boarded, the grapes spilled out, creating what a *New York Times* reporter described as "a reluctant squidginess between shoe and wharf," and leaving the docks smelling like a vineyard on the sea.

Any old grocery or pharmacy in Manhattan sold winemaking recipes and ingredients. At grape stands in the crowded markets, the vendors sang, "Marsigliana! Galante! Pir-i-go-ne!" The promise of alcohol sped up sales, as the sellers assured customers, "Succulent grape, signor. It makes sweet wine—and strong." Grape deliveries marked the start of autumn in the city, and the season ended around Election Day, when kids used the wooden grape crates to make bonfires in the streets. "Ya'd wait for the wop to get his grapes," recalled a man who grew up on the Italian East Side in the 1920s and '30s. "They would get deliveries of grapes on the sidewalks," he noted. "Whoosh! We'd grab 'em and run like bastards. The guinea would yell out, 'You son of a bitch. You son of a bitch.'"

. . .

"AW, jeez," Sal Meglio will say if you ask him how he first started making wine. You'll be sitting on a vinyl stool at the mirrored bar at the Red Hook VFW post, which Sal has tended for almost two decades. He'll take you downstairs to show you his collection of homemade red in Absolut and Bacardi bottles, cut up some Tuscan salami, break off chunks of grainy Parmigiano-Reggiano, and offer you a sip. "Knocks you on your ass, right?" asks Sal's friend Ralphie, pale-eyed, darkly bronzed, and tattooed with a ship at sunset. It's true, it's strong.

With a sheepish smile, Sal will tell you that he doesn't drink his own wine often, but when he does, he has a habit of calling up the neighborhood widows. They know his routine, says Sal. "They'll say, 'Sal, you drunk again?' 'Yes.' 'Is your wife in Atlantic City?' 'Yes.' 'You're all alone tonight?' 'Yes.' 'Okay, talk to you later.'"

"And they hang up!" says Sal, looking both indignant and forlorn. On the subject of wine, however, he is more assured. "You gotta see how it goes down the side of the glass," he says in the fluorescent-lit cellar, tilting his glass to swish a film of wine around the sides. "Goes down nice and smooth."

Sal is clean-shaven, pale, and wearing a pastel blue plaid short-sleeve cotton shirt. His thinning white hair is combed back and gelled down. "You'll never see me without a crease in my pants," he likes to say, sticking out his skinny leg in light blue jeans—creased. He never leaves the house without a handkerchief. He never wears sneakers. An heir to Old World tradition does not take short cuts.

For most of Sal's life, he worked for a family business importing California wine grapes for Brooklyn Italians, and he has been making wine himself since he was far too young to legally drink it. His father and mother came from the islands near Naples to Carroll Street, an island of Italians in Brooklyn. By the time Sal was born, the year after Prohibition ended, his family had moved to the heart of nearby Red Hook, a place with liquid edges and an overpopulation of longshoremen. His family rented the upper floor of a two-story, brown-brick box of a house on the main drag of Van Brunt, a few blocks from the piers where Sal's father worked as a winchman.

It was the Depression, and most everything was scarce. Yet in those days, you could almost live off the urban landscape. Sal's mother would grow tomatoes in the backyard, and buy more from a horse-and-wagon street vendor, for a year's worth of sauce. She would pour the sauce into quart-size glass soda bottles, cork them, and boil them in a fryer. She would collect pinecones and cook them on the stove to burst the shell and bare the seeds—pop, pop, pop, and out came pine nuts. Sal and his brother would roast coffee beans in a steel drum over a backyard bonfire fueled by wood they found in the street. Sal would ride his bike onto the ferry to Staten Island to go clamming or foraging for mushrooms. When he came home, his mother would make pasta with clam sauce. She would test the mushrooms by sautéing them with a shiny quarter—if the mushrooms were poisonous, the quarter would change color. (It never did.) Sal would pick persimmons and apricots straight off Guido the Undertaker's trees. His mother would grind a week's worth of sausage and throw the links over the clothesline in the yard, and if it transmitted the raw, pink smell of meat to the laundry that hung there later—no one noticed.

Even when there was no food but macaroni and beans, there was always homemade wine. Sal's mamma used to give him a bit mixed into a glass of cream soda. His pappa used to pull a gallon jar out from under the bed and take a swig in the morning before his feet even touched the floor. Sal's father made the wine himself, down in the cellar, standing in a barrel in his red-soled black rubber work boots and stomping down the grapes, with Sal's older brothers assisting. "One guy would throw in the grapes, half a barrel full, and my father would be crushing," says Sal. "They had a little hole where the juice is coming out, and you catch it with a pot." He would make four fifty-three-gallon barrels a year, along with a ten-gallon barrel of vinegar.

In Red Hook at the right time of year, you could walk down the street and smell the rich aroma of fermentation coming from most every home. *Un giorno senza vino è come un giorno senza sole,* goes the saying: A day without wine is like a day without sun. Landlords would give Italian families a spot in the cellar to keep their barrels. A kid sent downstairs to the barrel to fill a gallon jar to bring to the dinner table would tiptoe across the earthen floor. "You're not even supposed to talk around it! Makes it vibrate," Sal says. "Wine likes darkness and quiet."

"Air is wine's worst enemy," Sal tells me, his light hazel eyes wide and magnified through his glasses. Sometimes air would do the wine in. In time, the barrel of sweet red wine might turn acid, like vinegar, or moldy—to illustrate, Sal draws a diagram on the real estate section of the *Daily News:* "There's the wine," he points out as he draws a flat line in blue ink. "There's the air," he says, making little wavy lines coming down into the wine. "There's the white mold," he adds, carefully drawing little balls on top of the liquid. He looks up at me and shrugs his shoulders. "People would drink it anyway."

More circumspect winemakers, Sal says, would siphon off the wine from the barrel, bottle it, seal it with wax, and bury it in the backyard. It's hard to say how many wine bottles you might dig up in Brooklyn yards today. In the eighties, a friend of Sal's was gardening and hit his trowel against a five-gallon *damigiana*, or glass jug, containing some nicely aged red, which he took as a gift from Italians of yore. Sal helped him drink it.

IN the Red Hook of Sal's childhood, there was a don with one glass eye on Van Brunt Street, whose hand had to be kissed during visits. Crazy Joey Gallo, the mobster for the Profaci family, later known as the Gambino family, also lived nearby. Al Capone had gotten his start as a small-time criminal in the neighborhood, and the Mob leader Albert Anastasia still ran Murder, Inc., and the local waterfront. Grain barges from the Erie Canal and vessels carrying coffee, cocoa, and oil clustered just offshore, waiting to pull into the port. In the mornings, thousands of longshoremen would hurry to the docks to shape up, or present themselves to the hiring boss, who would pick out men to work that day. In the winter, dockworkers like Sal's father would stuff their denim coveralls and flannel shirts with newspapers to add another layer against the cold.

Hard-earned leisure came with homemade wine. Raffaele and Paolina sold it by the glass or the pitcher out of their compact grocery store to the men out back playing bocce ball, the hand game morra, or the card game brisk, or briscola. Manuel the Portuguese on Conover and King, and Sal's aunt Vittoria on Van Brunt, peddled it by the gallon or half gallon from their narrow little row houses. You would be mocked for the rest of your life if you were caught pouring store-bought wine into the barrel in the basement to present as homemade when the homemade ran out.

Kids would get drunk for the first time in their own cellars, giggling with their cousins in the damp cold as they used the siphon like a straw in the barrel and sucked and spat and sucked some more of their fathers' homemade red. In dimly lit apartments-cum–social clubs, with bedrooms furnished with nothing but card tables and chairs, men would buy homemade wine and fifty-cent dinners of mussels or tripe and stay up late into the night, gambling. At home, the osso buco and veal cutlets and eggplant Parmigiana on the table at dinner could simply not be swallowed without the accompaniment of wine. "A gallon would go *phtttt!*—like that," wrote Jerry Della Femina, a chronicler of Italian Brooklyn Sal's age. Homemade wine answered problems medical, sexual, cultural, wrote Della Femina. "If our neighbor Bellitti had cancer, which he did, and couldn't eat, the neighborhood advice was, 'Have a drink of wine.'"

Sal's father died when Sal was nine, when his two oldest brothers were already off in the service. His sister supported their mother and the four youngest on earnings from her thirteen-dollar-a-week job in a jam and jelly factory, and on her black market sales of the rationed sugar she would stuff into her pocketbook. After the war ended and the black market disappeared, Sal needed to contribute. Sal's *zio,* or uncle, Daniel Nito, had developed a profitable business selling wartime black market grapes as they came in on the freight cars. Now Daniel took the professional name Tony—it sounded more Italian—and focused his efforts on the seasonal business of providing *paesani* with California grapes to ferment into a hard red wine. When Sal was thirteen, Tony hired him. By the time Sal was in high school, he would finish his classes around noon and unload grapes till night, and on harvest weekends, he'd wake up at five in the morning and work all day.

All the labor made him preternaturally strong, with a good arm for baseball, which he rarely had time to play. He would turn over his weekly eight-dollar pay to his mother and keep the tips.

At that time, Tony Nito & Son (the son was Sal's cousin Joey) bought California grapes at auction in New Jersey, shipped them across the Hudson on a float to the rail yard in Brooklyn at Columbia and Baltic, and sold them right out of the freight cars. Sal would step up the metal stair, grab the handle, and swing himself into the car to unload thirty-six- and forty-two-pound wooden boxes of grapes. Hauling up into a given freight car, you could guess right away if the grapes were good. Often they would just smell fruity, which was a good sign. Sometimes the farmers would gas them with sulfur dioxide to preserve them for the journey, and if you could still smell the gas, you could bet the fruit would taste fresh. But sometimes—especially in those early days before refrigerated cars, when ice kept the grapes cool but also moist—they smelled of rot. Occasionally they arrived full of roll worms eating them from inside out.

The freight cars had no lights, and when Sal worked into the night, he would turn over a few wooden grape crates, melt some wax on top, and stick on some candles. He would unpack Muscats and Alicantes and Zinfandels in a flickering, uneven candlelight until ten, eleven, or twelve. Seven days a week, the grapes came in.

Loading grapes could be hard on the body. Sal had to get stitches in his head when a freight car door fell on him. When it was time for the stitches to come out, he walked into a tailor shop and asked a seamstress to remove them so he wouldn't have to bother with a doctor.

At least a half dozen grape sellers operated around that part of Brooklyn—each with his own turf—and many more worked other Italian neighborhoods. By the time Sal was eighteen, he started delivering the grapes himself, in a World War II "deuce and a half" army truck he drove without a license. "Jerkoff. You bastard," he'd say to traffic from the booth of the car. "*Vaffanculo!*" He had a string of other jobs, but always tried to take time off to work the grape season. Starting at eighteen, he worked at the White Rock Soda factory during the summer rush, only to leave in the fall for the grapes. Later, he labored on a construction crew building dams and bridges up and down the East Coast, only to quit in the autumn to be nearer home at harvest time. Eventually, Sal got a steady job at the city's Department of Sanitation, but would ask his boss for days off during the grape harvest. "Bastard guinea," his supervisor would say, but he would shut up when Sal paid him off in beer and the occasional bottle of homemade wine.

In the 1970s, Joey Nito bought a little bar called the Sky-way Tavern right in front of the Brooklyn-Queens Expressway, and gutted it to make a grape shop. Tony Nito & Son would sell thousands of boxes on a good day, stacked three high on the curb. The supplier out in California was the grower and winemaker Angelo Papagni, who later went to prison for passing off cheap wines as more expensive ones.

Grape crushing had its glam side, since the Mafia boys made wine too. Carlo Gambino, the crime family boss known for gifting friends with bottles of his homemade wine, would occasionally show up in his Cadillac to buy grapes from Joey Nito, Sal says. The dapper, black-hatted mobster would sit in his car and Joey would walk over to the window, Sal recalls. "He used to just tell my cousin, 'Send the grapes.'" It is not clear to Sal whether he made the wine himself or had "his monkeys" do it. "Crowd of geeps," Sal says, dismissively.

Of course, grapes sell only in the autumn, as they're picked, so Joey and Sal developed a tripartite business plan. As the grape supply thinned, Sal would sell Christmas trees out of the storefront. In January, Sal, a skilled mechanic, would fix up used cars for Joey to sell out of the same space. In September, Joey and Sal would again revert to the grapes. If Italian American manhood came to mean, in part, making wine in the basement, Sal helped make many an Italian American man.

Red Hook was a larger neighborhood then, including the present-day Carroll Gardens and Cobble Hill. But houses were knocked down to make way for highways in the 1940s, and workers with cranes and derricks and earthmoving machines dug giant trenches, which left mountains of dirt, where Sal would go sledding in the winter. Eventually, the highway overpasses, coughing exhaust and shuddering from compression brakes, split the neighborhood in two. Soon after, Brooklyn's cargo shipping industry moved across the river to New Jersey and left the longshoremen without jobs. Most of the winemaking families moved away. Carroll Gardens and Cobble Hill prospered while Red Hook was forgotten, hemmed between highway and water, an isolated hook of land jutting into the East River.

THE perception of taste is a function of moral ideals as well as of physical sensations. Philosophers have debated for millennia what good taste means. With wine, there is no consensus.

A microscopic fungus called yeast eats sugar and makes alcohol and carbon dioxide. Grape juice left alone contains yeast that will naturally turn it in to something like wine. But humans intervene, in processes more or less complicated, to achieve certain balances of flavor and alcohol. Some view the process as high art. Others view it as no more than a means to an alcohol end. Some view the whole thing—the crushing of the grapes, the drinking of the wine—as tradition.

Sal Meglio and Latif Jiji and even Leo Star and Meyer Robinson did not aim to make critically acclaimed wines. Their wines tasted good to their makers and the people whose glasses they filled.

"You and your group represent *zilch* population-wise!" said one of the Manischewitz sons-in-law to a reporter who cast aspersions on his wine. Americans liked his wine, and that's all that mattered. He muttered it again: "Zilch."

LATIF Jiji has transformed each step of the winemaking process into an annual ritual. The Making of Labels: Family and friends gather around the dining room table with paint, glitter, and glue to create handmade labels for the next vintage. The Cleaning of the Bottles: Latif rinses the previous year's bottles to prepare them to hold the coming year's wine. The Bottling: Latif siphons the wine from demijohns into bottles, leaving behind the chalky sediment. The Pruning of the Vine: He leans out windows to trim the weak and dead branches. Finally, the Harvest. Latif keeps a record each year in a blue-lined school notebook of how many pounds of grapes were plucked and who helped. Friends and family participate in the bounty; until her death, his mother used to stuff the grape leaves with meat and rice, just as she had done with the leaves of the vine that grew in their house in Basra when Latif was a child. A friend distills the leftover pomace to make grappa, just as he had in his native Armenia.

Latif's vine is more than a hundred feet long now, and still inching its way across the roof. The vine is so substantial that it is visible on the satellite view of Google Earth. A thick roof-top grapevine, it turns out, can lower electricity bills. Dry, brittle, and grapeless in the winter, it allows the sun to heat the roof and upper floor. In the summer, thick bunches of grapes provide shade that helps keep the house cool.

The taste and quality of the wine varies from year to year, but also from bottle to bottle. Some bottles develop a spiked grape juice taste. Mild and sweet, the wine usually tastes much like the grapes. The 2001 vintage is "very well balanced, but it still has the Latif character, its crispness," says Genio Rodriguez, Latif's crew chief and closest critic, who has cultivated an interest in wine since age sixteen, when he worked as a mover for a Queens mafioso who gave him a few nice bottles as partial payment.

In the Upper East Side, clusters of black Lexuses sleek as panthers move through streets full of art dealers and tax lawyers and face-lifts. There's nothing out there to suggest Latif's rambling, fairy-tale vineyard.

Standing on Latif's roof and looking out, it seems that all the backyards are under construction, everyone expanding their houses, maximizing their living space and property values. Cement decks take up entire backyards in a city of cement. Shallow reflecting pools decorate yards where no one goes to reflect. When a neighbor of Latif and Vera recently renovated his yard, he cut the roots of Latif's vine, which had twisted their way under the fence into his soil. The vine did not sprout as many leaves or grapes that year, or the next. But the following year the vine came back, bushy with grapes, and made a record harvest.

One day outside, Latif, leaning forward on his patio chair like some kind of backyard oracle, says to me: "There is magic in this vine."

A month after Prohibition was repealed, Meyer Robinson filed a certificate of incorporation for the Monarch Wine Company, Inc. Meyer's brother George Robinson and his partner, Leo Star, were ready to promote their Mount Zebo label. But George got sick and died of leukemia, and the blue-eyed, mustachioed, jokester brother Meyer took his place as a partner in the wine business. In time, Meyer married Roslyn Gross, a beautiful, fun-loving flapper, the daughter of a well-off Jewish flour miller who had managed to extract his family and his wealth largely intact from Vilna, Poland. Meyer and Roslyn moved to a two-bedroom apartment in an Art Deco building in Flatbush with pretty etched-glass mirrors in the lobby. They had a daughter, Gale, and a son, Samuel.

Meyer and Leo planned their business adroitly. They purchased equipment at bankruptcy sales, as a previous generation of kosher winemakers went bust after Prohibition. When they decided they needed a memorable brand name, they thought of Manischewitz. It was a solid, respected company in the Jewish world, named for a man who had slaughtered meat under a famed Lithuanian rabbi and who had arrived in the United States in 1886 to build a matzoh empire—one of the first trusted national Jewish brands. And so Meyer and Leo cut a deal with Manischewitz Food Products, Inc. The Monarch Wine Company would use the

Manischewitz name on its labels and pay a royalty on every bottle sold—the wine company is still paying today.

Manischewitz wine hit the market in an optimistic era when consumption and aspiration were rising. New York was the richest, biggest city in the world. Women wore new minks, men drove new cars, and all night long, the office towers of mid-Manhattan left the lights on, so their "glowing reflections hung like a canopy on the air when clouds were low." The subject of wine was approached with diffidence, and even the fashionable Cotillion Room at the Pierre Hotel was insecure enough to include this note on the wine list: "We have been fortunate in having the help of a Grand Officer of the noble 'Confrerie des Chevaliers du Taste Vin,' who assures us that many of the wines are of the type one finds in the great cellars of Europe." Wine snobbery was pervasive enough to be mocked. "It's a naïve domestic Burgundy without any breeding, but I think you'll be amused by its presumption," wrote one humorist.

Meyer and Leo had moved wine production in 1939 from Wooster Street to the Bush Terminal, a vast commercial and industrial complex along the Brooklyn waterfront, where they were able to build a highly automated production facility, far from the bubbis back on the Lower East Side. Monarch processing plants in upstate New York pressed the grapes into juice, froze it, and stored it until it was needed in the city winery. Most wineries spring into action once a year, during the grape harvest. Monarch made wine year round. Outside the Manischewitz factory, a 22,500-pound capacity Jack Frost truck would dump waterfalls of sugar into a chute that emptied straight into a large pool of wine in the middle of the factory floor. "An engine, its insides of gears and belts and wheels revealed, worked creakily away, poised over the center, stirring the sugar into the wine," wrote *Commentary* magazine in 1954, making "a deep purple whirlpool."

Meyer was Jewish in that peculiarly midcentury North American way, as the shtetl assimilated into suburbia. He kept a kosher home, sent his children to yeshiva school, and was president of the synagogue. Yet when he traveled into Manhattan, his favorite foods were lobster and Chinese—most unkosher. Producing the country's leading kosher wine as good as anointed him a community leader, and he served on the boards of the Anti-Defamation League, the Jewish Theological Seminary, the local United Jewish Appeal, and the United Synagogues of America. "Bad for business," Leo would mutter, when Meyer proposed unkosher food too publicly.

The rules of kashrut, codified by desert-dwellers thousands of years prior, could be tough on commercial winemakers. Only Sabbath-observant Jews could touch the wine from the time the grapes were crushed until the bottles were sealed with a cork—though there was an out. *Mevushal,* or cooked, wine is boiled, rendering it immune to the polluting fingers of gentiles. The grapes could not be processed on the Jewish Sabbath or the High Holidays of Rosh Hashanah and Yom Kippur—though these usually fall smack in the middle of the harvest.

There was always some question about just how kosher Manischewitz was. More orthodox producers refused to allow non-Jews to even look at the wine—their gaze could pollute it. Monarch, however, made no secret of hiring gentiles. The company followed obvious proscriptions—no work on the Sabbath, oversight by a rabbi. But Gale Robinson, Meyer's daughter, says that by the late 1960s and '70s, "the rabbis would say anything was kosher." For years the rabbis didn't even show up, said her husband, Marshall Goldberg, who worked for the company. His first task when he began was to fire the rabbis—a task everyone else had avoided—so the company could hire others who actually did their job.

Seeking to expand beyond the traditional ultrasweet Concord, Meyer and Leo converted a winery in Fowler, California, to kosher in order to produce muscatel, sherry, and port from grapes such as Carignanes, Palominos, Fresno Beauties, Feher Szagos, and Zinfandels. It turned out to be logistically challenging to make kosher wine at a distance from communities of Jews. An army of yeshiva students was brought in from hours away in Los Angeles to make the wine, and rabbis had to be flown in from Brooklyn to supervise.

Meyer didn't mind the inconvenience. He was a man who expected good things to happen. On the phone, he would ask, "Hi! How's everything? Great?" If his interlocutor demurred, he'd say, "Well, it'll get better. It'll get better!" He was so confident of his dominion that he would instruct his children, "If you ever have a problem—if somebody's following you or you get lost or you need money—go to a liquor store. Just tell them who you are."

Meyer and Leo were wine moguls of a different era. They decided early on that they had seen too many people in the liquor business become alcoholics, and so they rarely drank—except, of course, for Friday night kiddush over the Manischewitz. When his kids were little, Meyer would let them have Manischewitz diluted with seltzer. By the time Gale, the eldest, was offered the real thing at about age fifteen, she would comment, "Ugh! It's so sweet! Can't we ever serve something decent?" The even-keeled

Meyer would respond, "Don't bite the hand that feeds you!" and Roslyn would shoot her daughter a dirty look. Meyer would tour the great wineries of Italy and France and come home with little to say about the wine itself—instead he would be brimming with stories about the winemaking technology or the layout of the tasting room.

At a time when business owners paid off disc jockeys to mention their products ("I just had the best glass of Manischewitz wine!"), Meyer was friendly with Barry Gray, the brash, abrasive father of talk radio on WMIE, and William B. Williams, the silver-voiced host on WNEW who opened his show, "Hello, world!" He joined the Friars Club and joked with Borscht Belt comedians. Meyer would host off-the-record dinners at the winery—no women, no reporters—and invite the entire Dodgers team for a big Italian meal cooked by the head of Monarch's trucking division, accompanied, of course, by Manischewitz.

In the years immediately after Prohibition, Leo and Meyer had advertised that their wine was "like Mother used to make"— presumably from Concord grapes in some tenement basement. At that stage, advertising was simple. "Lifshitz wine! Lifshitz wine! Oy, how good," went one guileless Yiddish-language radio ad. "It's known by the greatest rabbis as the most kosher wine for Passover."

But by the 1950s, American taste was changing; a bottle of wine had become an attainable touch of class, and people were drinking more of it. Jews were assimilating, and their products were entering the mainstream: Hebrew National hot dogs, Levy's rye bread, the rise of the bagel. Monarch wanted to tap in to the broader audience, so a new ad agency worked to fix Manischewitz's most basic problem on the national market: its name.

People didn't know how to pronounce it—they would stumble and call it Manny, or even construct familiar-sounding words like "Mani-chevrolet."

"We concentrated on dinning the name into the heads of people," said the company's ad man, Charles E. Patrick. "We dropped almost all the visual advertising and took thousands of radio spot announcements all over the country just repeating over and over, 'Man, oh Manischewitz, what a wine.'" The next task was to override the American view of wine as a snobbish drink governed by difficult rules.

"You don't have to be a wine expert to enjoy it," read the text for one radio ad. "You don't have to worry whether to serve it before meals or after meals or when you entertain. For MANISHE-VITZ WINE is perfect *all the time.*"

"We want to bring drinking wine," Patrick said, "to the level of Coca-Cola."

Celebrities such as Lionel Hampton, the jazz musician, shilled for Manischewitz in black publications such as *Ebony* and the *Amsterdam News* in a special effort to reach African Americans, who had been early adopters.

The ad blitz worked, and soon in Los Angeles Manischewitz was competing neck and neck with the major California brand Gallo for the highest wine sales overall. In an advertiser's dream, while walking on the moon during the *Apollo 17* mission, the astronaut Eugene Cernan exclaimed in astonishment, "Man, oh Manischewitz." His comment was broadcast and rebroadcast back on Earth, and Meyer Robinson delighted in playing the recording for visitors to his office. "Isn't that amazing, on the moon!" Meyer would say, rising in excitement from his chair.

But trouble was brewing. The business partners had a falling out when Leo got divorced and moved to Florida with his new wife. The two principals barely spoke. Meyer would refuse to take a raise because then Leo would get one too. Instead, they survived on company credit cards, each trying to outdo the other in amounts charged, Meyer's son-in-law recalled.

At some point, as Americans became savvier about wine, Manischewitz became the butt of the joke. It was ridiculously sweet. Even the name somehow was funny. "Manishevevevitz," a man stuttered repeatedly on *The Jack Benny Program*. On St. Patrick's eve, Bob Hope introduced a quartet, all with Irish names, and announced that their sponsor was Manischewitz—hilarious. A record was released with the track "The Mambo-Shevitz," in which the refrain was "Man, oh man." Even the wine's spokesman began to look comical. Sammy Davis Jr. had been contracted to represent the company in the 1970s, but he was less and less the family entertainer one would wish to advertise one's kosher-for-Passover product, as he spent his time filling his Rolls-Royce with sex kittens and his schnoz with cocaine, as one journalist put it. Finally, the Manischewitz lawyers learned that the porn star Linda Lovelace had described in her memoir engaging Sammy in a foursome. Sammy Davis Jr. was soon out of a wine contract.

Monarch beat out Seagram's to import Tsingtao beer after Leo and Meyer managed to put aside their hostilities and travel all together with their families to China. Monarch imported the Italian beer Raffo and a Swedish beer called Kalback. A low-calorie wine, Manischewitz Light, debuted and was quickly dropped. The company also released Cream Anasetta, Cream Almonetta, and the best-selling Piña Coconetta, a piña colada–flavored wine cocktail that may have lacked a certain sacramental gravitas but sold 350,000 cases the year it was introduced. More

than 85 percent of Manischewitz consumers were not Jewish—
and 60 percent were black. Manischewitz was the number one
imported wine in Puerto Rico, and also sold in Cuba, Colombia,
Venezuela, Hong Kong, Belgium, and the Virgin Islands.

But poor management plagued the company. In 1984, a meeting was held with the sons-in-law on one side of the table, the
bankers on the other, and Meyer Robinson and Leo Star at either end. The bankers said, "You got six months to straighten this
business out," son-in-law Marshall Goldberg recalled.

Soon after, Meyer and Leo and the sons-in-law decided to
sell the Manischewitz brand for $20 million to the Canandaigua
Wine Company, one of the country's largest wine manufacturers, which moved production to the Finger Lakes area. When
the Brooklyn plant was closing down, Sal Meglio came over from
Red Hook and bought a hundred cases of Manischewitz wine
for five dollars a case, to sell for ten. Sal remembers a half-empty
warehouse and people making off like thieves with as many boxes
of wine as they could fit into their cars. The end of Manischewitz
was the last gasp for local winemaking: other commercial wineries closed in quick succession, and there followed a nearly wineless
period in New York City.

FOR most of Sal Meglio's career, there was a standard recipe for
wine among the Italians of Red Hook, as though everyone had
tasted everyone else's and developed a consensus. People would
mix twelve boxes of Alicante grapes, a couple boxes of Zinfandels,
and maybe a couple boxes of Muscat to give strength, and judge
the quality by how few glasses it took to get drunk, the faster the
better. But as the rents rose and the old Italians left Carroll Gar-

dens and Cobble Hill, the grape neighborhoods dispersed. New-comers began to edge out Italians in home winemaking prowess: Yugoslavs, Greeks, Romanians. Tony Nito was no more, and his son Joey polled the family about what to do with the business. Sal was in his sixties, Joey was in his seventies, Sal's brother who used to help out was in his eighties, and no one wanted to take over.

Look at the quiet, dead-end streets of the Red Hook neigh-borhood now and it's hard to imagine a place where each street was a vital artery for goods and people coming in from all over the world. Sal stayed still but the world he knew disappeared. Now he guesses he knows no more than half a dozen people in the old neighborhood who still make wine. Sal's not particularly religious; he goes to church for weddings and funerals. The ritual in his life for as long as he can remember has been winemaking. Every year he says he's too old, he'll quit. But he invariably joins his nephew and his brothers and cousins to make the next year's batch.

During wine season at the Brooklyn Terminal Market, crates of grapes still stack in piles, as SUVs pull up carrying young fami-lies with their Italian-speaking *nonnos*, or grandpas. "You got a better price for me? I always get a special price," someone will say. Quantities of grapes are stuffed into trunks, as carelessly and ef-ficiently as if the drivers were long-haul produce deliverers. Even now, a few people still attach big wooden blocks to the bottoms of their youngest kids' shoes and then drop the children into the barrel to crush. But most take shortcuts. There has been a switch from grapes to juice, to skip the step of crushing. The younger Italians think it's convenient. The older Italians think it's the enemy of tradition.

The great kosher wine industry of New York City may be

mostly gone, but Jews still buy grapes at the Brooklyn Terminal Market, and in the Orthodox Jewish neighborhood of Borough Park, everyone seems to know a home winemaker. Ephraim Grumet, a diamond manufacturer, dumps yellowish grapes he picks in his backyard into the blender for a few seconds, then pours the entire mixture—seeds, stems, and all—into a five-gallon glass jug. He ties a clean bedsheet over the opening and leaves it alone in the basement. Months later, he siphons the wine off the top and bottles it in a jug. It turns almost a rosé color from the seeds and skins, which makes it pretty when he gives it away at Purim.

IN Red Hook, Christopher Nicolson rinses out an oversize wineglass and shimmies up the racks of barrels to the topmost one, four levels up, by the ceiling, and offers a sample of the fermenting juice, leaning down, glass in hand. "You'll notice the smell is very exotic, like sandalwood, jasmine—kind of weird, curious," he calls from his perch atop the barrels, like a flying vintner. Then he dips his glass into the barrel, takes a sip, swishes it around in his mouth, spits it out onto the floor, and dumps the remainder back in the barrel. "It's antiseptic," he assures, as he climbs down, carefully placing his steel-toed Uniroyal boots patched with plastic wrap and duct tape around the ripped sole.

The small, commercial Red Hook Winery where he works opened in 2008 in a squat, brick former cannonball factory, just a few blocks from Sal Meglio's VFW bar—one of several new wineries in the city. Already Christopher's wine is selling to renowned Manhattan restaurants such as Blue Hill and Momofuku. Two leading California winemakers—Abe Schoener and Robert Foley—direct the process from a distance, and Christopher does the hard work on site of loading grapes, measuring recipes, monitoring air pressure and fermentation, and punching down the fermenting juice.

Many professional vintners in the state still won't make red wine out of local grapes because they are not naturally sweet enough—the specter of Manischewitz looms large. Rosé is the safe fallback. At Red Hook Winery, the winemakers experiment to discover the intrinsic character of Long Island–grown grapes. Every fermentation, they seek to uncover it, with rigorous experiments in grapes from Chardonnay, Sauvignon Blanc, Viognier, Cabernet Franc, Cabernet Sauvignon, Merlot, Petit Verdot, Gewürztraminer, and Riesling vines.

As new grapes come in one evening in September, there's a Willy Wonka feel to the whole operation: throttling, husking, desectioning, squirting, bubbling, frothing. Everything smells like purple grapes. Gooey stains of splatted grapes shape a gaudy mauve and violet on the stainless-steel machine that removes the stems and skins. Big silver machines are sucking out fruit juices and convection tubes are pumping the juices up across the room through various cylinders. There's a spring in everyone's step, all the way down the production line of volunteers who show up for the joy of making wine. Everyone seems happy. The B61 bus wheezes by, passengers staring out the window at the crates of grapes on the sidewalk. Colin Alevras, a bartender for Momofuku who has come to help shepherd the grapes through the machines, has a giant smile on his face as he says, "*This* is why New York is great."

. . .

AT the Jiji house on Ninety-Second Street, when the work is done and the weight of the harvest is called out—in recent years, 718 pounds, 712 pounds, 636 pounds—the backyard erupts in cheers.

"DINNER!" Latif's ten-year-old grandson Jake calls, and the crowd troops into the house, leaving black footprints and spilled juice on a runner of pink paper taped to the hardwood floor. Soon the yard will be hosed down, the winemaking apparatus dismantled, and the five-gallon jugs of golden wine-to-be moved to the chilled cabinet that will host its transformation.

Over the years, Latif assimilated. He forgot Arabic words as he perfected his English. By trial and error, he taught himself American practices like dating—for instance, when a girl agrees to a first date and says she'll spend the day with you, she doesn't mean for you to show up to pick her up at seven thirty a.m. Yet he also developed a lonesome nostalgia for all he left behind. His favorite Arabic poem—decades or hundreds of years old, he doesn't know—is about a man lost alone in the wilderness. The man weeps. He hears a dove weeping too. He says to the dove: "A stranger to a stranger is family." "That's how I feel," Latif says.

In truth, winemaking is a family activity. When a family disperses, and there's no one to crush with you and hold the jug for you, and eventually drink with you, you don't make wine. Latif hoped the converse would also be true: If you get people to crush grapes with you, and hold the jug for you, and maybe drink a bit of wine with you, you have family.

When Latif's children were little, he used to make up fantastical stories about his life in Basra that made it seem like a wondrous, funny place—in one, Latif was the pancake-maker for the queen of Iraq. A photo of Latif's childhood home hangs on the wall over the stairs, a large, beautiful brick building with tall, domed balconies, and a little boy in a white short-sleeve shirt standing out front, waving at the camera: Latif. "There were two more windows on the right side, four on the other," says Latif, tracing with his finger the missing pieces outside the edges of the photograph's frame.

Parents can spend their lifetimes trying to explain themselves to their children. Or they can offer experiences. In a way, the vine and the rituals around it are what Latif bequeaths.

"I want them to remember it, I want the grandchildren to," Latif says. "I'm trying to give them a sense of the memories I have and make them theirs."

"Part of it is being a refugee, not having my own home I grew up in," Latif says, leaning forward. "I'm not able to go back to my past and touch it and re-experience it, so I try to do something here that becomes my creation, that becomes part of what I am."

Fifteen years ago, Latif sent a sample to a winemakers' supply store in Pennsylvania and asked for advice on how to improve his wine, but the response was not useful; a friend in the chemistry department at City College offered to read up on pH and sugar content but never ponied up anything new. The wine tastes different each year and really there's no telling why. "I should spend some more time on ways to improve the quality," says Latif, in a tone that makes it clear he doesn't believe it. "You know how it is in this country," he says. "You're always looking for ways to make it better."

In truth, Latif—like Sal and many others in the city—is not

a critical oenophile. He makes wine to create ritual, to bind his family together year after year in a land without ritual or sense of family. He makes wine in tribute to his father and his own efforts with the vine. Latif makes wine as though to pour his past into a glass and share it.

EPILOGUE

IN the summer, Jorge Torres invites me to a Father's Day gathering in his garden in the Bronx. I bring two cartons of lemonade, two heavy watermelons, and two friends to help translate. Jorge breaks out in a huge smile as he talks about his childhood in Puerto Rico, and we while away the afternoon, eating cool watermelon in the heat, playing dominoes, splashing the kids in an inflatable pool, and listening to Jorge's classic Puerto Rican CDs. More people keep arriving with bags of chips and Cheez Doodles, sodas, and covered aluminum trays full of rice and beans, plantains, pasta, salad. Meanwhile, parts of pigs cook on a spit, sizzling and emitting bewitchingly porky scents. "Happy Father's Day," people say to Jorge, or simply: "Congratulations." It is a day to honor fathers, to honor him.

Toward the end of the afternoon, Jorge pulls the first of the *pernil* off the spit and beckons us over. "Where's the machete?" he calls into the casita, and someone brings it out and moves its enormous blade cleanly through the pork. As crisped skin falls, Jorge picks up pieces with his fingers and offers them to us. "Have some more," he urges, as he lays salty, fatty, tender meat on our plates.

As a person who has always managed on very little, Jorge knows well the role of food in survival. But he also understands the role of food in creating bonds, in telling stories, in building around himself the kind of family, the kind of neighborhood, the kind of city he wants. This feast and camaraderie were possible because Jorge carved space from a crowded Bronx neighborhood for growing things.

When I began work on this book, I thought I would be spending time with people who had been shunted to the edges of an overdeveloped city. But over time, meeting people and reading history, I started to realize that people who produce food draw others around them; they are not isolated, but among the most connected. As much as any other group of laborers and artists, they *are* the culture of New York. They are the ones who wrangle space to manufacture foods and to share them at feasts and ceremonies—the things that help weave the unruly, disparate strands of the city into something uniquely itself.

During the time I was reporting this book, Michelle Obama planted an organic vegetable garden on the White House lawn, and keeping chickens in the backyard became a minor national pastime. Beekeeping was legalized in New York City and a spate of wineries and breweries and new butcher shops specializing in humanely raised meat opened up around town. Little Brooklyn companies now make enough pickles and preserves to fill entire shops.

People are experimenting in urban agriculture in ways few imagined when I began writing. A Manhattan-based firm called BrightFarms specializes in building greenhouse farms on the roofs of supermarkets. In the Greenpoint neighborhood of Brooklyn, Gotham Greens has built a hydroponic greenhouse on top of an old bowling alley. On the 40,000-square-foot roof of the old Standard Motor building in Queens, Ben Flanner grows hundreds of thousands of organic plants in neat rooftop beds. A former marketing manager at eTrade, he now kneels in the dandelion greens, before the geometric grays of Midtown Manhattan, working a mix of lightweight soil and compost created from local coffee chaff and cocoa husks and leftover fruit pulp from juice bars—"developing the terroir," Ben likes to call it. He starts at five-thirty a.m., and he is sometimes tired enough to fall asleep with his head on the bar when he goes out at night. He gets by on less than $30,000 a year and his ability to survive is, for him, the test of the farming experiment: "If my bank account gets down to zero, I know something's got to change."

Universities have produced urban utopians who look into the future and want the city to feed itself. Each day New York City receives dozens of tons of food from trucks and ships and airplanes by the best estimate of the Port Authority—an amount that would be near impossible to produce locally. But analysts make more modest calculations: If you take the city's 5,701 flat, strong, large rooftops, you'd have 3,079 acres to plant vegetables. If you take 10 percent of the city's backyards and farm them modestly, you could feed about 72,000 people. If you build a thirty-story high-rise vertical farm on a whole city block, 50,000 people could eat each year. This last comes from Dickson Despommier, a Columbia University medical ecologist who believes cities must become self-sufficient. "I think a city is the equivalent of a parasite," he says. "A big, giant parasite that's living off of this landscape, and as the parasite's needs increase, and the landscape remains the same, it creates huge problems for this parasite to maintain itself," he says. "So how can you turn a parasite into a symbiont, that's the big question."

Over the time I was writing, I saw Willie Morgan settle into his new, permanent garden, after years of tending unwanted land. I followed David Selig as he savored his bees' odd honey and unlocked one small mystery of city life. I watched Tom Mylan open a butcher shop and then move beyond it, as he developed the ambition to tear down the whole rotten, soul-sucking system of factory farmed meat. I saw that food can change people. It can change places, too.

Writing this book revealed to me a rich and complicated city that I didn't know existed. New York had a brilliant agricultural past, which it cast away, then an even more brilliant manufacturing past, which it also cast away. For generations, planners have sought to move food production out of the city, but people have persisted in tending, growing, fermenting, butchering, and manufacturing basic foods to eat and share and sell—because they need to and because they want to. People think that New York City is not a place for growing things, but it turns out to be absolutely a place for growing things. It is a place where people practice alchemy, taking the stress and hardship of city life and turning it into something nourishing.

The city, with its size, heft, and momentum, can seem to obliterate individual stories and the collective past. Yet just as personalities are built by layers of experiences, so the city is built on the memories and knowledge of those who live here. The guy at the deli used to raise goats in Yemen. A woman across the street hopes to open a winery. The taxi driver plans to go back to Haiti and keep bees. A colleague at work catches crabs for her mother's

Trinidadian curry. Delivery trucks from the meat markets barrel through Midtown. The bar down the street offers beer made up the block. This all adds up to our collective experience. We build wineries, breweries, vegetable farms, beehives, sugar refineries, butcheries, and fishing piers, and the city reflects the needs we work to fulfill. People find ways to impose their hunger, their desires and dreams on the cityscape, seeking fulfillment from what they find nearby.

"Have some," says Jorge Torres, another day in his garden, standing by his sugarcane plant. And he slashes into the stalk, carves out a pretty piece, and I taste the sweet juice produced in the soil of this city.

ACKNOWLEDGMENTS

Thanks first of all to the people of the Bronx, Queens, Brooklyn, Manhattan, and Staten Island, who made food and drink with me, who trusted me with their stories, and who in many cases became my friends.

Special thanks to David and Kate Morrison, who showed me that things could grow in New York City, and to Dave Vogel, who helped me to imagine writing about it. This book would not exist without them.

Only one name appears on the front cover—but many, many people contribute to a book. Jane Ziegelman invited me to her home for a crash course in historical research, jumpstarting my search through old newspapers, magazines, and archives. John Waldman discussed with me the fates of fish and oceans. Just after dawn one morning, John Lipscomb steered me down the Hudson and through the oily waters of Newtown Creek, and Mitch Waxman shared observations about its beauty and horror. Edie Stone gave me her cell phone number and for years, answered questions whenever I called, and also generously opened up her files at GreenThumb. John Ameroso engaged in extended explanations of urban garden history, pH, and other matters of soil. K. Jacob Ruppert graciously invited me to Louisiana to page through his family collection of records; Gale Robinson did the same on Central Park West; and Harry W. Havemeyer on the Upper East Side. Ellen Pehek helped me to discover the natural world of city parks. Daniel Bowman Simon shared ideas and old newspaper clippings about urban agriculture. Yoni Brook gave me the rundown on city slaughterhouses. Buildings wizard Tony Robins helped me make geographic sense of the historical city.

Many thanks to Andrew Coté, David Selig, and the other beekeepers. Willie Morgan and many other gardeners. Classie Parker showed me how to cook handpicked peaches and spike them with bourbon to make magical preserves. Ben Flanner took me from rooftop to rooftop as he developed more ambitious urban farms. Gracias a Juana Cariño, mujer extraordinaria, quien compartió la cosecha de su jardín conmigo. Ian Marvy, Marlene Wilks, and Kennon Kay offered their thoughts, techniques, and their city farms. Tom Mylan and his butcher colleagues shared knowledge and philosophy, pork and gin drinks. Jake Dickson brought me to a pig roast. Muchas gracias a Jorge Torres quien me abrió las puertas de su casita y me contó su historia. Jon Conner and Josh Fields patiently gave many long-distance brewing explanations. Ben Granger asked me to his yard to snip hops plants. Kelly Taylor shared his beer and his many insights. Jane Borock, Michael Louie, and Ben Sargent took me fishing late at night in Brooklyn, and Naima Rauam took me to the late-night wholesale fish market in the Bronx. Ellen Zachos got me slightly drunk on delicious homemade wines made of amelanchier and linden flowers. Sal Meglio and Latif Jiji both invited me back again and again to share their amazing lives. There are many others, and I'm grateful to them all.

Food people, I've learned, are generous. More thanks to Anne Mendelson, Zak Pelaccio, David Rosengarten, Robin Ottaway, Garrett Oliver, Robert La Valva, Baron Ambrosia, Ethan Millrod and Karen Frillman, Vera and Jessica Jiji and their family, Annalee Sinclair, Robert Ambrosi, Karen Washington, Jonathan Bach, Ken Davies, Glenn Evans, Allen Katz, Linda LaViolette, Kathleen McTigue, Owen Taylor, Haja and Cindy Worley, Wendy Kosofsky, Michael Grady Robinson, Joe Crimi, Christopher Nicholson, Charlie Milan, Dennis Richards, Adrian Miller, Rav. Phillip Herzog, Ralph Lelia, Shirley Moss, Frank Prial, Richard Riggio, Lou Venich, Angie Blackwell, and Bert Silk for contributing important bits and pieces that have added up to this book.

Many people read versions of this book and made it better. The gifted editor George Hodgman, with his intuitive sense for the way stories should unfold, and his appreciation for beauty and oddness, pushed me to develop the narrative. The capable Lucinda Bartley always had my back, as she queried facts and carried statements to their logical conclusions. Marjorie Braman dispensed elegant solutions. Tom Engelhardt read several chapters with his X-ray vision for what works and what could work better. Jonathan Cobb kindly helped me to rethink an early draft.

The spectacular writer Cara Hoffman inspired and buttressed me, read many drafts of the manuscript, and showed me how to work toward the soul of the story. For years, I've been talking with Megan Hester about this book and everything else, so I know her rare gift for listening closely, and for figuring out both what is wrong and how to make it right. Still she surprised me by proving herself—though not a professional editor—one of the most talented editors I know.

The gifted Lyssa Rome was my first writing partner, setting me on a path toward a book. Writing sessions with Doug Merlino helped put my ideas on the page, then he blazed the trail I followed. Conversations with Annia Ciezadlo in one week in Beirut helped develop this book, and she too led by example, showing me that writing ostensibly about food can be brilliant and funny and powerful enough to tell the story of everything else. Griff Witte read chapters and shared his practical approach to clean, simple, beautiful storytelling. Dan Morrison, Fariba Nawa, and Tracie McMillan proved once again that good books can be written.

My agent, Rebecca Friedman, has been a ray of light and a friend, and she made this book happen. My wonderful editor, Jenna Ciongoli at Crown, believed in this idea from the start and worked patiently and attentively to make sure every part of it came together. The impressive team at Crown put together a beautiful cover and design, came up with great ideas for publicity, and otherwise worked hard to make this book work.

The talent and dedication of my research assistants John Peng, Desmond Cole, Jason Bell, and Nate Blum propelled the project forward. Elena Suslov and Clarissa León also contributed. The skilled journalist Eileen Markey stepped in towards the end to whip up missing facts. My assistant Clara Potter's intelligence, curiosity, and drive contributed enormously to spot research and sustained fact-checking. Thanks also to Jennifer Alzate, intrepid transcriber.

Mohamad Bazzi made sense of my imperfect oral renditions of Arabic poetry. Katya Pischalnikova got on the phone to Moscow to talk about beekeeping. Andrea and Lucia Bernagozzi translated from the Brooklyn Italian. Ana Campoy investigated obscure horticultural terms of southern Mexico. Marie-Hélène and Alexa Pratley translated nineteenth-century beer talk from the German. Evie Groch translated old Yiddish radio ads. Natalia Agüeros-Macario, Héctor Arce, and Ana Melendez trekked to Bronx gardens to translate the Spanish of rural Puerto Rico.

My extraordinary mentors fed, advised, and encouraged me. Orville Schell gave all kinds of useful nuts and bolts suggestions about bookwriting. Tom Engelhardt, editor beyond compare, made me believe that I could write a book. Michael Powell had a smart idea for every dead end. Mark Danner offered his support by e-mail. Michael Pollan sat me down and brainstormed with me as I conceived the book. Wayne Barrett was always ready to talk shop over pierogies. Thanks to Steve Coll for allowing me to absorb his breakneck brilliance as he wrote his own book, and for believing in me. All of these people elevated my aspirations and it's hard to imagine this process without them.

Many people who have dedicated their careers to topics I address in this book were kind enough to share their ideas. With some, I had extended and ongoing conversations: José O. Solá, Ismael García-Colón, John J. McCusker, Joshua B. Freeman, Thomas C. Pinney, John Waldman, Kenneth T. Jackson, Mike Wallace, Edwin G. Burrows, Suzanne Wasserman, Roger Horowitz, Jeff Pettis, Kevin Matteson, Dennis Maika, Charlie Gehring, Teresita Levy, Peter Rose, John T. Edge, Jane P. Cleaver, Robert Maass, Norman Brouwer, Charlie Bagli, Jane Weissman, Joe Flood, Caledonia Jones, Basil Seggos, John Calcagno, James Ortenzio.

Good people I met in the *Washington Post* newsroom helped

me along: Tom Wilkinson, Gabe Escobar, David Hoffman, Phil Bennett, Sewell Chan, Anthony Shadid, Karl Vick, Julie Tate, Ann Gerhart, David Finkel, Robin Givhan, Keith Richburg, Peter Goodman, David Segal, Tiffany Harness, Lynn Medford, Dale Russakoff, Helayne Seidman, Barbara Vobejda, Ernesto Londoño, Josh Partlow. Same thing at the *New York Times*: Jim Dwyer, Tony DePalma, Clyde Haberman, Ethan Bronner, Jenny 8. Lee, Wendell Jamison, Greg Winter, Christine Hauser. Thanks too to June Thomas.

Librarians are the hidden force behind historical nonfiction. Jay Barksdale set me up with a work space in the Allen Room of the New York Public Library. Hannah Miryam Belinfante at the NYPL went out of her way to help, as did Eric Robinson and Debra Bach at the New-York Historical Society, and Louisa Watrous at the Mystic Seaport Museum.

The skilled David Kaplowitz flew in from London for a whirlwind four-borough tour to make a beautiful video.

Friends have offered support and love without which this long project would not have been possible, and have been patient while I disappeared from them to write: Helena Wright, James Baldwin, Galit Seliktar and On and Tamuz Barak, Megan, Ty and Zora Citerman, Poppy Burke, Katya Pischalnikova, Rania Jawad, Irene Shen, David Kaplowitz, Nadir Abdessemed, Rebecca Miller, Jean-Louis Racine, Emilie Cassou, Vlasta Vranjes, Filipe Ribeiro, Marwan Kanafani, Kaoru Watanabe, Mohamad Bazzi, Annia Ciezadlo, Ana Campoy, Ruxandra Guidi, Michelle Hester, Emma Blijdenstein, Matthew Price, Kim Ghattas, Griff Witte, Yam Greenstein, Klancy Miller, and Tomoeh Murakami Tse (who also adorned me with her handmade jewelry).

Thanks to my inspiring family: Paula, Lee, Brian, Rachel, and

Allison David; Eric, Ava, and Oren David and Yen Tov; Ilana David, Jean Vecina, and Noa David-Vecina; Sheila Mudrick, Stephanie Myers and Gillian Batt, and Natasha Myers and Dorion Sagan; Tallulah and Berenicci Hershorn; and the rest of the clan, whose support has sustained me. Thanks too to Debby Kaplan.

And most especially, thanks to my perceptive, brave, wickedly funny, amazing sister, Leslie Shulman, and my generous and grounded mother, Barbara Shulman, who have shown me what to strive for.

My father, Arthur Shulman, loved books, food, history, and cities. I wish he had lived to see this book, and so much else.

Thanks to the Callerys, the Blakemores, the Owens, David and Wendy Kemp, Carol and Art Gray, and Celine Cooper and family; thanks to Kitty Francis, Rochelle Smith, and the very special Linda Wolburgh. Thanks to Karen and Carolina Rivera.

Thanks to Jack Morrison, Cora and Joe Morrison, and Ida and Mac Morrison, for choosing to be my family.

Thanks to Jack Agüeros, Marie-Hélène and Alan Pratley, and to Natalia Agüeros-Macario and Cris Macario, to Lee Scheingold, Grace McCabe, and Glenda Rosenthal, for welcoming me into their family.

Finally, thanks to Marcel Agüeros for accompanying me to pig roasts in the Bronx and beer parties in Brooklyn, for dissecting many drafts of the book with surgical precision, for making me laugh and for keeping me steady and for otherwise standing by me during years of hard work.

NOTES

A complete list of sources is available at www.robinshulman.com.

A small number of books and documents broadly shaped my understanding of the issues, the foods, and the places I wrote about. The exhaustive WPA accounts of New York City's food supply, *Feeding the City*, available at the Municipal Archives, provide a snapshot of an entire food system in the 1930s and early '40s. Edwin G. Burrows and Mike Wallace, in their sweeping narrative account of New York City, *Gotham: A History of New York City to 1898*—1,236 pages long and never boring!—helped place many of the issues in context. Jeff Kisseloff in his incredible oral history of Manhattan, *You Must Remember This*, tells personal stories in the voices of the people who lived them. Luc Sante in *Low Life: Lures and Snares of Old New York* showed me how to write about a hidden city. Jane Ziegelman in her fascinating and intimate history of the food culture of a single building, *97 Orchard*, showed impacts of food on tenement life. Hasia Diner in *Hungering for America* and Donna Gabaccia in *We Are What We Eat* provided scholarly accounts of immigrant food histories. I am indebted to all of these works.

1. HONEY

This chapter was based largely on interviews, contemporary and historical newspaper accounts, and scientific papers on bees and the environment.

25 *"Like human beings":* Neil Ulman, "Hobbyists Say Bees Are More Fun Than A Barrel of Monkeys," *Wall Street Journal*, January 23, 1967.

37 *"see it taken from the combs":* "Keeping Bees in Chicago," *New-York Tribune*, October 28, 1900.

37 *The manager of a beekeeping supply store:* Meyer Berger, "Secretary of 5th Ave. Association Leaves at 70 After 35 Years and Stacks of Memories," *New York Times*, June 1, 1956; Meyer Berger, "Beekeeping Is a

Dwindling Hobby in the City, but Fanciers Still Abound in Suburbs,"
New York Times, May 28, 1956.

46   *Once, a tropical storm ripped:* Emily S. Rueb, "In Rescue of Beehive Exposed by High Winds, Honey and Rancor," *New York Times,* August 31, 2011.

2. VEGETABLES

Interviews and historical newspaper accounts of gardening shaped this chapter. Laura Lawson's wonderful and well-researched book *City Bountiful* gave a great overview of the urban gardening movement in history. Access to the files of GreenThumb, New York City's community garden program, helped tell the city's more recent urban community gardening story. *Of Cabbages and Kings County,* by Marc Linder and Lawrence S. Zacharias, describes the evolution and decline of Brooklyn farming. Gilbert Osofsky's *Harlem: The Making of a Ghetto* is an amazing book, which every other book on Harlem seems to cite or repeat. Joe Flood, in *The Fires,* tells the story of why and how the city burned in the 1970s, which is the prequel to how the city came to grow vegetables on vacant lots.

58   *"The finest farmlands in America":* Daniel M. Tredwell, quoted in Marc Linder & Lawrence S. Zacharias, Of Cabbages and Kings Country (Iowa City: University of Iowa Press, 1999), 1.

59   *"So far as possible":* M. B. Levick, "In the Hidden Gardens of Manhattan," *New York Times,* April 19, 1925.

61   *Lenape Native Americans cultivated:* Anne Mendelson, "The Lenapes: In Search of Pre-European Foodways in the Greater New York Region," in *Gastropolis: Food and New York City,* ed. Annie Hauck-Lawson and Jonathan Deutsch (New York: Columbia University Press, 2009), 15–33; Gerard T. Koeppel, *Water for Gotham: A History* (Princeton: Princeton University Press, 2000), 8–9.

66   *"Dear Charlie":* Letter from Booker T. Washington to Charles W. Anderson, January 26, 1907, Washington Papers, Library of Congress, Box 35. Quoted in Gilbert Osofsky, *Harlem: The Making of a Ghetto, Negro New York, 1890–1930* (New York: Harper & Row, 1963).

66   *One Grady C. Houston:* Charlayne Hunter, "An Entrepreneur's Trucks Bring Southern Soul Food to Harlem," *New York Times,* December 20, 1971.

66   *Pig Foot Mary, née Lillian Harris:* Osofsky, *Harlem: The Making of a Ghetto: Negro New York, 1890–1930* (New York: Harper & Row, 1963).

67   *A woman named Nora Mair:* Jeff Kisseloff, *You Must Remember This: An Oral History of Manhattan from the 1890s to World War II* (San Diego: Harcourt, Brace Jovanovich, 1989), 328.

67   *"snare a carrot":* Mildred Adams, "City Gardens in a Setting of Stone," *New York Times,* August 28, 1927.

68   *suitcases filled with fresh peaches:* Isabel Wilkerson, *The Warmth of Other Suns: The Epic Story of America's Great Migration* (New York: Random House, 2010), 296.

68   *"Music too tight.":* Jervis Anderson, *This Was Harlem, 1900–1950* (New York: Farrar, Straus, Giroux, 1981), 152.

68   *"There'll be plenty of pig feet":* Frank Byrd, "Rent Parties," in *A Renaissance in Harlem: Lost Essays of the WPA,* by Ralph Ellison, Dorothy West, and Other Voices of a Generation, ed. Lionel C. Bascom (New York: Amistad, 1999).

68   *Thelonious Monk wore:* John T. Edge, *Southern Belly: The Ultimate Food Lover's Companion to the South* (Athens, GA: Hill Street Press, 2002), 19.

68   *Uptown manufacturing jobs were evaporating:* Jonathan Gill, *Harlem: The Four Hundred Year History from Dutch Village to Capital of Black America* (New York: Grove Press, 2011), 409.

68   *about 14 percent of Harlem residents:* Eric C. Schneider, *Smack: Heroin and the American City* (Philadelphia: University of Pennsylvania Press, 2008), 121–22.

69   *more than half of Harlem's economy hinged:* Fred J. Cook, "The Black Mafia Moves into the Numbers Racket," *New York Times,* April 4, 1971.

72   *"I hope":* "Tanner's Column," *New York Amsterdam News,* July 1, 1967.

73   *FDNY veterans still call:* Most of these incredible anecdotes about fires in the 1970s are from Joe Flood, *The Fires: How a Computer Formula, Big Ideas, and the Best of Intentions Burned Down New York City—and Determined the Future of Cities* (New York: Riverhead, 2010).

73   *From 1970 to 1980:* Ibid.

73   *"Something happened":* Leslie Maitland, "Air of Uncertainty Dogs Coney Island," *New York Times,* November 3, 1975.

73   *"Stretches of empty blocks":* Roger Starr, "Making New York Smaller," *New York Times Magazine,* November 14, 1976.

78   *"Parts of New York City":* "Crowded Streets and Empty Lots," *New York Times,* September 1, 1983.

78   *Booker T. Washington described the farm:* Osofsky, *Harlem: The Making of a Ghetto: Negro New York, 1890–1930* (New York: Harper & Row, 1963), 44.

78   *Eldridge Cleaver noted:* Eldridge Cleaver, "The Land Question and Black Liberation," in *Confrontation vs. Compromise: 1945 to the Present: African American Political Thought,* vol. 2, ed. Marcus Pohlmann (New York: Routledge, 2002).

80   *"This is a step to improve":* Murray Schumach, "1,000 'Farms' Planned on Lots in New York," *New York Times,* April 26, 1977.

80   *His Cornell University Cooperative Extension Program:* "Harvest Time in City Lots Where Rubble Grew," *New York Times,* September 6, 1979.

81   *Ameroso soon found that keeping the pH:* Tom Fox, Ian Koeppel, and
      Susan Kellam, *Struggle for Space: The Greening of New York City 1970–
      1984* (New York: Neighborhood Open Space Coalition, 1985), 19.

81   *"The fact of the matter is":* "Talk of the Town: Green," *The New Yorker,*
      June 26, 1978, 21–22.

82   *"Sign right by the X":* Ibid. 23

84   *sprouted as many as 1,000 gardens:* Estimates vary wildly. This conforms
      to estimates given by Ken Davies and John Ameroso in separate inter-
      views.

85   *"Mr. Governor, if you have this taken away":* "Whites Planning to Take
      Over Numbers in Harlem," *New York Amsterdam News,* April 16, 1977.

86   *"This is a free market economy":* Robert Polner, "Rudy: Sales Will Go
      On," *Newsday,* January 12, 1999.

87   *"No gardens, no peas!":* Monica Polanco, " 'No Gardens, No Peas,' Cry
      Protesters in Park," *New York Daily News,* April 11, 1999.

88   *Several NYU researchers proved:* Ioan Voicu and Vicki Been, "The Effect
      of Community Gardens on Neighboring Property Values," *Real Estate
      Economics* 36 (2008): 241–83.

3. MEAT

Roger Horowitz's informative and well-written book *Putting Meat on the
American Table* was singularly helpful, and his other articles were great too.
Two books by nineteenth-century butcher Thomas De Voe, *The Market Book*
and *The Market Assistant,* both available online, were time capsules that
helped me to understand the world of a butcher in a bow tie and top hat. De
Voe's *Abattoirs* gave a sweeping history of slaughterhouses. Various reports
of the Greenwich Village Society for Historic Preservation were helpful to
cobble together a history of the Fourteenth Street meat market, as was the
1962 study of the Fourteenth Street Market by the USDA, and interviews
with lawyers, landlords, and meatpackers who remember it. Joshua B. Freeman's *Working-Class New York* gives a sense of the manufacturing city that
is no more. Butcher Tom Mylan's various writings, on blogs and in myriad
publications, helped tell his personal story.

94   *a "rock star butcher":* Kim Severson, "Young Idols With Cleavers Rule
      the Stage," *New York Times,* July 7, 2009.

98   *"scattered over many populous districts":* Quoted in Roger Horowitz, *Put-
      ting Meat on the American Table: Taste, Technology, Transformation* (Bal-
      timore: Johns Hopkins University Press, 2006), 29.

98   *"offensive odors":* Horowitz, Ibid., 25.

98   *one reporter unrolled a map:* "Plague Spots in the City," *New-York Tri-
      bune,* December 26, 1880.

99   *"The meat was exceedingly tender":* Jasper Danckaerts, *Journal of Jasper
      Danckaerts, 1679–1680,* 51.

99   *On the journey across the ocean:* Peter G. Rose, trans. and ed., *The Sensible Cook: Dutch Foodways in the Old and the New World* (Syracuse University Press, 1989). 24.

100   *"the heads of sheep":* Raymond A. Mohl, *Poverty in New York, 1783–1825* (Oxford University Press, 1971). Quoted in Donna R. Gabaccia, *We Are What We Eat: Ethnic Food and the Making of Americans* (Cambridge: Harvard University Press, 2000), 59.

103   *"To get a proper crust":* Myspace.com, Tom Mylan blog, www.myspace .com/tommylan/blog/201517708.

104   *"While I haven't made it":* Myspace.com, Tom Mylan blog "How to Cook an Expensive Steak," www.myspace.com/tommylan/blog.

104   *"Sorry I bled everywhere":* Rebecca Marx, "More Mylan Mayhem: Mylan Injured, but Still Able to Type," *Village Voice*, July 27, 2009. blogs.villagevoice.com/forkintheroad/2009/07/more_mylan_mayh .php.

104   *"a 6x8 box, outdoors":* the-meathook.tumblr.com/post/220333571/oh -helll-yesss-were-going-to-be-on-the-brian.

105   *"These are mostly masculine fantasies":* Bonnie Powell, "Having a Ball in Tunisia," *Meatpaper*, Issue 3, Spring 2009.

106   *Hog riots broke out in 1825:* This entire account from Edwin G. Burrows and Mike Wallace, *Gotham: A History of New York City to 1898* (New York: Oxford University Press, 1999), 477.

106   *Despite officials' best efforts:* Jane Ziegelman, *97 Orchard: An Edible History of Five Immigrant Families in One New York Tenement* (New York: HarperCollins Publishers, 2010), 113–14.

106   *"Our wives and daughters cannot walk abroad":* Cadwallader Colden, quoted in Burrows and Wallace, *Gotham: A History of New York City to 1898* (New York: Oxford University Press, 1999), 477. The description of pigs in this paragraph is also from *Gotham*.

106   *"Here is a solitary swine":* Charles Dickens, "American Notes for General Circulation," in *Writing New York: A Literary Anthology*, ed. Philip Lopate (New York: Library of America, 2008), 58.

107   *"putrefy on the dealer's hands":* Robert Milham Hartley, *An Historical, Scientific, and Practical Essay on Milk: As an Article of Human Sustenance; with a Consideration of the Effects Consequent upon the Present Unnatural Methods of Producing It for the Supply of Large Cities* (Jonathan Leavitt, 1842), 147.

108   *They had marched in civic parades:* Roger Horowitz, "The Politics of Meat Shopping in Antebellum New York City," in Paula Young Lee, ed., *Meat, Modernity and the Rise of the Slaughterhouse* (Durham: University of New Hampshire Press, 2008).

109   *the 320,500 cattle, 1.2 million hogs:* "The Board of Health: An Important Meeting Yesterday," *New York Times*, September 3, 1874.

109 *"The lowing and moaning of the cattle":* Albert H. Buck, ed., *A Treatise of Hygiene and Health, vol. 2* (New York: William Wood & Co., 1876), 404.

109 *"Slaughtering establishments are just as essential":* "As to Slaughter-houses," *New York Times,* April 2, 1899.

110 *"Please tune in":* The Meat Hook blog, October 15, 2009. the-meathook .tumblr.com/post/213737668/at-10-30-at-night-my-phone-rings-its -harry (accessed September 14, 2011).

111 *"I spend every waking moment":* getcurrency.com/dining-travel/tom -mylan-butcher-and-co-owner-the-meat-hook-brooklyn. Web site no longer available.

112 *"era of cheap beef":* Quoted in Horowitz, *Putting Meat on the American Table,* (Baltimore: Johns Hopkins University Press, 2006), 29.

112 *"to give the impression":* Hasia R. Diner, *Hungering for America: Italian, Irish, and Jewish Foodways in the Age of Migration* (Cambridge: Harvard University Press, 2003), 164.

112 *The Centennial Brewery converted:* Gansevoort Market Historic District Designation Report, New York City Landmarks Preservation Commission, 2003, 15. www.thehighline.org/about/neighborhood-info.

113 *As late as 1929, a full third:* Donna R. Gabaccia, *We Are What We Eat: Ethnic Food and the Making of Americans* (Cambridge: Harvard University Press, 2000), 70.

118 *"I definitely look at everyone":* Tom Mylan, "Sex Advice from Butchers," September 10, 2009, Nerve.com. www.nerve.com/advice/sex-advice -from/sex-advice-from-butchers?page=2.

118 *in 1932, a second tunnel was constructed:* "Appendix K: Archaeological Resources, Hudson Yards FGEIS," www.nyc.gov/.../hyards/app_k _archaeological_text_fgeis_final.pdf.

119 *workers finally built:* For a detailed account of events in this paragraph, see Clarence Dean, "West Side Ending Cattle Run Epoch," *New York Times,* November 13, 1955.

120 *"It's Saturday night":* Sarah DiGregorio, "Chatting with Tom Mylan: Date-Night Butchery, the Word 'Hipster,' and Why Butchering Is Not as Cool As You Think It Is," *Village Voice,* November 16, 2009. blogs.villagevoice.com/forkintheroad/2009/11/chatting_with_t.php.

125 *"take the skill out of every step":* A. D. Anderson, *Newsweek,* 1965. Quoted in Betty Fussell, *Raising Steaks: The Life and Times of American Beef* (Orlando: Harcourt Books, 2008), 182.

125 *The small, aging multilevel shops . . . were struggling:* "Meat Plants Here Face U.S. Upgrading," *New York Times,* March 4, 1968.

125 *The market was so congested:* Robert L. Holland and Donald A. Bowers, "The Fourteenth Street Wholesale Market for Meat and Poultry in New York City," *Marketing Research Report,* No. 556, U.S. Department

of Agriculture, Transportation and Facilities Research Division. November 1962.

126   *the city had acquired:* "Bronx Getting Co-Op Meat Market," *New York Times,* April 30, 1973.

126   *"the stench of slaughterhouses":* Joe Flood, *The Fires: How a Computer Formula, Big Ideas, and the Best of Intentions Burned Down New York City* (New York: Riverhead, 2010), 131.

127   *New York in 1947:* Joshua B. Freeman, *Working-Class New York: Life and Labor Since World War II* (New York: New Press, 2000), 8.

127   *a queerness about the city's small semi-industrial concerns:* Jan Morris, *Manhattan '45,* (New York: Oxofrd University Press, 1987), 230.

127   *"The sidewalks run with rivulets":* Shaila K. Dewan, "After Blood and Guts, Seeking Landmark Glory," *New York Times,* June 4, 2001.

135   *"a collective cackle":* Joseph Berger, "A Slaughterhouse in Brooklyn, and Misery Next Door," *New York Times,* June 10, 2011.

136   *"for a soothing experience":* Lisa Colangelo, "Queens Farm Museum Stops Selling Pork at Farmers Markets, Restaurants," *New York Daily News,* June 22, 2011.

137   *"Everything from feed to breed":* Tom Mylan, "Hi, My Name is Tom and I'm a Farmaholic," *Gilt Taste,* September 7, 2011, http://www.gilttaste.com/stories/1804-hi-my-name-is-tom-and-i-m-a-farmoholic.

4. SUGAR

Documents from the history of the Domino sugar plant in Williamsburg were available at the New York Historical Society and the Brooklyn Historical Society. Harry W. Havemeyer, the last of his family to be apprenticed in the sugar business, has painstakingly documented his family story in books available at the New York Historical Society (and sometimes on Amazon). Noel Deerr's classic two-volume book *The History of Sugar* contained fascinating arcana. The collected works of Sidney Mintz—books, articles, and chapters in books—were helpful for an overview of sugar history, and particularly for vivid descriptions of life among Puerto Rican sugar workers. The book *Slavery in New York,* edited by Ira Berlin and Leslie M. Harris, was very helpful, as was the book *Nueva York, 1613–1945,* which accompanied an exhibit at El Museo del Barrio. The New Netherland Project has translated and posted online incredible records from the Dutch West India Company, which offered direct access to their concerns. The accounts of eighteenth-century sugar-house owners and *The Weekly Post-Boy* and *New-York Gazette,* two of the city's earliest newspapers, at the New York Historical Society, also provided a window onto a previous version of the city. The dissertation of José O. Solá, on the sugar planters near Caguas, Puerto Rico, was helpful in understanding Jorge Torres's story. On Caribbean sugar and migration, I consulted the works of César J. Ayala, including his book *American Sugar Kingdom* and his article "The Decline of the Plantation Economy and the

Puerto Rican Migration of the 1950s," and other articles. On Puerto Ricans in New York, Virginia Sánchez Korrol's *From Colonia to Community* gave a helpful overview, and I really enjoyed Ruth Glasser's great book *My Music Is My Flag.*

140   *Planters and mill owners:* Noel Deerr, *The History of Sugar: Volume One* (London: Chapman and Hall, Ltd., 1949), 105.

142   *"Mr. Torres . . . has the overwhelming support":* Letter from Ivine Galarza, District Manager, Bronx Community Planning Board #6, to Chris Meyers, Assistant Director, NYC Operation GreenThumb, December 11, 1995.

144   *"a reed" that "brings forth honey":* Sidney W. Mintz, *Sweetness and Power* (New York: Penguin, 1986), 20.

144   *"The sugar canes, the few that were":* Christopher Columbus, Giuliano Dati, Diego Alvarez Chanca, Diego Méndez, "Memorial of the Results of the Second Voyage of the Admiral, Christopher Columbus, to the Indies, drawn up by him for their Highnesses King Ferdinand and Queen Isabella; and addressed to Antonio de Torres, from the City of Isabella, the 30th of January, 1494," in *Select Letters of Christopher Columbus, with Other Original Documents, Relating to His Four Voyages to the New World,* vol. 43.

145   *Beginning in the 1500s, Europeans imported:* Sidney W. Mintz, "Pleasure, Profit and Satiation," in *Seeds of Change,* eds. Herman J. Viola and Carolyn Margolis (Washington, D.C.: Smithsonian Institution Press, 1991), 121.

145   *"A hatchet was kept in readiness":* David Brion Davis, *Inhuman Bondage: The Rise and Fall of Slavery in the New World* (New York: Oxford University Press, 2006), 108.

146   *"clever and strong":* Ira Berlin and Leslie M. Harris, "Introduction," in *Slavery in New York,* eds. Ira Berlin and Leslie M. Harris (New York: New Press, in conjunction with the New-York Historical Society, 2005), 51. Also Edward J. Sullivan, ed. *Nueva York, 1613–1945* (New York: New-York Historical Society, in association with Scala Publishers, 2010).

146   *when the English took Manhattan: Volume 17–Curaçao Papers 1640–1665,* (New Netherland) www.nnp.org/nnrc/Documents/curacao/index.html#/1/.

146   *The quantity of these articles:* Anne Grant, *Memoirs of An American Lady,* 113. Quoted in Peter G. Rose, trans. and ed., *The Sensible Cook: Dutch Foodways in the Old and the New World* (Syracuse University Press, 1989), 28.

146   *"a noise of trumpets":* Russell Shorto, *The Island at the Center of the World: The Epic Story of Dutch Manhattan and the Forgotten Colony That Shaped America* (New York: Vintage Books, 2005), 64.

146 *little bag of sugar could buy:* "Account left by Mr. Josua and Mordakay Enriques, the first of the month of January 1656." New Netherland Project, the New Netherland Institute, *Resolution Book of Curaçao,* 1643 and 1644, no. 58, MM, article 37. www.nnp.org/nnrc/Documents/curacao/index.html#/1/.

146 *Boil black cherries in wine:* Peter G. Rose, trans. and ed., *The Sensible Cook: Dutch Foodways in the Old and the New World* (Syracuse University Press, 1989), 103.

147 *Dutch West India Company officials:* "Inventory of the Caribbean Muscovado Sugar Sent Aboard the Galiot *Nieuw Amstel . . .*" New Netherland Project, article 48a, the New Netherland Institute, www.nnp.org/nnrc/Documents/curacao/index.html#/1/.

147 *the men on board subsisted mainly:* Robert C. Ritchie, *Captain Kidd and the War Against the Pirates* (Cambridge: Harvard University Press, 1986), 29.

147 *"such an excessive Rain":* Edward Ward, *A Trip to Jamaica: With a True Character of the People and Island* (London, 1698). Quoted in Thomas W. Krise, ed., *Caribbeana: An Anthology of English Literature of the West Indies, 1657–1777* (Chicago: University of Chicago Press, 1999), 85.

147 *"notwithstanding her husband's presence":* Ibid., 62.

147 *"what he was doing":* Ibid., 83–84.

147 *New York increased molasses imports:* John James McCusker, Jr., "The Rum Trade and the Balance of Payments of the Thirteen Continental Colonies, 1650–1775," (PhD dissertation, University of Pittsburgh, 1970), 444.

148 *You could also drink a calibogus:* List of drinks from Wayne Curtis, *And a Bottle of Rum: A History of the New World in Ten Cocktails* (New York: Broadway Books), 2007.

148 *alcohol consumption for white men:* John James McCusker, Jr., "The Rum Trade and the Balance of Payments of the Thirteen Continental Colonies, 1650–1775," (PhD dissertation, University of Pittsburgh, 1970), 468.

148 *"Dam'd fine girl":* Christine Stansell, *City of Women: Sex and Class in New York, 1789–1860* (Urbana: University of Illinois Press, 1987), 27.

149 *Caribbean seasonal rhythms:* This whole description of the New York waterfront is from Burrows and Wallace, *Gotham: A History of New York City to 1898* (New York: Oxford University Press, 1999), 122-123.

149 *only one sugarhouse in that early period:* Mary Louise Booth, *History of the City of New York: From Its Earliest Settlement to the Present Time* (New York: W. R. G. Clark and Meeker, 1859).

149 *"PUBLICK NOTICE":* New-York Gazette, August 17, 1730.

150 *"We are of Opinion Good Bright Muscovado":* "Letter from John and Henry Cruger to Jeremiah Piniston, New York, August 19, 1766," *John*

> *and Henry Cruger: Letter Book June 18, 1766–August 11, 1787,* New-York
> Historical Society.

150 *Newsmen at the* New-York Gazette: *New-York Gazette,* 1726, 1750.

151 *"all kinds of sweet meats, sugar work":* A 1796 advertisement in Rita
Susswein Gottesman, ed., *The Arts and Crafts of New York, 1800–1804:
Advertisements and News Items from New York City Newspapers* (New
York: New-York Historical Society, 1965), 310. Quoted in Cindy R.
Lobel, "Consuming Classes: Changing Food Consumption Patterns
in New York City, 1780–1860," (PhD dissertation, City University of
New York, 2003), 76.

151 *The* Witte Paert *sailed:* Leslie M. Harris, *In the Shadow of Slavery: African Americans in New York City, 1626–1863* (Chicago: University of
Chicago Press, 2003), 15.

151 *Fully a fifth of the city's people:* Ibid., 49.

152 *"as much good sugar and rum":* James A. Rawley with Stephen D. Beh-
rendt, *The Transatlantic Slave Trade: A History,* revised edition (Lincoln:
University of Nebraska Press, 2005), 338.

152 *suggested the maple tree as a "boundless" source: Daily Advertiser,* March 8,
1790. Quoted in David N. Gellman, *Emancipating New York: The Politics of Slavery and Freedom, 1777–1827* (Baton Rouge: Louisiana State
University Press, 2006), 92.

152 *"the lash of cruelty on our fellow creatures":* Ibid., 93.

154 *Fine hairs on the cane stalk:* Edward A. Suchman and Raul A. Muñoz,
"Accident Occurrence and Control Among Sugar-Cane Workers,"
Journal of Occupational Medicine 9 (1967): 407.

157 *"It is really now one of the most rucketing":* Eric Homberger, *The Historical
Atlas of New York City: A Visual Celebration of Nearly 400 Years of New
York City's History* (New York: Henry Holt, 1994), 70.

157 *"I have been here only 3 days":* Letter from Frederick Havemeyer to his
wife, London, June 8, 1839. Reproduced in Henry O. Havemeyer, *Bio-
graphical Record of the Havemeyer Family, 1600–1943, more particularly
the descendants of Frederick Christian Havemeyer (1774–1841), and their
sugar refining interests* (New York: privately printed for Henry Osborne
Havemeyer, 1944).

158 *"confectionary and gew-gaws":* Philip Hone, Diary, January 26, 1838.
Quoted in Phillip Lopate, ed., *Writing New York: A Literary Anthology*
(New York: The Library of America), 1998.

158 *Per capita consumption of sugar leapt:* Cindy R. Lobel, "Consuming
Classes: Changing Food Consumption Patterns in New York City,
1780–1860," (PhD dissertation, City University of New York, 2003), 78.

159 *"Bones is hard business now":* "Walks Among the New York Poor: The
Rag and Bone Pickers," *New York Times,* January 22, 1853.

159　*you could get burned and bruised:* "Incidents and Accidents," *New York Daily Times,* January 3, 1853; "Williamsburgh," *New York Times,* August 10, 1865; "A Laborer's Horrible Death; Caught in an Elevator Shaft and Frightfully Crushed," *Brooklyn Eagle,* November 17, 1884; "The Hottest Place in Town; If You Don't Like the Weather of the Last Few Days, Try a Sugar Refinery," *New-York Tribune,* August 7, 1896.

159　*You could stab yourself:* "Scalded by Boiling Sugar," *Brooklyn Eagle,* January 18, 1899; "Foot Crushed," *Brooklyn Eagle,* April 26, 1875; "Bags of Sugar Fell on Him; Frederick Senft Probably Fatally Hurt at the Havemeyer Refinery," *Brooklyn Eagle,* December 31, 1900.

159　*the intense, 110-degree heat:* "Incidents and Accidents"; "Sugar Workers Stricken," *New-York Tribune,* July 30, 1892.

159　*burn an unlucky worker "to a crisp":* "A Victim Found and Identified," *New York Times,* June 18, 1887.

160　*"I cannot grant your request, boys":* "Havemeyers and Elder Lose Their Firemen and Boilermen," *New York Times,* June 15, 1893.

160　*"Get it down as a fact":* Draft manuscript of Harry W. Havemeyer, *Henry O. Havemeyer: The Most Independent Mind* (New York: privately printed, 2011), 44.

161　*"He considered him a brute":* John E. Parsons, the trust's lawyer, in testimony to the Hardwick Committee. Quoted in Richard Zerbe, "The American Sugar Refinery Company, 1887–1914: The Story of a Monopoly," *Journal of Law and Economics* 12, no. 2 (October 1969).

161　*called their job "hell":* "Death in the Refineries: How the Slaves of the Sugar Trust Work, Suffer and Die," *New York Tribune,* July 22, 1894.

161　*"a conscienceless octopus":* "Mr. Havemeyer Not Guilty," *New York Times,* May 28, 1897.

161　*"I think it is fair to get out":* Cesar J. Ayala, *American Sugar Kingdom* (Chapel Hill, NC: University of North Carolina Press, 1999), 31.

161　*"with all the enthusiasm of a schoolboy":* "H. O. Havemeyer Dies at L.I. Home," *New York Times,* December 5, 1907.

162　*"So far as the coffee end of the war is concerned":* "End of Sugar War Not Near; President Havemeyer Aware of No Arrangement Looking to That End; Few Developments To-day," *Brooklyn Eagle,* April 3, 1900.

162　*"Do you see any possible way":* "War of the Sugar Kings," *Washington Post,* March 30, 1900.

162　*a near total monopoly that controlled 98 percent:* Jack Simpson Mullins, "The Sugar Trust: Henry O. Havemeyer and the American Sugar Refining Company" (PhD dissertation, University of South Carolina, 1964), 157; Harry W. Havemeyer, *Merchants of Williamsburgh: Frederick C. Havemeyer, Jr., William Dick, John Mollenhauer, Henry O. Havemeyer* (New York: privately printed, 1989).

162   *U.S. Navy gunships quietly floated:* Julian Go, *American Empire and the Politics of Meaning: Elite Political Cultures in the Philippines and Puerto Rico During U.S. Colonialism* (Durham: Duke University Press, 2008).

162   *"Every man, woman, and child":* "Trade of Porto Rico," speech on the bill H.R. 8245, Hon. Jacob Ruppert, Jr., in the House of Representatives, Wednesday, April 11, 1900, Washington, D.C.

163   *Puerto Rico's annual production of sugar jumped tenfold:* José Solá, "'The Funnel System in Which His Is the Little End': The Technological Transformation of the Sugar Industry and American Protectionism in the Emergence of the Colonos in Caguas, Puerto Rico, 1898–1928" (PhD dissertation, University of Connecticut, 2004), 89.

163   *that single crop provided:* Nydia R. Suarez, "The Rise and Decline of Puerto Rico's Sugar Economy," in *Sugar and Sweetener,* S&O/SSS-224/December 1998. Economic Research Service/USDA, 22.

163   *little Puerto Rico became the second largest:* Luis A. Figueroa, *Sugar, Slavery, and Freedom in Nineteenth-Century Puerto Rico* (Chapel Hill: University of North Carolina Press, 2005), 49.

164   *"These traders almost never see":* John Mitchell, "Price," Feeding the City, WPA, The Municipal Archives, New York.

164   *a group of men including Frederick Havemeyer:* Harold van B. Cleveland and Thomas F. Huertas, *Citibank, 1812–1970* (Cambridge: Harvard University Press, 1985), 42.

164   *They raised funds to build their own, independent* central: Solá, "The Funnel System."

165   *"four cents more than the food expense":* Cesar J. Ayala, *American Sugar Kingdom* (Chapel Hill, NC: University of North Carolina Press, 1999), 182.

166   *Political agitators against Spain established:* Virginia E. Sánchez Korrol, *From Colonia to Community: The History of Puerto Ricans in New York City* (Berkeley: University of California Press, 1983), 13.

166   *They bought winter coats on credit:* The first stop for many migrants, especially those who came in winter, was Old Man Markofsky at 106th and Second Avenue, a "clothier on the long, long installment plan," wrote one of his customers. *Gráfico,* March 27, 1927, p. 2. Quoted in Korrol, Ibid., 64.

166   *Salaries in Puerto Rico stayed roughly level:* Clarence Senior and Donald O. Watkins, "Toward a Balance Sheet of Puerto Rican Migration," United States-Puerto Rican Status Commission Report, 1966, Washington, D.C., p. 749. Quoted in Korrol, Ibid., 38.

166   *"Job and Home in New York":* Alfredo López, *Doña Licha's Island: Modern Colonialism in Puerto Rico,* (Boston: South End Press, Boston: 1987), 96.

167   *Thrift Flight from San Juan to Idlewild cost only $52.50:* Great descriptions

of the journey are found in Dan Wakefield, *Island in the City: The World of Spanish Harlem* (New York: Arno Press, 1975), 29.

167   *by the 1950s, 43,000 people:* César Ayala, "The Decline of the Plantation Economy and the Puerto Rican Migration of the 1950s," *Latino Studies Journal* 7, no. 1 (Winter 1996), 63.

167   *Sugar production on the island peaked:* Suarez, "The Rise and Decline of Puerto Rico's Sugar Economy," in *Sugar and Sweetener,* S&O/SSS-224/December 1998. Economic Research Service/USDA, 24.

167   *the sugar industry laid off 42,000 Puerto Rican workers:* Ayala, "The Decline of the Plantation Economy," *Latino Studies Journal* 7, no. 1 (Winter 1996), 80.

171   *When the Fanjuls announced three years later:* Winifred Curran, "Gentrification and the Nature of Work: Exploring the Links in Williamsburg, Brooklyn," Environment and Planning A 36 (2004): 1254.

171   *"relics from a bygone era":* Ibid.

171   *"Out of huge barrels loom red sugar cane":* John Walker Harrington,"Food That Tempts Harlem's Palate," *New York Times,* July 15, 1928.

172   like sugarcane in February: Sayings contributed by Jorge Torres in New York, Hector Luis Freire in Cidra, Puerto Rico. Others from Cristino Gallo, *Language of the Puerto Rican Street: A Slang Dictionary,* (Book Service of Puerto Rico, 1980).

173   *"I can see from here/the cane fields":* Cesar J. Ayala, *American Sugar Kingdom* (Chapel Hill, NC: Unversity of North Carolina Press, 1999), 249.

5. BEER

The collections and files of K. Jacob Ruppert were incredibly helpful in writing this chapter, as were extensive newspaper and magazine accounts. Older books on the history of brewing include Stanley Baron's *Brewed in America* and Herman Schlüter's *The Brewing Industry and the Brewery Workers' Movement in America.* Dorothee Schneider's *Trade Unions and Community* vividly describes brewery structures and working conditions. Maureen Ogle's *Ambitious Brew* gave a more contemporary history of beer in America. For the history of Manhattan's early German neighborhood, I turned to *Little Germany,* by Stanley Nadel.

178   *Beer-loving Germans:* Stanley Nadel, *Little Germany: Ethnicity, Religion, and Class in New York City,* 1845-80 (Urbana and Chicago: University of Illinois Press,), 41.; For the number of breweries, see Bill Harris and Jorg Brockmann, *One Thousand New York Buildings* (Black Dog and Leventhal, 2002), 320. Also Fred Ferretti, "Where Have All the Breweries Gone?" *New York Times,* August 9, 1978.

181   *"[They] brew as good beer here":* Stanley Baron, *Brewed in America: A History of Beer and Ale in the United States* (Boston: Little, Brown, 1962).

181   *a quarter of all:* Hermann Schlüter, *The Brewing Industry and the*

Brewery Workers' Movement in America (Cincinnati: Press of S. Rosenthal & Co., 1910), 31; Burrows and Wallace, *Gotham: A History of New York City to 1898* (New York: Oxofrd University Press, 1999), 33.

182   *Later laws also limited times for brewing:* Dorothee Schneider, *Trade Unions and Community: The German Working Class in New York City, 1870–1900* (Urbana: University of Illinois Press, 1994).

183   *where he could drill seven hundred feet:* George Ehret, *Twenty-Five Years of Brewing with an Illustrated History of American Beer* (self-published, 1891), 48, 84.

184   *Milwaukee and St. Louis combined:* Maureen Ogle, *Ambitious Brew: The Story of American Beer* (Orlando: Harcourt, 2006), 55.

184   *"The little boy, who is just tall enough":* Georg Techla, *Drei Jahre in New York,* 100–101. Quoted in Stanley Nadel, *Little Germany* (Urbana and Chicago: University of Illinois Press, 1990), 105.

184   *"Sometimes he is presented life size":* Charles Dawson Shanley, "Signs and Show-Cases of New York," *Atlantic,* May 1870.

185   *"naked goddesses, grim knights, terrific monsters":* George C. Foster, *New York by Gas-Light* (Berkeley: University of California Press, 1990, reprint of 1856), 157.

185   *"We Germans do not mingle with Americans":* Burrows and Wallace, *Gotham: A History of New York City to 1898* (New York: Oxford University Press, 1999), 989

185   *A dining room mural portrayed:* "Decoration & Furniture; New Houses—Indoors and Out," *The Art Amateur: A Monthly Journal Devoted to Art in the Household,* March 1883, 4, 8.

185   MALZ UND HOPFEN/GIBT GUTE TROPFEN: "Two Highly Interesting Rooms; A 'Kneipstube' in the House of Jacob Ruppert and the Pompeiian Parlor of Nathan Strauss," *New York Herald Tribune,* December 6, 1903.

191   *"Wealth . . . is rushing in upon us like a freshet":* Lopate, *Writing New York* (New York: The Library of America), 191.

191   *"We brewery workers have already":* *New Yorker Volkszeitung,* February 18, 1881. Quoted in Dorothee Schneider, *Trade Unions and Community: The German Working Class in New York City, 1870–1900* (Urbana: University of Illinois Press, 1994), 136.

192   *When finally the workers tried to form unions:* Herman Schlüter, *The Brewing Industry and the Brewery Workers' Movement in America* (Cincinnati: Press of S. Rosenthal & Co., 1910), 156.

192   *"Show this apprentice no favors":* "Beer and Baseball," *The New Yorker,* September 24, 1932.

192   *"polluted harpies that, under the pretense":* Jervis Anderson, *This Was Harlem* (New York: Farrar, Straus, Giroux, 1981), 13.

192   *his father kept the brewery lawyer Congressman Ashbel Fitch happy:* Letters of Ashbel Fitch, 1890. Courtesy of K. Jacob Ruppert.

193   *New Yorkers disliked the dense flavor:* "The Million's Beverage," *New York Times,* May 20, 1877.

194   *"black pearls in oysters":* Burrows and Wallace, *Gotham* (New York: Oxford University Press, 1999), 1073.

194   *chop suey houses or hole-in-the-wall saloons:* Luc Sante, *Low Life: Lures and Snares of Old New York* (New York: Farrar, Straus, Giroux, 1991), 121.

194   *fellow members held a stag dinner at Sherry's:* M. H. Dunlop, *Gilded City: Scandal and Sensation in Turn of the Century New York* (New York: William Morrow, 2000), Chapter Five: "Girls."

194   *received her father's gift of a fully furnished house:* "Miss Ruppert Married; She Becomes the Wife of Herman Adolph Schalk—Other Weddings Yesterday," *New-York Tribune,* May 1, 1895.

194   *Amanda wore orange blossoms:* "Dinner, Opera, and Wedding Gowns," *New York Times,* January 19, 1902.

195   *"Chap 1.—How the Lover Robbed the Brewer":* "Bridegroom and Father to Fight for the Dead Bride," *New York Journal,* December 12, 1897.

195   *"running an automobile beyond the lawful speed limit":* "Two Congressmen Arrested," *New York Times,* March 26, 1902.

196   *"Adolphus Busch would drop into town":* Gerald Holland, "The Beer Barons of New York," *American Mercury* 23, no. 92 (1931): 402, 406.

199   *"aggressive step":* Damon Runyon, "They Call the Colonel 'Jake.'" King Feature Syndicate, 1924.

199   *the widow of Bible printer Daniel Fanshaw:* "The Will of Daniel Fanshaw Anti-Tobacco Legacy," *New York Times,* June 6, 1860; "The Late Daniel Fanshaw; Proceedings of the New-York Typographical Society," New York Times, March 1, 1860 interviews.

199   *Witness after witness testified:* "Is Lager-Bier Intoxicating?" *New York Times,* February 5, 1858.

199   *"If it takes a pail-full of bier":* Ibid.

200   *"the scum of the Old World":* Burrows and Wallace, *Gotham* (New York: Oxford University Press, 1999), 1164.

200   *Jacob Jr. developed the capacity to produce:* Gerald Holland, "The Beer Barons of New York," *American Mercury* 23, no. 92 (1931): 406.

200   *"You may walk the streets":* "For Excise Revision; Jacob Ruppert, Jr., Says New York Law Is Best, However," *New-York Tribune,* November 13, 1908.

200   *beer was safer than milk:* Gerald Holland, "The Beer Barons of New York," *American Mercury* 23, no. 92 (1931) 407.

200   *"aged in glass enameled tanks":* "Method of Brewing Beer," *New-York Tribune,* March 7, 1909.

201   *"I drank beer from little up":* Jeff Kisseloff, *You Must Remember This: An*

Oral History of Manhattan from the 1890s to World War II (San Diego: Harcourt, Brace Jovanovich, 1989), 101.

201 *"You couldn't walk the street":* Ibid., 118.

201 *government investigated Jacob Jr.'s closest relatives:* Letter from Chief to Leland Harrison, Office of the Counselor, State Department, November 2, 1917. Letter from Chief Agent 78448 to W. Offley, November 2, 1917.

201 *The State Department was concerned:* Letter from Chief Agent 78448 to W. Offley, November 2, 1917.

201 *her son George and his wife, Emma:* Notes from DOI files, February 18, 1918.

202 *"George Ruppert's wife met Count Von Bernsdorff":* Notes from DOI files, author and date unknown.

202 *"Enemy Propaganda Backed by Brewers":* "Enemy Propaganda Backed By Brewers," *New York Times*, November 21, 1918.

203 *In* Jacob Ruppert vs. Caffey: K. Jacob Ruppert, "In Re John Barleycorn: The Role of the NYCLA in the Repeal of Prohibition," *New York County Lawyer*, November 2005.

203 *The Supreme Court dismissed Jacob Jr.'s injunction:* "Ban on 2.75 Beers in Wartime Upheld by Supreme Court," *New York Times*, January 6, 1920.

203 *The answer was extensive: New York Telegram*, 1929. Quoted in Luc Sante, *Low Life: Lures and Snares of Old New York* (New York: Farrar, Straus, Giroux, 1991), 138.

204 *the Cotton Club in Harlem:* Jervis Anderson, *This Was Harlem, 1900–1950* (New York: Farrar, Straus, Giroux, 1981); Jim Haskins, *The Cotton Club* (New York: Random House, 1977), 29–30.

204 *"thundering up the cobbled pavement":* "Schultz Reigned on Discreet Lines," *New York Times*, October 25, 1935.

204 *an elaborate system to pipe its beer underground:* "Dry Raid on Garage Reveals 'Beer Line,'" *New York Times*, August 8, 1930.

204 *Gangsters waged beer wars with spectacular violence:* "Schultz Reigned on Discreet Lines," *New York Times*, October 25, 1935.

205 *They would stalk drivers and payroll men:* Ibid.

205 *"in a sporting spirit":* Jacob Ruppert, "The Ten-Million-Dollar Toy," *Saturday Evening Post*, March 28, 1931.

206 *the power to make immigrant children American:* Steven A. Riess, *Touching Base: Professional Baseball and American Culture in the Progressive Era* (Urbana: University of Illinois Press, 1983), 29.

206 *the Yankees . . . shouldering their bats like guns:* Glenn Stout, *Yankees Century: 100 Years of New York Yankees Baseball* (Boston: Houghton Mifflin Company, 2002), 71.

206 *"He shivers, turns up the collar":* Damon Runyon, "They Call the Colonel 'Jake.'" King Feature Syndicate, 1924.

211   *"They are not sure their salesmen can meet:* "Brewers Tell Fear of Gang Rivalry," *New York Times,* November 24, 1932.

212   *3.2 percent beer, at least, returned:* "Bottling to Start Now," *New York Times,* March 23, 1933.

212   *ordered members across the country:* "Chicago Ready for Zero Hour," *New York Times,* April 6, 1933.

212   *"Beer may not be intoxicating":* "Friday Morning Beer," *Washington Post,* April 6, 1933.

212   *"an uptown brewery":* "Broadway Disappointed," *New York Times,* April 7, 1933.

212   *the form of six Clydesdales:* "Six Big Horses Bring Smith a Case of Beer," *New York Times,* April 8, 1933.

213   *George Ehret had never recovered:* "Ruppert Acquires Ehret Brewery," *New York Times,* April 6, 1935.

213   *"Take it from an old-timer":* Display Ad 14, *New York Times,* July 18, 1933.

214   *"The dainty glass bottle of Ruppert's":* Display Ad 11, *New York Times,* October 12, 1935.

214   *only twenty-three breweries left in the city:* Fred Ferretti, "Where Have All the Breweries Gone?" *New York Times,* August 9, 1978.

214   *Across the country, the great brewing families:* Ibid.

214   *Hijackers kidnapped:* "Beer Truck Seized in Hijacker's Raid," *New York Times,* May 3, 1933.

214   *A Ruppert employee exchanged shots:* "Brewery Payroll Saved in Hold-Up," *New York Times,* September 6, 1934.

214   *A Brooklyn barkeep was terrorized:* "Beer Thugs Wreck Brooklyn Resort," *New York Times,* September 13, 1933.

217   *"Colonel Jacob Ruppert says men marry only":* "Bachelor Apartment," *Bachelor* magazine.

217   *he ordered all home games thereafter:* Jay Maeder, "Jacob Ruppert: The Old Ball Game," *New York Daily News,* March 2, 1999.

217   *The Colonel said one word:* "Ruppert Dies at 71," *New York Times,* January 14, 1939.

6. FISH

John Waldman's amazing book *Heartbeats in the Muck* was an accessible and impressive overview of New York City's harbor. Joseph Mitchell's *Up in the Old Hotel* provides such a ravishing account of the Fulton Fish Market and other watery locales that decades later, it's hard to find any more to say. The book *Manahatta* by Eric W. Sanderson, and his article with Marianne Brown, "Manahatta: An Ecological First Look at the Manhattan Landscape Prior to Henry Hudson," helped me to imagine the waterways of Manhattan of yore. Various articles in scientific journals helped elucidate the problem of local contaminants that fishers consume with the fish. *Seaport Magazine,*

Winter/Spring 1990, an issue dedicated to New York Harbor, was helpful, as was Clyde L. MacKenzie, Jr.'s *The Fisheries of Raritan Bay*, which tells everything you ever wanted to know about fishing on the bay that abuts Staten Island, including offering an oral history of the last fishermen there. *The Report of the Metropolitan Sewerage Commission of New York* in 1910 gave vivid detail about early contamination.

222 *a poll of two hundred women:* Laura Anne Bienenfeld, Anne L. Golden, and Elizabeth J. Garland, "Consumption of Fish from Polluted Waters by WIC Participants in East Harlem," *Journal of Urban Health* 80, no. 2 (June 2003).

222 *"This was the first time the U.S. EPA":* Jason Corburn, "Combining Community-Based Research and Local Knowledge to Confront Asthma and Subsistence-Fishing Hazards in Greenpoint/Williamsburg, Brooklyn, New York," *Environmental Health Perspectives* 110, supplement 2 (April 2002): 245.

222 *A community group spent several months:* Ibid.

223 *Once, seventy miles of streams:* Eric W. Sanderson and Marianne Brown, "Mannahatta: An Ecological First Look at the Manhattan Landscape Prior to Henry Hudson," *Northeastern Naturalist*, 14(4), 2007, 545.

223 *the lobby of an apartment building:* Nick Paumgarten, "The Mannahatta Project," *The New Yorker*, October 1, 2007.

223 *"When my sister picked me up":* Jeff Kisseloff, *You Must Remember This: An Oral History of Manhattan from the 1890s to World War II* (San Diego: Harvourt, Brace Jovanovich, 1980), 272.

224 *"The bulk of the water in New York Harbor":* Joseph Mitchell, "The Bottom of the Harbor," *Up in the Old Hotel and Other Stories* (New York: Vintage Books, 2008), 465.

226 *A vast underground lake of contamination:* Daphne Eviatar, "The Ooze," *New York Magazine*, June 3, 2007.

226 *"Like the Blob":* Ibid.

227 *"Exceedingly refreshing":* Edward Neufville Tailer Diaries, May 26, 1848; June 3, 15, 17, 24, 1848; New-York Historical Society.

227 *a survey of industry along the creek noted:* Jason Corburn, "Combining Community-Based Research and Local Knowledge to Confront Asthma and Subsistence-Fishing Hazards in Greenpoint/Williamsburg, Brooklyn, New York," *Environmental Health Perspectives* 110, supplement 2 (April 2002): 242.

228 *"It is not possible to describe":* Jasper Danckaerts, "Journal of Jasper Danckaerts, 1679–1680."

228 *"I had to try some of them raw":* Ibid., 51.

228 *In his day, tuna, perch, sturgeon:* Gerard T. Koeppel, *Water for Gotham: A History* (Princeton: Princeton University Press, 2000), 9. Also Meta F.

Janowitz, "Indian Corn and Dutch Pots: Seventeenth-Century Foodways in New Amsterdam/New York," *Historical Archaeology* 27, no. 2
(1993).

228 *"With all the interlacing of waterways":* Anthony Hiss, "Love Among the
Ruins," *The New Yorker*, March 17, 1980.

229 *They built homes facing the water:* Russell Shorto, *The Island at the Center
of the World: The Epic Story of Dutch Manhattan and the Forgotten Colony
That Shaped America* (New York: Vintage Books, 2005), 106.

229 *The original charter for the Trinity Church:* Stokes 1915–1928, quoted in
Eric W. Sanderson and Marianne Brown, "Mannahatta: An Ecologi-
cal First Look at the Manhattan Landscape Prior to Henry Hudson."
Northeastern Naturalist 14, no. 4 (2007).

230 *"He-e-e-e-e-e-ere's your fine Rocka-a-way clams":* Jessica B. Harris,
High on the Hog: A Culinary Journey from Africa to America (New York:
Bloomsbury, 2011), 126.

230 *the son of Mr. and Mrs. Moles Lynn:* William N. Zeisel, Jr., "Shark!!!
And Other Sport Fish Once Abundant in New York Harbor," *Seaport
Magazine*, Winter/Spring 1990.

230 *In 1800, oyster houses advertised:* John Waldman, *Heartbeats in the Muck:
The History of Sea Life and Environment of New York Harbor* (New York:
Lyons Press, 1999), 40–41.

230 *"All along the East River are places":* Ingersoll, 1881. Quoted in Clyde
L. MacKenzie Jr., *The Fisheries of Raritan Bay* (New Brunswick, N.J.:
Rutgers University Press, 1992), 66.

230 *"anyone with a length of string":* William N. Zeisel Jr., "Shark!!! And
Other Sport Fish" *Seaport Magazine*, Winter/Spring 1990.

231 *When the mackerel:* Norman Brouwer, "The New York Fisheries," *Seaport Magazine*, Winter/Spring 1990.

231 *"Hey, best here!":* Harpo Marx, with Rowland Barber, *Harpo Speaks . . .
About New York* (New York: Little Bookroom, 1961).

235 *The Dutch built deep canals:* Gerard T. Koeppel, *Water for Gotham*
(Princeton: Princeton University Press, 2000), 14.

235 *Over time, the streams and ponds:* Eric W. Sanderson and Marianne
Brown, "Mannahatta: An Ecological First Look at the Manhattan
Landscape Prior to Henry Hudson," *Northeastern Naturalist*, 14, no. 4
(2007), 545.

235 *Human waste filled the waterways:* Ibid., 547.

235 *Dead horses and cows:* Benjamin Miller, *Fat of the Land*. Quoted in
Philip Lopate, *Waterfront: A Journey Around Manhattan* (New York:
Crown Publishers, 2004), 96–97.

236 *The people who came in from the water:* Burrows and Wallace, *Gotham*
(New York: Oxford University Press, 1999), 322.

236   *Waterfront districts earned names:* Luc Sante, *Low Life* (New York: Farrar, Strauss, Giroux, 1991), 18.

236   *"amidst the stench of the oozing":* W. O. Stoddard, "New York Harbor Police," *Harper's New Monthly Magazine* 45, no. 269 (October 1872).

237   *"rising and breaking of sludge bubbles":* Joseph Mitchell, "The Bottom of the Harbor," *Up in the Old Hotel and Other Stories* (New York: Vintage Books, 2008), 465.

237   *"Children grow pale and languish":* "Death and Hunter's Point," *Harper's Weekly,* August 13, 1881.

237   *"the stenches began asserting themselves":* Andrew Hurley, "Creating Ecological Wastelands: Oil Pollution in New York City, 1870–1900," *Journal of Urban History* 20, no. 3 (May 1994): 340.

237   *the area had become an ecological wasteland:* Ibid.

237   *open the spigots for thousands of gallons of oil:* "Fierce $1,000,000 Fire on East Tenth Street," *New York Times,* November 29, 1901; "Bronx Fire Near Motor Truck Plant," *New York Times,* February 10, 1919.

238   *flames a hundred feet tall leapt from a gasoline barge:* "Gasoline Lighter Ablaze in Hudson," *New York Times,* March 5, 1916.

238   *"lighted by some strange grotesque sun":* "Three Men Die in Oil Ship Fire," *New York Times,* October 11, 1912.

238   *new indoor plumbing efficiently piped raw waste:* Wilbur N. Torpey, "Response to Pollution of New York Harbor and Thames Estuary," *Journal (Water Pollution Control Federation),* 39, no. 11 (November 1967), 1797–1809.

238   *Chemicals and sewage made for a toxic brew:* John Waldman, "How to Make New York City Seafood Local Again," talk at the South Street Seaport Museum, November 18, 2010.

238   *People caught typhoid fever:* John Waldman, *Heartbeats in the Muck: The History of Sea Life and Environment of New York Harbor* (New York: Lyons Press), 42.

238   *"have been grumbling considerably recently":* "Mass Meeting of Fishermen Called," *New York Times,* March 14, 1899.

238   *The fishermen decided to propose bills:* "League of Salt-Water Fishermen Meets—Central Road Accused," *New York Times,* December 19, 1899.

239   *"The life of the bobtail clam":* Quoted in Kevin Bone, *The New York Waterfront: Evolution and Building Culture of the Port and Harbor* (New York: Monacelli Press, 1997), 166.

239   *"a smelly black substance":* "New York's Polluted Waters," *New York Times,* July 27, 1919.

240   *"in which V is the velocity of the ascending sewage":* Report of the Metropolitan Sewerage Commission of New York: Sewerage and Sewage Disposal in the Metropolitan District of New York and New Jersey, April 30, 1910, 457.

240   *"black in color from sulfide"*: John Waldman, *Heartbeats in the Muck: The History of Sea Life and Environment of New York Harbor* (New York: Lyons Press), 86–87.

240   *Fields of sewage surrounded Manhattan:* Ibid.

241   *Mr. Charles H. Townsend:* Ibid., 481.

244   *Soon, steamships and railroads routinely carried fish cargoes:* Cindy R. Lobel, "Consuming Classes," (PhD dissertation, University of New York, 2003), 69.

244   *"All the fisheries in New York harbor are nearly destroyed":* Quoted in Thomas De Voe, *The Market Book: Containing a Historical Account of the Public Markets in the Cities of New York, Boston, Philadelphia and Brooklyn, Etc.* Google eBook, 203–4.

245   *"rattling and jolting along":* Patrick Cirincione, "Impressions of Fulton Fish Market," WPA, Feeding the City WPA Project, Municipal Archives.

245   *But increasingly, even the boats:* Philip Lopate, *Waterfront: A Journey Around Manhattan* (New York: Crown Publishers, 2004), 257.

245   *"Ho! Clahmmmmmmmmmms!":* Terry Roth, "Street Cries and Criers of New York," WPA, November 3, 1938.

245   *He would invent fish-related lyrics:* Clyde (Kingfish) Smith, Marion Charles Hatch, November 29, 1939. WPA. American Memory, Library of Congress. memory.loc.gov/ammem/index.html (accessed June 9, 2011).

246   *the* Times *ran recipes for shad:* "News of Food," *New York Times,* April 22, 1947.

247   *"Scarcely anything but weak-fish":* "Fresh Fish," *Appletons' Journal of Literature, Science and Art* 5, no. 108 (April 22, 1871).

247   *the* Felicia, *a Brooklyn-built wooden dragger:* Norman Brouwer, "The New York Fisheries," *Seaport Magazine,* Winter/Spring 1990.

250   *"His face was dead gray":* Saul Bellow, *Humboldt's Gift* (New York: Penguin Classics, 1996), 53.

250   *"Inshore, it's dead":* "Pollution Wrecking Inshore Fishing," *New York Times,* September 8, 1977.

250   *State Department of Environmental Conservation banned:* "Hudson-Harlem Eels Banned as Hazard," *New York Times,* August 4, 1977.

252   *"I was nearly hanged":* Josh Barbanel, "Council Panel Backs Ban on Fishing from Some City Bridges," *New York Times,* December 16, 1984.

253   *Fish can be contaminated at levels:* Bridget Barclay, "Hudson River Angler Survey: A Report on the Adherence to Fish Consumption Health Advisories Among Hudson River Anglers," Hudson River Sloop Clearwater, Poughkeepsie, New York, 1993, 35–36.

253   *"I think if we do not reach out":* Virginia Flaton, co-chair, Citizens

Advisory Committee, Harbor Estuary Program, "Hearing of the Committee on Waterfronts," City Council, City of New York, June 17, 2002.

254 *A pilot study by the Mount Sinai School of Medicine:* Anne Golden, M.D., et al., "Biomarkers of Human Health Risk in the Hudson River: The Hudson River Anglers Health Study (Pilot Stury 1999–2000)," presentation, Rutgers University, May 1, 2001.

7. WINE

William Prince's *A Treatise on the Vine* and Alden Spooner's *The Cultivation of the American Grape Vine* are both available online and helpful in laying out nineteenth-century Brooklyn winery history. Leon D. Adam's *The Wines of America* offers a basic summary of New York State wines. *Dry Manhattan,* by Michael Lerner, was a fabulous rundown of New York during Prohibition. This chapter also relied extensively on newspaper accounts, interviews, and the private collection of Gale Robinson, who allowed me to examine business records belonging to her father, Meyer Robinson. The article "Wine Like Mother Used to Make" from *Commentary* magazine in May 1954 provided a snapshot of the people of Manischewitz wine.

263 *"shining in its glass like a sun":* Rina Drory, *Models and Contacts: Arabic Literature and Its Impact on Medieval Jewish Culture* (Leiden: Koninklijke Brill, 2000).

265 *"very suitable . . . for planting vineyards":* Jasper Danckaerts, *Journal of Jasper Danckaerts, 1679–1680.*

265 *elsewhere in Manhattan, European vines withered:* Gerard T. Koeppel, *Water for Gotham: A History* (Princeton: Princeton University Press, 2000), 33.

266 *Isabella Gibbs from the Carolinas:* William Prince, *A Treatise on the Vine: Embracing Its History from the Earliest Ages to the Present Day, with Descriptions of Above Two Hundred Foreign and Eighty American Varieties; Together with a Complete Dissertation on the Establishment, Culture, and Management of Vineyards . . .* (New York, 1830). Also Thomas Meehan, ed., *The Gardener's Monthly and Horticultural Advertiser,* vol. 2 (Philadelphia, —1860).

266 *"They were much injured":* Alden Spooner, *The Cultivation of American Grape Vines and Making of Wine* (E. B. Spooner & Co., 1858), 69.

266 *Another Brooklyn experimenter:* Letter from Zachariah Lewis, Esq., to Alden Spooner, April 20, 1832, Brooklyn. Quoted in Spooner, *The Cultivation of American Grape Vines,* 70.

266 *an elderly Frenchman named Monsieur Thiry:* "A Grower of Grapes and Savings Banks," *New York Times,* September 8, 1901.

268 *Ephraim Wales Bull, of Concord, Massachussetts:* "Found the Concord

Grape; Recent Death of Dr. Ephraim W. Bull in Concord, Mass."
New York Times, October 13, 1895.

268 *"I looked about to see:* "Grape, Raisin and Wine Production in the United States," George C. Husmann, in *Yearbook of the United States Department of Agriculture, 1902.* Washington Government Printing Office, 1903, 408.

268 *Concord grape production doubled:* "Wine-Making Along the Hudson; Magnitude of the Fruit-Growing Business and Its Results," *New York Times,* October 25, 1883.

268 *"Scores of speculators":* "A Great Grape Crop," *New York Times,* September 6, 1888.

268 *uncovered whiskey barrels:* "Fruit Growers Are Happy; The Crops This Season Along the Hudson Have Been Fairly Good," *New York Times,* October 8, 1890.

268 *three and a half tons per acre:* "How the Grape Industry Grew," *Independent,* November 19, 1891.

268 *a favorable record against the Catawba:* "Grapes for the Million," *American Farmer,* March 15, 1893.

269 *"pious old graybeards":* Michael Gold, *Jews Without Money* (New York: Carroll & Graf Publishers, 1930), 114.

269 *"The Hebrews do not seem to be":* "Residents of East Side Make Their Own Wine," *New York Tribune,* November 29, 1903.

270 *Vintners would pay a rabbi:* "Dry Raiders Seize Sacramental Wine," *New York Times,* September 13, 1922.

270 *"sacramental wine business among the Gentiles":* "Dry Agents Seize $500,000 in Wine," *New York Times,* November 12, 1921.

270 *hundreds of shady wineries:* "Dry Raiders Seize Sacramental Wine," *New York Times,* September 13, 1922.

270 *"Dry Agents Plan War upon Illicit Rabbis":* Michael Lerner, *Dry Manhattan: Prohibition in New York City* (Cambridge: Harvard University Press, 2008), 121.

270 *"He was a bootlegger":* Michael Cooper, "Charming Wine You Can Cut," *New York Times,* March 31, 1996.

271 *the kosher wine industry was born:* Leon D. Adams, *The Wines of America,* 3rd ed. (New York: McGraw-Hill Book Company, 1973), 489.

271 *"as they would make bread":* Michael Lerner, *Dry Manhattan* (Cambridge: Harvard University Press, 2008), 106.

271 *Italian households spent:* Ibid.

272 *the gutters in front of tenements:* Ibid.

272 *shipments of California wine grapes:* "Wine Grapes Must Debark in New Jersey This Fall," *New York Times,* October 19, 1924.

272 *"a reluctant squidginess":* Ibid.

272   *recipes and ingredients for wine making:* Ibid.

272   *"Succulent grape, signor":* Michael di Liberto, "Wine Time in East Harlem," *New York Times,* November 8, 1931.

272   *"They would get deliveries":* Jeff Kisseloff, *You Must Remember This: An Oral History of Manhattan from the 1890s to World War II* (San Diego: Harcourt, Brace Jovanovich, 1989), 411.

277   *"A gallon would go* phtttt!": Jerry Della Femina, *An Italian Grows in Brooklyn* (Boston: Little, Brown and Company, 1978), 20.

280   *Italian American manhood:* Laura Schenone, *A Thousand Years Over a Hot Stove: A History of American Women Told Through Food, Recipes, and Remembrances* (New York: W.W. Norton & Company, 2003), 218.

281   *"You and your group":* Steven Flax, "Let Them Keep Laughing," *Forbes,* September 28, 1981.

283   *Meyer Robinson filed a certificate:* Certificate of Incorporation, Monarch Wine Company, State of New York, January 12, 1934. Courtesy of Gale Robinson.

283   *purchased equipment at bankruptcy sales:* January 7, 1942, Monarch Wine meeting minutes, early Monarch Wine documents. Courtesy of Gale Robinson.

283   *Meyer and Leo cut a deal:* Minutes of a meeting of the Board of Directors of the Monarch Wine Company, Inc., June 15, 1944. Courtesy of Gale Robinson.

283   *use the Manischewitz name on its labels:* Laura Manischewitz Alpern, *Manischewitz: The Matzo Family: The Making of an American Jewish Icon* (Jersey City, N.J.: KTAV Publishing House, in association with the American Jewish Historical Society, 2008), 186.

284   *the office towers of mid-Manhattan:* Jan Morris, *Manhattan '45* (New York: Oxford University Press, 1989), 52.

284   *"We have been fortunate":* Ibid., 212.

284   *"It's a naïve domestic Burgundy":* Ibid., 213.

284   *"An engine, its insides of gears and belts":* Morris Freedman, "Wine Like Mother Used to Make," *Commentary,* May 1954.

287   *"like Mother used to make":* Ibid.

287   *people were drinking more of it:* Harold D. Watkins, "Californians Reassess American Tastes, Pour Out Many New Flavors," *New York Times,* September 17, 1958.

288   *"We dropped almost all the visual advertising":* Freedman, "Wine Like Mother Used to Make," *Commentary,* May 1954.

288   *"We want to bring drinking wine":* Ibid.

288   *Manischewitz was competing:* Ibid.

288   *"Man, oh Manischewitz":* NASA video of the Apollo 17 mission at http://next.nasa.gov/alsj/a17/a17v.1424550.mpg.

289   *Sammy Davis Jr. had been contracted:* David Usborne, "The After-life of Sammy Davis Jr.," *The Independent*, June 23, 2007.

289   *More than 85 percent of Manischewitz:* Ibid.

EPILOGUE

299   *you'd have 3,079 acres:* "The Potential for Urban Agriculture in New York City," Urban Design Lab at the Earth Institute, Columbia University, 2011.

299   *10 percent of the city's backyards:* Interview with Nevin Cohen, assistant professor, environmental studies, The New School.

299   *"A big, giant parasite:* "The Sustainable City: Farming Upwards," podcast of the New York Academy of Sciences, http://www.nyas.org/Publications/Media/PodcastDetail.aspx?cid=9abc4f6d-2489-48ea-b088-bf5c5ef69c27.

Robin Shulman grew up in a farming town in tobacco country in Ontario, Canada, and several moves later, arrived in New York City at age sixteen. She has a bit of rural and a lot of urban in her.

As a journalist, Shulman has reported for news outlets including the *Washington Post*, the *New York Times*, the *Los Angeles Times*, *Slate*, and the *Guardian*. She has worked in rural, suburban, and urban America and in the Middle East. She lives in New York City.